T0301839

Immigration and Nation Building

MONASH STUDIES IN GLOBAL MOVEMENTS

Series Editor: John Nieuwenhuysen, *Director, Monash Institute for the Study of Global Movements, Monash University, Australia*

This series is an important forum for the publication of new research on global movements sponsored by Monash University. It presents a multidisciplinary perspective on global movements of people, resources and ideas in their diverse economic, social, political and cultural dimensions. The series makes a valuable contribution to our understanding of some of the most important trends and challenges arising in an increasingly globalised world.

Titles in the series include:

Privatization and Market Development
Global Movements in Public Policy Ideas
Edited by Graeme Hodge

Globalisation of Accounting Standards
Edited by Jayne M. Godfrey and Keryn Chalmers

Counter-Terrorism and the Post-Democratic State
Edited by Jenny Hocking and Colleen Lewis

New Global Frontiers in Regulation
The Age of Nanotechnology
Edited by Graeme Hodge, Diana Bowman and Karinne Ludlow

Nations of Immigrants
Australia and the USA Compared
Edited by John Nieuwenhuysen and John Higley with Stine Neerup

Terrorism and Social Exclusion
Misplaced Risk – Common Security
Edited by David Wright-Neville and Alina Halafoff

Immigration and Nation Building
Australia and Israel Compared
Edited by Andrew Markus and Moshe Semyonov

Immigration and Nation Building

Australia and Israel Compared

Edited by

Andrew Markus

*Australian Centre for Jewish Civilisation,
Monash University, Australia*

and

Moshe Semyonov

*Department of Sociology and Department of Labor Studies,
Tel Aviv University, Israel*

MONASH STUDIES IN GLOBAL MOVEMENTS

Edward Elgar

Cheltenham, UK • Northampton, MA, USA

Published by
Edward Elgar Publishing Limited
The Lypiatts
15 Lansdown Road
Cheltenham
Glos GL50 2JA
UK

Edward Elgar Publishing, Inc.
William Pratt House
9 Dewey Court
Northampton
Massachusetts 01060
USA

A catalogue record for this book
is available from the British Library

Library of Congress Control Number: 2010926003

ISBN 978 1 84980 063 1

Typeset by Servis Filmsetting Ltd, Stockport, Cheshire
Printed and bound by MPG Books Group, UK

Contents

Contributors

Majid Al-Haj is Vice President and Dean of Research at the University of Haifa, Israel, where he is Professor of Sociology and head of the Center for Multiculturalism and Educational Research. Majid Al-Haj received his doctorate from the Hebrew University of Jerusalem and pursued post-doctoral studies at Brown University, Providence, RI, USA. His most recent work focuses on education and multiculturalism in Israel and the impact of Russian immigrants on Israeli culture and ethnic politics. He has published extensively on the social and political structure of the Palestinians in Israel, Palestinian refugees, immigration in Israel, and freedom of expression. Recent publications include *Immigration and Ethnic Formation in a Deeply Divided Society: The Case of the 1990s Immigrants from the Former Soviet Union in Israel* (2004), *Education among the Palestinians in Israel: Between Control and Culture of Silence* (2006), and the co-edited *Cultural Diversity and the Empowerment of Minorities: The Israeli and the German Cases* (2007).

Karin Amit is the Academic Committee Coordinator at the Institute of Immigration and Social Integration and a senior lecturer in the Department of Business Administration at Ruppin Academic Center, Israel. She received her PhD from Tel Aviv University, Israel. Her research interests include immigration and leadership and she is a member of the Metropolis International Steering Committee.

Olena Bagno is a Neubauer Fellow at the Institute for National Security Studies at Tel Aviv University and a post-doctoral fellow in the Department of Political Science at Stanford University, USA. She completed her PhD dissertation in the Department of Political Science at Tel Aviv University, Israel. Her research interests focus on immigration, politics, security and civil society.

Allan Borowski is Professor of Social Work and Social Policy at La Trobe University, Melbourne, Australia. He obtained his doctorate in 1980 from Brandeis University, Waltham, MA, USA. Upon completion of his PhD he worked in Canada as a senior policy analyst with the Province of Ontario's Ministry of Community and Social Services; he has also held positions as Research Manager of the Australian government's Bureau of

Immigration, Multicultural and Population Research, as Chair in Social Work at The University of New South Wales, Australia, and in The Hebrew University of Jerusalem's Paul Baerwald School of Social Work. He has served as a consultant to a variety of public and non-profit organizations in the United States, Israel, Indonesia and Australia and was a visiting professor at universities in Israel, England, Hong Kong, Canada and Sweden. He was elected a Fellow of the Gerontological Society of America in 1997 and of the Academy of the Social Sciences in Australia in 2006. Borowski has produced over 100 publications, including the co-edited *Immigration and Refugee Policy: Australia and Canada Compared* (1994) and *Longevity and Social Change in Australia* (2007).

Na'ama Carmi is a teacher in the faculty of law at the University of Haifa, Israel. Carmi is a member of the National Privacy Protection Council. She has also served on The National Committee for Social Sciences (2002–05) and was Chairperson of the Association for Civil Rights in Israel (2001–02). Carmi's publications include *The Law of Return: Immigration Rights and their Limits*, Tel-Aviv University Press (2003, in Hebrew).

Anne Daly is Associate Professor of Economics at the University of Canberra, Australia, and holds a PhD in Economics from the Australian National University, Canberra. Her thesis compared age-earnings profiles for men and women in Australia, Great Britain and the United States. She currently teaches Microeconomics and Labour Economics at the University of Canberra. She has considerable experience in working in interdisciplinary research teams on such topics as the position of Indigenous Australians in the labour market, women in the workforce and the relationship with the welfare system, and transitions between education and working life for young people. She has maintained a research interest in international comparisons of labour market outcomes and her work has recently been published in the *Australian Review of Public Affairs* and the *Economic Record*.

Sergio DellaPergola is one of the world's leading demographers and a specialist in world Jewry. A former Chairman and Professor of Population Studies at the Hebrew University of Jerusalem, he now holds the Shlomo Argov Chair in Israel-Diaspora Relations at the university. DellaPergola is also a senior fellow at the Jewish People Policy Planning Institute, an independent think tank in Jerusalem. He has published numerous books and hundreds of papers on topics including Jewish identification and population projections in the diaspora and Israel. Recent publications include the co-edited *Jewish Intermarriage Around the World* (2009) and *Papers in Jewish Demography* (series).

Yitchak Haberfeld is Associate Professor of Labour Studies at Tel Aviv University, Israel. His research areas include economic assimilation of immigrants, gender, ethnic and racial-based earnings differentials, and industrial relations systems. He has published extensively on the status of immigrants in the labour market. His work has been recently published in the *European Sociological Review, Demography* and *Work and Occupations*.

Andrew Jakubowicz is Professor of Sociology and Co-director of the Cosmopolitan Civil Societies Research Centre at the University of Technology, Sydney, Australia. He has undertaken research on the politics of cultural relations since the late 1960s. He has worked in the multicultural city of Bradford in the UK, and headed the Centre for Multicultural Studies at the University of Wollongong, Australia. He has published on the media, racism and cultural diversity, social policy and cultural diversity, and ethnic politics in Australia. He has a particular interest in the interrelationship between ideas about imperialism and the socio-political structures that emerge in post-colonial societies. As an educator he runs the award-winning website Making Multicultural Australia (http://multiculturalaustralia.edu.au) designed to use multimedia to engage with the widespread ramifications of cultural pluralism. Recent publications include entries in the *Encyclopedia of Race Ethnicity and Society* (2008) and the *Encyclopedia of Religion* in Australia (2009).

Siew-Ean Khoo is Senior Fellow in the Australian Demographic and Social Research Institute, Australian National University, Canberra, and is former Executive Director of the Australian Centre for Population Research at the Australian National University. A graduate of Harvard University, Cambridge, MA, USA, she has worked with the East-West Population Institute at the East-West Centre in Honolulu, HI, USA, and the Bureau of Immigration, Multicultural and Population Research in Australia. Her current research focuses on Australia's population and demography, particularly in relation to international migration and the settlement outcomes of immigrants and their children. She was the lead author of a study on *Second Generation Australians* that was commissioned and published by the Australian Government's Department of Immigration and Multicultural Affairs in 2002. Other published papers have examined intermarriage patterns, educational and occupational outcomes and language maintenance among the second generation in Australia. Recent journal articles have also included studies of skilled temporary migration to Australia, based on an Australian Research Council-funded research project in collaboration with the Department of Immigration. She is co-editor and contributing author of two recent books: *The Transformation of Australia's Population: 1970–2030* (2003) and *Public Policy and Immigrant Settlement* (2006).

Susan Kneebone is Professor of Law and Deputy Director of the Castan Centre for Human Rights Law, Faculty of Law, Monash University, Melbourne, Australia. She teaches courses on Forced Migration and Human Rights, International Refugee Law, and Citizenship and Migration Law, which incorporates discussion of citizenship theory. She is the author of many articles on these issues and editor and co-editor of books which consider interdisciplinary and comparative perspectives, including *The Refugees Convention 50 Years On: Globalisation and International Law* (2003), *New Regionalism and Asylum Seekers: Challenges Ahead* (2007), and *Refugees, Asylum Seekers and the Rule of Law: Comparative Perspectives* (2009). She has made a number of submissions to public enquiries and frequently handles media enquiries on these issues, including a submission in 2007 on the legislation to introduce the citizenship test.

Andrew Markus holds the Pratt Foundation Research Professor of Jewish Civilisation in the Australian Centre for Jewish Civilisation, Monash Univeristy, Melbourne, Australia, and is a past Director of the Centre. He has researched Australian immigration and indigenous history and contemporary issues since the 1970s and currently heads four major research projects. These include an ongoing project measuring attitudes to immigration issues and social cohesion, an attitudinal study of the contemporary Jewish communities of Australia and a cross-generational study of Yiddish speaking immigrants and their descendants in Melbourne. He is the author or co-author of a number of books and reports, including *Race: John Howard and the Remaking of Australia* (2001), *Mapping Social Cohesion: The Scanlon Foundation Surveys* (2008, 2010) and *Australia's Immigration Revolution* (2009).

Rebeca Raijman is Associate Professor in the Department of Sociology and Anthropology at the University of Haifa, Israel. She received her PhD in Sociology from the University of Chicago, USA. Her research focuses on international migration (in Israel and the US) with special emphasis on migrants' modes of incorporation into host societies. She is currently conducting comprehensive research regarding the socio-political and religious organization of undocumented migrants' communities, the politics and policy of labour migration in Israel, and the social mechanisms underlying the emergence of prejudice and discrimination against subordinate ethnic minorities in modern societies. Her work has been recently published in *Social Problems* and the *International Journal of Comparative Sociology*.

Moshe Semyonov holds the Bernard and Audre Rapoport Chair in the Sociology of Labor at Tel Aviv University, Israel. He teaches in the Departments of Sociology and of Labor Studies, and is also Professor of Sociology at the University of Illinois at Chicago. He received his PhD in Sociology from the State University of New York at Stony Brook, USA. Semyonov's main research interests lie in the areas of labour market inequalities, labour migration in the global economy, and comparative social stratification. His current research focuses on structural sources of ethnic, gender and socio-economic inequality (mostly in the labour market) and on the status of labour migrants across societies. He is co-editor of *Stratification in Israel: Class, Ethnicity and Gender* (2004) and his work has recently been published in the *American Sociological Review* and *Social Problems*.

Haya Stier is Associate Professor of Sociology and Labor Studies at Tel Aviv University, Israel. She received her PhD from the University of Chicago, USA. She is conducting research in the areas of immigration, gender, family and social policy. She has published extensively in sociological journals on issues related to immigration, family and social policy, with recent publications in *Research on Aging* and the *European Sociological Review*.

Acknowledgements

This volume was made possible by the vision of Professor John Nieuwenhuysen, Director of the Monash Institute for the Study of Global Movements, Monash University, Australia and Dr Sam Lipski, CEO of the Pratt Foundation, Melbourne, Australia, and through the financial support of their organizations. The meeting of the authors, held in April 2009 at the European campus of Monash University in Prato, Italy, was facilitated by Ms Sahar Sana, Administrator of the Monash Institute for Study of Global Movements and Ms Irene Thavarajah, Manager of the Conference and Events Management Office, Monash University. Professor Loretta Baldassar, Director of the Monash University Prato Centre, and her staff made possible the smooth running of the meeting of the authors. We thank Alex Pettifer, Editorial Director, Edward Elgar Publishing, for recognizing the importance of this project.

Introduction

Andrew Markus and Moshe Semyonov

Australia and Israel are nations of immigrants, with the highest and second highest proportion of overseas-born amongst the industrialized nations. Some 34 per cent of Israel's population were born outside the country, compared to 24 per cent in Australia, 19 per cent in Canada, 12 per cent in the USA and 9 per cent in the UK. Despite a number of similarities, the two societies differ considerably in the composition of their populations, in the scope and history of migration flows as well as in their size, economic structures and in their social and migration policies.

In 2009 Israel's population numbered an estimated 7.5 million, Australia's population 21.8 million. While the differential in the populations of the two countries is in the ratio 3:1, the differential on many economic indicators is of the order of 4:1 or 5:1. Thus Israel's GDP is 25 per cent of Australia's, its budget revenues are 20 per cent of Australia's. The Israeli labour force of 2.95 million workers is 26 per cent of Australia's 11.21 million workers. Per capita income in Israel at US\$28 200 is 75 per cent of the Australian per capita of US\$37 700. Public debt as a proportion of GDP is 15.4 per cent in Australia and 75.7 per cent in Israel.

The purpose of this book is to examine similarities and differences in the incorporation of immigrants into the two societies. It considers the relative positions of the native born and the immigrant both within and across the two societies, and the extent to which societal and economic conditions and migration policies have produced differential patterns of social, political and economic integration of the immigrants to the country.

Both countries have substantial subordinate indigenous populations. Approximately 20 per cent of the Israeli population (1.2 million) are Arab. Most Israeli Arabs have lived in the region for generations, although some migrated to Palestine in the late nineteenth and early decades of the twentieth century, as economic opportunities increased in the wake of Jewish immigrants. The Arabs living within Israel have citizenship rights and participate in the political system. Palestinians that live in the West Bank or Gaza Strip or in neighbouring countries claim the geographical area of Israel as their legitimate homeland.

1

Australia has an indigenous population estimated at 517 200, or 2.5 per cent of the total, in 2006. This population is rapidly increasing, having grown from 458 500 in 2001, or by 12.8 per cent. The largest numbers live in New South Wales (148 200) and Queensland (146 400). Thirty-one per cent of the indigenous population live in major cities; 45 per cent in regional Australia; and 25 per cent in remote areas.

Modern Israel has characteristics typical of settler societies, for example in the pattern of relations between its immigrant and indigenous populations, Australia is a settler society. Jewish immigrants to Mandatory Palestine and the state of Israel have seen themselves, whatever their motivation, as returning to the land of their forefathers, to a land inscribed with historical and religious links extending over more than 3000 years. By contrast, the history of white Australian settlement, which had its beginnings as a British convict outpost, spans less than 250 years. Until the 1950s Australians of the middle and upper classes typically saw themselves as exiles and yearned to return to mother England and what they termed 'civilization'. To the present most immigrants arrive in Australia with little knowledge of the country, drawn solely by economic opportunity and the prospect of improved quality of life.

Dispossession of the indigenous population in Australia began with the first settlement in 1788 and continued well into the twentieth century. As late as the 1950s, in some cases at later dates, small bands of traditional Aboriginal people were being expelled from their lands. Indeed, both Aboriginal and Palestinian people have unsettled claims for sovereignty and for financial and other forms of compensation.

The relative scale of current conflict, which is much less in Australia, is explained not simply by the extent of problems and unresolved issues, which are substantial in both countries, but also by the smaller number and more limited resources of the Aboriginal and Torres Strait Islander populations and their relative lack of militancy. Also of importance for the failure to advance a range of Australian indigenous claims is the lack of support received, compared to support of Palestinians by Muslim nations and interest groups in the west, evident in the priority accorded their status in the forums of the United Nations and the mainstream media. This level of support often fails to meet Palestinian expectations, but is of a different magnitude to that provided to Australia's indigenous peoples.

ISRAEL

Israel is a multi-ethnic society inhabited by Jews who immigrated to the country from practically every corner of the globe, by non-Jews (mostly

Arabs who lived in the region for generations), and by overseas labour migrants who have begun arriving particularly in the last decade. Whereas Arabs can be viewed as indigenous to the region, the overwhelming majority of the Jewish population is composed of either first- or second-generation immigrants. Most of the Jewish immigrants who arrived from the 1930s to the 1960s were refugees who came with little belongings and from a wide variety of countries of origin. The labour immigrants to Israel are part of the recent ever-growing flows of global migrants who arrive from a variety of less-developed and poor countries in search of better economic opportunities. Similar to other societies, labour immigrants in Israel have become a source of cheap labour mostly used to fill low-status and low-paying menial jobs. As will be argued and demonstrated in this book, the changing population of Israel and the immigration flows have resulted not only in a change in the composition of the population but also in rising socioeconomic inequalities among sub-populations and among ethnic groups.

Of Israel's 7.5 million residents, 75 per cent are Jews, 20 per cent are Arabs (mostly Muslims) who are citizens of Israel and the remaining are non-Jewish immigrants, including approximately 200 000 labour migrants who are neither permanent residents nor citizens. When these figures are put in an historical perspective, the dramatic increase in the population of Israel becomes apparent. Sixty-one years ago, when Israel gained its independence, its population numbered only 600 000 Jews and 156 000 non-Jews (mostly Muslim and a relatively small proportion of Christian Palestinian Arabs). Thus within six decades the population of Israel has increased by almost ten-fold and has become considerably more heterogeneous. Immigration has accounted for over 40 per cent of Israel's population growth and for approximately 50 per cent of the growth of the Jewish population.

Israel was established as the 'homeland for the Jewish people'. Consequently, the state of Israel relies on the criterion of *jus sanguinis* to determine the status of immigrants, providing for total inclusion and immediate acceptance of Jewish immigrants and their family members and exclusion of non-Jews. Unlike other immigrant societies, migration of Jews to Israel is viewed as a returning Diaspora rather than an economic migration. The returning Diaspora is characterized by two distinct features: first, immigrants feel affinity and sense of belonging with the host society even prior to immigration; second, the receiving society grants new immigrants immediate and unconditional acceptance.

The *jus sanguinis* system of inclusion is embodied in the Law of Return (1950) and the Nationality Law (1952), according to which every Jew (and family members of Jewish immigrants) has the right to settle in Israel and to be awarded Israeli citizenship upon arrival. New arrivals are also provided with financial and institutional support to facilitate the transition from country of origin to country of destination. By contrast, Israel makes it almost impossible for non-Jewish immigrants to become permanent residents, let alone Israeli citizens. The definition of Israel as the homeland of the Jewish people and the supporting institutional structures are responsible for a large degree of the social, political and economic inequalities between Jews and Israeli Arabs and between citizens and non-Jewish labour migrants.

The Flows of Jewish Immigrants, Geocultural Disparities and the Role of Government

Since immigration has become a central defining characteristic of Israeli society and a major component of its collective identity one cannot understand social processes, especially the emergence of socio-economic inequalities and the stratification system in Israel, without considering the roles that immigration and immigration policies have played. There are five major periods of immigration and immigration policies that can be distinguished. These five periods are defined by specific historical periods associated with the establishment and development of the state. They are: pre-statehood immigration (until 1948); mass immigration immediately after the establishment of the state (1948–52); sporadic migration during the following three decades (1953–89); and mass migration of Soviet immigrants following the downfall of the Former Soviet Union (FSU) (1989–1995); scattered and declining Jewish immigration coupled by an increase of inflows of non-Jewish labour migrants (from 1996 to date).

The early flows of Jewish immigrants to Palestine came mostly from East and Central European countries at the turn of the nineteenth century with the ideological goal of establishing the homeland for the Jewish people. These early immigrants have settled throughout Israel and established, for the most part, their own rural and urban communities as well as the pre-state political, civic and economic institutions. Although the Jewish institutions and communities were largely separated from the Arab community inter-ethnic competition over land and labour began early, many years before the establishment of the state of Israel. While the nature of the competitive relations between Arabs and Jews has changed over the years, it is still one of the major features of Arab–Jewish relations in Israel and one of the sources of inequality between Jews and Arabs in Israel.

The pre-state era of Jewish immigration to Israel was characterized by low levels of societal and economic resources and by a low level of centralized control. However, in 1948, when Israel came into being, the state became intensively involved in shaping and implementing immigration and absorption policies. The central role of the state was apparent in all spheres of immigrant life, especially during the period of mass migration immediately after the establishment of the state and after the war of independence (1948–52). During this period Israel was flooded by a massive influx of refugees from two major geo-cultural regions. The first comprised European survivors of the Holocaust and the second comprised refugees from Muslim countries in the Middle East and North Africa. In a little over four years, the Jewish population of Israel was almost tripled, from 600 000 to 1.5 million. In the history of the state, the largest numerical intake of immigrants occurred immediately after its establishment.

Far-reaching state involvement was required to cope with the combination of huge numbers, destitution among the refugees and ethnic diversity. During this period the immigrants were highly dependent on the state, which established tent towns and then large housing projects, mostly on the outskirts of major cities. Later, the state adopted a population dispersion policy which directed new immigrants (disproportionately from the countries of North Africa) to newly established development towns in the peripheral northern and southern regions. These towns were characterized by labour intensive industries and by manual low-skilled and low-paying jobs. To date, these towns disproportionately house immigrants of North African and Middle Eastern origin, have a scarcity of high-skilled and high-paying jobs, and are viewed as one of the major sources of ethnic disparity in Israel.

Post-1948 immigrants from Europe were able to advance more rapidly. Their smooth economic and social integration, relative to Asian-Africans, can be attributed to several factors including favourable treatment from their compatriots who were in positions of power and influence, better social networks and connections, and more suitable cultural orientation and professional skills that were needed in the expanding and growing modern Israeli economy. By contrast, immigrants from Central Asia and North Africa suffered multiple disadvantages. They lacked the social connections in the new country, they were directed to peripheral communities, they were often looked down upon as their cultural orientation and customs were deemed inappropriate and 'inferior' by the dominant population. They also lacked the formal education that was required for high-paying jobs.

During the following three decades (1953–88) immigration to Israel declined, but the state's capacity to assist the newly arrived considerably increased. A range of financial benefits were generously allocated to assist integration. They included language instruction, job training, stipends and cash grants, subsidies to purchase a home, loans on favourable terms and tax exemptions. The immigrants who arrived during this period came from a wide range of countries and their choice of Israel as their destination was mainly influenced by push factors in their country of origin (for example, political unrest in countries such as Argentina, South Africa and Iran). Indeed, during this period there was relatively less pressure on the labour and housing markets and immigrants enjoyed relatively smooth incorporation into the economy and society.

The year 1989 marked a turning point in immigration to Israel. Following the downfall of the Soviet Union, Israel became the destination for almost one million Jewish immigrants and their family members (400 000 of whom arrived within two years, 1989–91). During less than one decade the population of Israel increased by 20 per cent. Although the new immigrants were highly educated and many had professional occupations they experienced substantial difficulty finding jobs appropriate to their qualifications.

To assist the immigrants the state established and enacted a new policy of 'direct absorption'. Immigrants received a 'basket of absorption' – cash and services – and had more freedom than earlier immigrants to decide how to utilize the available support. The 'basket of absorption' included a financial payment of approximately $10 000 (depending on the size of the family), monthly rental support that could be converted for mortgage payment, tax exceptions, free academic education for qualified students, Hebrew language courses and retraining programs. The immigrants could choose from one of a number of retraining programs, where to live, whether to buy an apartment or to rent one, whether to buy a car, Hebrew classes and when to enter the labour market. Although Soviet immigrants have experienced downward occupational mobility upon arrival, intermediate assessments suggest that they are closing the gap with Jews of Asian-African origin and have already passed the Arab population.

In 1991, when immigrants from the FSU were arriving in massive numbers, Israel was actively rescuing tens of thousands of Ethiopian Jews (joining those who were rescued in 1984). The Ethiopians, unlike the 'Russians' had a very low level of formal education and professional training and came from a region characterized by adherence to traditional values. Similar to the Soviet immigrants, the Ethiopians received generous government support, somewhat larger than that given to the 'Russians' and with more supervision by the government. They continue to face considerable difficulty adjusting to Israeli society.

Non-Jewish Labor Migrants and Asylum Seekers

In recent decades Israel has become a destination for a large number of global labour migrants. Similar to many European societies, Israel has begun importing and recruiting non-citizen 'guest workers' to fill low-paying and low-status menial jobs that the local population is reluctant to take. Israel began relying on non-citizen labour after the 1967 six-day war, as increasing numbers of Palestinians from the West Bank and Gaza Strip joined the Israeli labour force. The non-citizen Palestinian workers were concentrated in a few industrial sectors and were highly segregated in a relatively small number of blue-collar and low-status occupations. The Palestinians from Gaza and the West Bank were day workers, mostly employed in construction, agriculture and services. By 1987 the number of daily commuters reached over 150 000 persons and comprised about 10 per cent of the Israeli labour force.

Following the first 'Intifada' (the Palestinian uprising in 1987) Israel enacted a policy of recruitment of foreign guest workers to replace Palestinian workers whose employment in Israel had become more problematic. Temporary guest workers from Romania, Turkey and later from China were recruited for construction; workers mostly from Thailand were brought in for agricultural jobs; and workers from the Philippines were imported for domestic services and care of the elderly. In 1987, the number of work permits issued to foreign workers by the Israeli Ministry of Labour numbered 2500, increased to 9950 in 1993 and reached over 100 000 by 1996. Along with the documented contract workers, many labour migrants from African, Latin American and several Asian and East European countries began arriving without work permits. Most of the undocumented foreign workers in Israel live in the Tel Aviv metropolitan area with very little possibility of becoming citizens.

Although non-citizen labour migrants have become an integral part of Israeli society and have established their own organizations and associations, they do not benefit from the Israeli welfare system. The foreign workers live in the poorest neighbourhoods of the city; work in the least desirable occupations; take low-paying menial jobs, quite often below the minimum wage and without any benefits. Not only do they suffer from the worst working conditions, but the undocumented are also under a constant threat of deportation. Nevertheless, similar to the experience of other labour-importing countries, labour migrants and asylum seekers (mostly from Darfur) continue to arrive, changing the ethnic composition of the Israeli labour force. Currently the number of guest workers in Israel is estimated as 200 000 (10 per cent of the Israeli labour force), half of whom are undocumented.

In recent years the number of asylum seekers, arriving mostly via Egypt, has increased markedly: from a recorded 502 in 2005 to 7703 in 2008. The issue is regarded as a 'temporary problem'. Some nationals, including Eritreans and Sudanese, are treated as deserving of asylum; others, when captured, are taken to their supposed point of entry and simply expelled, as were 122 people during June 2009. In 2008 it was planned to remove some 3000 illegal immigrants from Eilat, but an appeal to the High Court stalled the expulsion. In public discussion there is a blurring of the categories of asylum seekers and illegal labour immigrants.

AUSTRALIA

Over 40 per cent of Australians are either immigrants (24 per cent), or Australia-born with one or both parents born overseas (18 per cent). The overseas-born number 4.4 million, a majority of whom (62 per cent) have come from outside the main English speaking countries.

Like Israel, Australia had a very high intake in the immediate post-war years, its highest in per capita terms in the second half of the twentieth century – but whereas this intake more than doubled Israel's population between 1948 and 1952, the Australian intake over the same period, of a similar magnitude in numerical terms, increased the population by under 10 per cent. At only one time in Australia's history was there immigration on a scale to match Israel's intake in the period 1948–52; this occurred during the gold-rushes of the 1850s, when the population of the colony of Victoria increased sevenfold from 76 000 to 540 000.

In the more than 60 years since 1945, Australia's population tripled. The peaks in the intake were in the immediate post-war years, the late 1960s, the middle years of the 1980s and since 2003.

While Australia's years of peak intake have matched Israel's, the low points of the intake have not been as marked. In Israel the annual intake fell below 20 000 on 13 occasions, with a low of 9500 in 1986. In Australia the net annual intake since 1947 has fallen below 40 000 in only four years and below 60 000 in only 11 years.

Refugees and Selection Policy

Both countries have had a large intake of refugees since 1945, but the proportion was higher in Israel in the first decade after Independence. Australia's refugee intake was also at its peak in the post-war years, with the arrival of 170 700 displaced persons from Europe during 1947–52, compared to 199 000 refugee arrivals over the next two decades. There was, however, no open door to refugees, who had first to pass a strict selection process and in the initial post-war period accept employment as directed by government officials. In the period 1975–85, 95 000 refugees were admitted from Indo-China, most of whom came from Vietnam. Since 1985 Australia has maintained an annual humanitarian quota in the range of 11 000 to 13 000 for refugees and asylum seekers.

The problem of uninvited asylum seekers reaching the north-west of Australia in small boats (primarily from ports in Indonesia) has been a major political issue. Australia's policing of borders is perhaps the most rigid (and effective) in the western world, with an estimated 48 500 undocumented residents in Australia in 2008.

To deal with the small number of asylum seekers arriving by boat, since 1992 Australian governments (both Labor and Conservative) have developed the most draconian deterrent policies in the democratic world. These policies are rarely extended to those who arrive in Australia by air and having been admitted for a short-term visit to lodge claims for asylum. The elements of the policy have included mandatory detention of asylum seekers (including women and children) behind barbed wire and in remote locations while their claims to asylum were assessed (a process that could take up to three years). Detention centres were located inland, thousands of kilometres from major cities, and on islands off the Australian mainland, including a detention centre in Nauru. Those who were released into the community and subsequently lodged an appeal following adverse primary determination of their right to asylum were denied the right to work and to obtain welfare pending the outcome of their appeal – they survived on the support of church groups and others. While elements of the policy have been liberalized since 2005, mandatory and offshore detention remained in place in 2009.

For much of its history, while it focused on recruitment from the UK, Australia (like Israel) had difficulty in attracting sufficient numbers of immigrants and was required to invest heavily in recruitment and in providing subsidised travel. The quest for immigrants from the UK began in the 1830s and continued in times of high labour demand for 140 years. In the 1920s there were attempts to attract immigrants by the promise of cheap land, in the 1950s and 1960s government campaigns were based on the attractions of the Australian climate and £10 ($20) fares.

Australia did not have a Law of Return, but a *jus sanguinis* policy that bore similarity with Israel's criteria: where one policy was based on religion, the other was based on race (as understood at the time). Preference was particularly directed to nationals of the founding group, the British. By contrast, the peoples of Asia, Polynesia and Micronesia, Australia's immediate neighbours, were excluded, together with peoples from other parts of the world designated 'coloured'. Alongside the British, the so-called Aryan peoples of Europe were welcomed; other Europeans were barely tolerated until after World War II, when a racial policy of 'Populate or Perish' led to admittance of large numbers of low-status 'white' immigrants from southern and eastern Europe to provide unskilled labour for economic growth and the human stock to make the country more defensible should future wars in the Asian region threaten.

Responding to international currents which made overt racial discrimination unacceptable by the 1960s, Australia avoided the pariah status imposed on the South African apartheid regime, gradually repealing the discriminatory legislation which controlled the lives of the indigenous peoples and the administrative practice which denied permanent residence to 'coloured' immigrants. A high point of change was reached in 1975 with the enactment of the Racial Discrimination Act section 9(1), which made it unlawful for any person to do any act:

> involving a distinction, exclusion, restriction or preference based on race, colour, descent or national or ethnic origin which has the purpose or effect of nullifying or impairing the recognition, enjoyment or exercise, on an equal footing, of any human right or fundamental freedom in the political, economic, social, cultural or any other field of public life.

In the 1960s and 1970s Australian policy thus underwent substantial change, in contrast with the lack of change in Israel, where major regional wars and their consequences dominated life in these years. While overt racial discrimination was removed from Australian legislation, vestiges remained in immigration policy and in the treatment of Aborigines and Torres Strait Islanders. While some states passed legislation restoring land to indigenous Australians, the promise of uniform national legislation remained unfulfilled and the hoped for formal reconciliation of peoples did not eventuate.

Australia, like almost all countries of immigration, has adopted a policy which is designed to ensure that its established traditions are not altered as a consequence of immigration. Thus, applications for settlement in Australia begin with a statement of principles:

> The English language, as the national language, is an important unifying element of Australian society. Australian society is also united through the following shared values: respect for the freedom and dignity of the individual; freedom of religion; commitment to the rule of law; Parliamentary democracy; equality of men and women; a spirit of egalitarianism that embraces mutual respect, tolerance, fair play and compassion for those in need and pursuit of the public good; equality of opportunity for individuals, regardless of their race, religion or ethnic background.

Those seeking citizenship must take an oath to uphold the democratic traditions of the country and must pass a test taken in English requiring some knowledge of the country's history and culture.

There is a further element little recognized in the context of the discussion of the Australian settlement policy. One national group, has automatic right of residence in Australia, subject to health and character test: New Zealanders – citizens of another nation – need only to present their passport to gain entry and ongoing residence. No visa or selection test is involved. There are some 7 million Jews living outside Israel who have automatic right of settlement in Israel; there are over 4 million New Zealanders who have automatic right of residence in Australia, but they are, of course, not the only group entitled to permanent residence and citizenship. In 2008 there were an estimated 521 000 New Zealanders resident in Australia.

As Australia removed discriminatory racial criteria from its immigration policy it found that there was no longer a need to provide financial assistance to attract sufficient numbers in preferred immigrant categories. Indeed, the numbers seeking settlement in Australia have consistently exceeded the number of available visas. Australian governments have consequently been free to focus on developing selection criteria to maximize the economic benefit of immigration. Israel, with its priority to protect the Jewish character of the state, has been largely dependent on the operation of push factors.

A market driven change in both countries is the introduction of visas for workers admitted on a temporary basis to work in specific occupations. A major difference is that labour immigration in Israel is focused on unskilled and semi-skilled occupations, a major component of Australia's long-stay program is directed to meeting labour demand in a range of skilled occupations.

State Involvement in Immigration and Settlement

Immigration and settlement programs in Australia and Israel have been characterized by a high level of direct government involvement, but at a higher and more sustained level in Israel.

The peak of Australian government involvement was in the post-war decades. The government tightly regulated industry, supported new developments with tariffs, sent recruitment and selection teams overseas, provided on arrival accommodation for British and refugee immigrants, controlled employment placement of refugees and provided English language programs free of charge. Although some categories of immigrants were directed to work in rural areas in their first years, in the long term the great majority settled in the capital cities. There were no development towns to house immigrants on the Israeli model, although the urban centres have become increasingly segmented into immigrant and native born regions, particularly in Sydney and Melbourne with their combined population in excess of 8 million and with the overseas born comprising over 30 per cent of the total.

Since the 1970s there has been a decrease of direct state involvement in the Australian economy and in the settlement (although not selection) of immigrants, with the exception of the refugee program. The family reunion program requires support from family members and the skilled intake operates on the basis that those admitted have immediately employable skills and will establish themselves with minimal assistance from the state. There is no Australian equivalent to match the generosity of the 'basket of absorption'.

Status Hierarchies

There are hierarchies in all immigration programs. Hierarchies are based on ethnicity (or race), language, educational attainment, recognizable occupational qualifications, and cultural proximity to the dominant socio-economic groups of the host society. In the immediate post-war period the high status immigrant groups in Australia were Anglo-Celtic and northern European, more highly regarded than the immigrants recruited to fill unskilled and semi-skilled occupations from southern and eastern European countries and some countries of the Middle East, notably Lebanon and Turkey.

When immigration became possible from Asian countries the status hierarchy underwent some modification. For a time Asian immigrants were, in the eyes of many, assigned the lowest rung on the hierarchy, particularly while refugees from Indo-China dominated the intake from Asia and sparked a major debate in 1984. A broad range of Asian countries have been represented in the intake of the last two decades. Significant numbers of these immigrants have qualifications which fit them for middle-rung occupations and many have come with capital sufficient to enable purchase of housing distant from traditional immigrant suburbs. The hierarchy was further disrupted over the last decade by the association in the public mind of the threat of terrorism and Islam. Surveys indicate that there has been a shift in the status hierarchy, with the lowest ranking of immigrants from the Middle East and Muslim countries.

CONCLUSION

Immigration has posed greater challenges for Israel than Australia, which is not to downplay the major difficulties faced in Australia in the management of its large immigration program. Israel's immigration intake at its peak from 1948–52 and 1989–94 was higher than the peak intake in Australia, measured in terms of per capita and, in some years (1949, 1990), in absolute numbers.

Israel has been less selective than Australia in its Jewish intake; indeed, selectivity in its settlement program has been almost entirely limited to encouragement of immigration from specific countries rather than selection from amongst an eligible pool of applicants, given the entitlement of all Jews to settle. As a consequence, Israel has had to integrate large numbers of immigrants with very little economic resources, some national groups characterized by low educational attainment and poor employment prospects. Further, Israel has had to meet these greater challenges with a markedly less developed economy, particularly in the immediate post-war decades.

Australia's harsh asylum policies developed in the 1990s point to a similarity with Israel. In both countries there is a long-standing fear of being swamped, in Australia by uncontrolled movements of peoples from Asia, in Israel from the Arab world, most immediately from the Palestinian population resident in the occupied territories and neighbouring countries. Israel has more immediate justification of fear in the context of ongoing armed conflict. Rigid policies adopted in Israel include the denial of residence to those Palestinians who fled their homes during war (notably during 1947–48) and the prevention of family reunion. The fear of being swamped is triggered differently in the two societies and manifests itself in different policies. In Australia disproportionate reaction is triggered by the arrival of unauthorized boats. In Israel there is no short-term trigger, rather an established policy which has its origin in war and conflict of long duration.

Australia's fear of Asia no longer leads to a denial of the right of immigration – indeed, in recent years immigrants from Asian countries have made up more than 30 per cent of the intake. The issue is now one of control (and fear of the loss of control) rather than the exclusion of whole categories of people. In Israel a total ban on the right of re-settlement and settlement to Palestinians and non-Jewish immigrants from the Arab world remains in place.

The major streams of immigration to Israel have resulted from push rather than pull factors – as in the case of the waves of refugees in 1948 and years immediately following and the migration following the collapse of the Soviet Union. Since 2000 immigration has been a result of the linked factors of economic difficulty and antisemitism in South America, South Africa and Europe. Israel has, however, far from monopolized Jewish migration, even at times when the push factors were of maximal force. Thus, the United States attracted a higher proportion of immigrants with high educational qualifications from the Former Soviet Union than Israel. In recent years Australia has been the country of first choice for Jewish emigrants from South Africa.

In Australia pull factors are the key determinants. Given its attractiveness to immigrants, Australia is in a position to select carefully those best qualified to meet its immediate labour needs and it rejects more applications than it accepts. Its immigration system has become ever more market driven, with many costs transferred to the would-be immigrant. Thus applicants wishing to migrate to Australia must pay a fee for assessment of their application, entitlements of immigrants have been cut back, and new long-stay visa categories have been introduced.

In Australia, unlike Israel, those with temporary long-stay visas have the right to apply for permanent residence. This option facilitates optimal selection of permanent residents, for those with temporary visas have been able during their period of residence to provide evidence of capacity to integrate, unlike those selected overseas and without experience of Australia. Israel's denial of the option of permanent residence to labour immigrants may protect the Jewish character of the state, but it further compounds the difficulties of meeting labour demand with the best available workers. Australia's developing selection policy thus enhances the prospect of selecting 'quality' entrants, understood in terms of human capital and level of education and qualification, to meet the immediate needs of the labour market. Israel bears much higher recruitment and integration costs per settled immigrant, and immigration is less geared to optimize economic performance. Rather, it continues to focus on ethnicity as the basis for nation building, maintaining a process which once defined Australian policy.

1. Demography – trends and composition

Karin Amit, Allan Borowski and Sergio DellaPergola

Demographic forces can have profound impacts on societies – social, economic, political and environmental. This chapter focuses on international migration, a demographic force which has played a major role in shaping the societies of both Australia and Israel – two major immigrant-receiving countries.

While many countries experience population inflows of various types (for example, refugees and asylum seekers, tourists, seasonal workers, and so on), Australia and Israel are among only a handful of countries (others include, for example, the USA, Canada and New Zealand) which have long sought immigrants for permanent settlement. Their historic and contemporary imperatives for doing so, however, are quite different. These differences are reflected in the comparative analysis presented in this chapter.

Australia emerged from World War II greatly concerned, following near-invasion by Japan during the war, about the capacity of her small population to secure such a large island-continent. 'Populate or perish' was the slogan of the times. Population growth was also seen as vital for economic development and immigration was to be a major driver. In Israel's case, at the close of World War II the state was yet to be established. What existed in British Mandatory Palestine was a *yishuv*, a Jewish settlement, living among a larger Arab population. However, in order to ensure that any state established as the national Jewish home in parts of Palestine (as initially proposed by the 1917 Balfour Declaration, as provided for under the UK's 1922 League of Nations Mandate over Palestine and as voted for by the United Nations General Assembly in resolution 181 on 29 November 1947) would be viable, immigration was vital. Thus, in the case of Australia, post-war immigration variably impacted on the size and characteristics of the population of an existing nation state. In Israel's case, by contrast, immigration was a prerequisite for national existence and, rather than 'merely' impacting on an existing society, it played a major role in shaping it from the outset. In Australia the overriding policy concern was the contribution of migration to further population growth while in Israel it was migration per se in order to 'create' a population of a sufficiently viable size to ensure both the emergence of the nascent Jewish state and then its continued survival.

The focus of this chapter is upon select demographic aspects of immigration to Australia and Israel. Demographic analysis is concerned with the study of the components of population variation and change. Thus, this chapter begins by overviewing the size and growth of Australia's and Israel's populations and then, in the next section, turns to an examination of the components of population growth. In the first part of the second section the chapter focuses on the roles played by natural increase and net migration in contributing to Australian population growth. This approach to the analysis of the components of population growth, while quite common in Australian studies, would not sit completely comfortably with a comparative analysis in which Israel was taken as the departure point. Hence, both in this section and others in this chapter it is neither always possible nor appropriate to provide a comparative analysis of demographic aspects of migration to the two countries that covers completely identical dimensions.

In the third section the chapter explores the categories of immigrants who may be admitted to Australia and Israel under their migration programs. The chapter then turns to an examination of the impact of immigration on the composition of Australia's and Israel's populations. Here particular attention is given to the role of immigration in diversifying the population in terms of ethnicity and race, language and religion. Consideration is also given to the impact of immigration on the geographical distribution of the Australian and Israeli populations. The last section offers some concluding comments.

POPULATION SIZE AND GROWTH

Australia

Since the federation of six former British colonies to form the Commonwealth of Australia in 1901, Australia's population has increased more than six-fold, from 3.4 million to an estimated population of 21.78 million at the end of the March quarter 2009 (Australian Bureau of Statistics 2008a; 2009a). Indeed, Australia's population has grown each year since white settlement in 1788 with the exception of four years (Australian Bureau of Statistics 2008a; Pink 2009: 2).

Australia experienced some of the highest population growth rates during the post-World War II baby boom (1947–64). As the beginning of the baby boom began soon after the commencement of Australia's post-war migration program in 1945 and was shortly followed by the founding of the modern State of Israel in May 1948, much of the data presented in this chapter spans the period since the mid to late 1940s.

At the beginning of the baby boom the Australian population numbered 7.64 million. By the time the baby boom had ended (1965) it stood at 11.51 million. Annual population growth rates during this period ranged from a low of 1.6 per cent at the beginning of the boom to a high of 3.3 per cent. By the tail end of the baby boom, however, annual population growth rates were about 2 per cent.

Since then annual population growth rates have ranged between 1 and 2 per cent per year except for 1969, 1970 and 1971 when they were marginally above 2 per cent. Over the course of the last decade (1998–2008), annual population growth rates have averaged 1.3 per cent (Australian Bureau of Statistics 2008a).

In the most recent years, however, the annual population growth rate has increased significantly. The most recent data published by the Australian Bureau of Statistics and released in March 2010 relate to the end of the September quarter of 2009. In that year Australia's population grew by 451 900 people – a number well in excess of the resident population of the city of Canberra and the largest addition on record to the Australian population in any one year – representing a population growth rate of 2.1 per cent (Australian Bureau of Statistics 2010). This population growth rate is the peak of a broadly upward trend that began in 2005 and is the highest rate since the late 1960s/early 1970s. It was also well in excess of both the world average of 1.2 per cent and the growth rates of such countries as India, Indonesia and the UK, for example.

Israel

Like Australia, Israel has experienced rapid population growth. Indeed, Israel's population growth has been one of the fastest in the world. The total population, estimated at 805 600 at independence on 14 May 1948, grew to 2 841 000 at the end of 1968, 4 477 000 at the end of 1988, and 7 472 000 by September 2009 – an increase of eight and half times within the space of 61 years. Israel's total population annual growth rate over the six decades to 2008 was 3.8 per cent – 3.6 per cent for Jews and 4.2 per cent for Arabs and others. Between 1948 and 1960, the Jewish population grew at an annual rate of 9.2 per cent – quite a unique growth rate in a global perspective. In more recent years growth rates have settled at a lower level

– in 2008 it was 1.8 per cent – 1.6 per cent among Jews and 2.6 per cent among Arabs.

In contrast to Australia, issues of Israel's population size and growth have been at the core of political debates in a part of the world that has been the focus of an enduring and unresolved conflict. The issue of a population majority and, for that matter, the size of the Jewish majority within the State of Israel, has been of constant policy concern and a recurring theme in political discourse (DellaPergola 2003). International migration has been one of the crucial drivers of actual population change and a key focus of policy debates. Policies crucially determined the main strategy of unlimited, maximum possible, non-selective Jewish immigration, but the actual volume of immigration was more often than not determined by the external circumstances that affected Jewish communities outside of Israel rather than by Israel's own immigration policies (Friedlander and Goldscheider 1979; DellaPergola 2009a). In recent years, the higher rate of Arab population growth compared to Jewish population growth and its consequent effect on the sociocultural profile of Israeli society as well as some new types of international population movements (described later in this chapter) have led some to advocate a more coherent approach to Israel's immigration policies (Rubinstein et al. 2009).

COMPONENTS OF POPULATION GROWTH

Australia

Population growth occurs when there is an excess of births over deaths (natural increase) and/or an excess of immigrants over emigrants (net migration). Fluctuations in the rates of natural increase and net migration, in turn, cause fluctuations in population growth rates. While Australia and Israel are today among the fastest growing developed countries in the world, the scale of the contribution of natural increase and net migration to population growth in each country was different.

Since the 1940s, the contribution of natural increase to Australian population growth was generally greater than the contribution made by net migration. But net migration made a greater contribution to population growth than natural increase in 1949, 1950, 1982, 1988, 1989, 2001 and in each year since 2005. Thus, in 2007 and the year ending 31 March 2009, net migration contributed 59 per cent and 63 per cent respectively to total population growth (Borowski and Shu 1992: 2; Australian Bureau of Statistics 2008b, 2009a).

These recent sizable increases in both the size of the Australian population and its population growth rate are attributable to high fertility rates (and record low death rates) and high levels of net migration due to high immigration intake targets ('planning levels') set by the Federal Government for Australia's immigration program.

Natural increase
After World War II the Total Fertility Rate (TFR) in Australia rose each year from 2.98 babies per woman of child-bearing age in 1948 until 1961 when it peaked at 3.54. This was followed by a sharp decline to 2.88 in 1966, stabilization until the early 1970s and then a dramatic decline during the 1970s. The fertility rate fell below replacement (2.1) in 1976 (to 2.06) and at no time since then has replacement level fertility been achieved. TFR stabilized somewhat during the 1980s but resumed a more gradual decline in the 1990s. The fertility rate reached a low of 1.73 in 2001 but has increased since then. The total fertility rate was 1.97 in 2008 (the highest since 1977 when it was 2.01) and 'yielded' 296 600 births (Borowski and Shu 1992: 12; Australian Bureau of Statistics 2008c, 2009a). The recent TFR increase has been attributed to economic prosperity as well as family benefits (such as the Baby Bonus which, until January 2009, was a universal payment to mothers of newborn babies) and other supports for women in the workforce (Borowski and McDonald 2007).

While Australian fertility fluctuated, mortality rates (the number of deaths per 1000 population) have been in a state of steady decline over the 100 or so years since federation. The crude death rate, which stood at 12.2 in 1901, had declined to 7.5 by 1985 and still further to 6.4 20 years later. In the year to March 2009 there were 143 700 deaths (the highest on record) representing a standardized death rate (which eliminates the effects of the changing age structure on the population) of just over six, close to the lowest on record (Australian Bureau of Statistics 2009a).

The large excess of births over deaths indicates that Australia's population would have continued to grow, albeit at a slower rate, even in the absence of immigration.

Net migration
Compared with the contribution of natural increase to population growth, the contribution of net migration has fluctuated much more widely. For example, net migration was 149 507 in 1950, 89 090 in 1960, 111 784 in 1970, and 13 515 in 1975. Each successive year between 2005 and 2009 witnessed a marked increase in net migration. The most recent figure, for the year ending 31 March 2009, was 278 200, the largest number ever recorded although the adoption of a new definition serves to exaggerate the extent

of change (Borowski and Shu 1992; Australian Bureau of Statistics 2008d, 2009a; Markus et al. 2009: 58).

These wide fluctuations in net migration levels are due to the fact that the overall intake level of Australia's immigration program and the migrant mix (the numerical targets for each of the 'streams' or categories under which immigrants may seek admission) are established on an annual basis by the Federal Government. Many factors shape the government's decision-making in establishing these planning levels, for example, foreign policy considerations and obligations under international conventions to which Australia is a signatory. The most salient factor is the state of the economy. A recent example of this phenomenon was the announcement on 16 March 2009 by the Minister for Immigration and Citizenship, Senator Chris Evans, of a reduction of 14 per cent in the 2008–09 permanent skilled migration stream intake from 133 500 to 115 000 in view of the impact of the Global Financial Crisis (GFC).

Emigration
The important role played by immigration in the population growth of such major immigrant-receiving countries as Australia and Israel can easily mask the population flows that take place in the opposite direction, namely, emigration.

Australian statistics on emigration are based on information provided by air and ship passengers as they leave Australia and who declare their intention to depart permanently (for at least 12 months). Errors in these data arise from temporary 'departers' who actually leave permanently and permanent departers whose absence turns out to be temporary.

Over the last three or so decades the number of permanent departures has ranged from a low of 18 100 in 1985–86 (Borowski and Shu 1992) to a high of 76 923 in 2007–08. Permanent departures as a proportion of permanent arrivals was lowest in 1987–88 (14.3 per cent) and highest in 2001–02 (54.3 per cent) (Department of Immigration and Citizenship 2008a).

The Australian experience has been that, for the overseas-born, high (or low) levels of emigration have been associated with high (or low) levels of immigration two years earlier, that is, a small but significant number of immigrants choose to leave within two years of their arrival. Thus, in 2007–08, when 40.9 per cent of permanent departures were born overseas, 13.7 per cent had lived in Australia for less than two years while 69.3 per cent had resided in Australia for five years or more. The largest group of overseas-born departures were the New Zealand-born followed by the UK-born, Chinese-born, Hong Kong SAR-born and Vietnamese-born. A majority of immigrants returned to their country of birth.

Large numbers of Australian-born, including the Australian-born children of former immigrants, also emigrated. In 2007–08, 39 144 Australian-born people left permanently. The major destinations for 49.1 per cent of all Australian-born emigrants who left in 2007–08 were the UK, New Zealand or the US. The next most popular destinations were Singapore (7.6 per cent) and the United Arab Emirates (UAE) (6.1 per cent).

Emigration from Australia represents a substantial loss of human capital. Of all permanent departures in 2007–08, 65.7 per cent were employed prior to leaving. The largest group (20 042 or 39.7 per cent) were professionals, followed by managers and administrators (8651 or 17.1 per cent) and intermediate clerical, sales and service workers (6024 or 11.9 per cent) (Department of Immigration and Citizenship 2008a, 2008b).

Israel

Any meaningful analysis of the contribution of net migration to Israel's population growth, especially the high levels of immigration during the formative years of the state, must recognize the role played by international migration in the global Jewish historical experience. The main trends of world Jewish migration between 1880 and 2008 are presented in Figure 1.1. They show cyclical patterns of mobility.

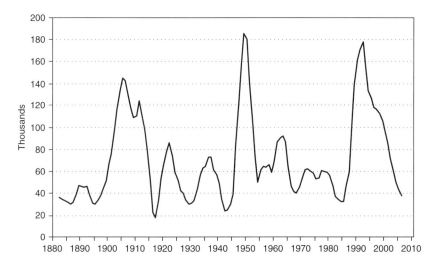

Source: DellaPergola (2009a).

Figure 1.1   World Jewish immigration, 1880–2008 – five year moving averages

Between the second-half of the nineteenth century and the beginning of the twenty-first century, over 9 million Jews moved from, to, and across many countries and continents. The scope of this movement is underscored by the world Jewish population estimates of 10.5 million in 1900, 16.5 million in 1939, 11 million in 1945 and 13.3 million in 2009 (DellaPergola 1998, 2007). The periodical ups and downs reflect major changes in political and socio-economic conditions and the sensitivity of Jewish communities to those changes. Thus, the upturns in movement were a concomitant of a significant worsening in the status of Jews relative to other citizens in the main migration sending countries fuelled by old and new anti-Semitic prejudice and rapid Jewish population growth. The consequent highly unstable and risky conditions for local Jewish populations stimulated, where feasible, large-scale emigration.

The aggregate data presented in Figure 1.1 summarize the patterns of movement of about four million Jewish migrants between 1881 and the eve of the establishment of the State of Israel in 1948, most of whom moved from Eastern Europe to the USA. They also summarize the patterns of movement since World War II, a period during which a further five million Jews migrated from a variety of countries of origin – 1.9 million between 1948 and 1968; 1 million between 1969 and 1988, and 2.1 million between 1989 and 2008. Of these, 45 per cent moved from Eastern Europe, 29 per cent from Asia and Africa, 14 per cent from Israel, and 12 per cent from Western countries. The latter include return migration of former Israeli emigrants, among them the foreign-born children of Israeli citizens who entered Israel for the first time as immigrant citizens. Overall between 1948 and 2008 Israel received 63 per cent (the majority) of the world's Jewish migrants while 37 per cent went to Western countries. Israel attracted 65 per cent of all migrants from Eastern Europe, and 74 per cent of those from Asia and Africa.

Net migration
Figure 1.2 shows the percentage contribution of net migration and net Jewish migration to Israel's total population size at various points in time. Over 3 million immigrants provided a crucial push to overall population growth, especially during the first two decades of Israel's existence and again during the early 1990s.

Migration contributed 38 per cent of Israel's total population growth while natural increase accounted for the remaining 62 per cent. Among the Jewish population the contribution of net migration was more significant and reached 45 per cent compared with 55 per cent due to natural increase. Between 1948 and 1960 migration contributed 69 per cent of total Jewish population growth, declining to 7 per cent in the 1970s, rising again to 65

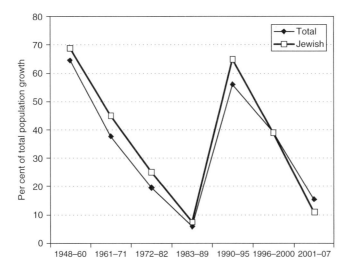

Figure 1.2   International migration balance as a percentage of total population growth, Israel 1948–2007

per cent in the early 1990s, and again declining to 11 per cent after 2000. Among Arabs and others, population growth relied almost exclusively on natural increase. The impact of immigration on Israel's non-Arab non-Jewish population mostly reflected the recent addition of non-Jewish members of immigrant Jewish households from the Former Soviet Union (FSU) – about 80 per cent of the growth over the last ten years. A modest migration inflow among the Arab population occurred in the mid-1990s following the signing of the Oslo Agreements in 1993.

Natural increase
Fertility rates in Israel have been relatively high and steady for such a highly developed country. In the mid-1990s, the TFR among Israeli Jews was 2.6, down from its highest level of 4 in 1951, and higher than among the total population of any other highly developed country. In 2008, the TFR was 2.98 while for Jews it was 2.88, 3.84 for Muslims, 2.11 for Christians, 2.49 for Druze and 1.57 for persons not classified by religion (DellaPergola 2009b). Overall Jewish fertility levels in Israel are the product of a significant lowering of the fertility of immigrants from Asia and Africa, on the one hand, and measurable increases in fertility among immigrants from Europe and America, on the other. During the 1990s and the first half of the first decade of the 2000s the Jewish TFR was quite stable, and after 2005 it tended to increase again.

The TFR among Israel's Christians, mostly ethnic Arabs, was initially similar to that of Jewish immigrants from Asia and Africa, but decreased to a level significantly lower than that of Jews standing at 2.11 in 2008. Israel's Druze started their fertility transition later, in the second-half of the 1970s, but converged to the Jewish fertility level in what seemed to become a sustained level (2.49 in 2008). Israel's Muslims were the main exception to this pattern of convergence toward the fertility of the Jewish mainstream. Their TFR was briefly above 10 during the 1960s, declined to 4.6–4.7 by the mid-1980s, and remained steady at that level thereafter until after the year 2000, passing from 4.74 in 2000 to 4.03 in 2005, and 3.84 in 2008. It is too soon to judge whether this is the beginning of a phase of convergence toward the fertility patterns of the majority. In fact nearly all of the noted fertility reduction reflects changes among the southern Bedouin sub-population, while the majority of Israel's Muslims maintain quite stable fertility patterns (DellaPergola 2009b).

Israel's mortality patterns mirrored those of the small group of highly developed countries with high life expectancies. A youthful age structure stemming from relatively high fertility and also partly reflecting past international migration (see below) in turn generated low death rates and contributed to high rates of natural increase.

Immigration

With regard to migration to Israel, Jewish immigrants arrived in a sequence of flows and waves that began at the end of the nineteenth century and has continued until the present. Semyonov and Lewin-Epstein (2003) distinguish between five major periods of immigration over this period:

1. Immigration prior to statehood (until 1948);
2. Mass immigration immediately after the establishment of the state (1949–52);
3. Intermittent migration during the following three decades (1953–59), with a significant divide in 1968 after the June 1967 war;
4. Mass immigration following the downfall of the FSU (1989–95);
5. Sporadic immigration from western countries such as Argentina, France and the USA, along with continuing and declining immigration from Ethiopia and declining immigration from the FSU – still the main component (1995–2010).

Over the course of these five periods, there were two immigration peaks. Figure 1.3 captures the rhythm of the inflow of immigrants in terms of absolute numbers and rates per 1000 inhabitants in Israel and shows

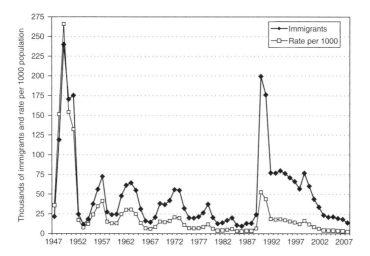

Note: *Not including immigrant citizens.

Source: Israel Central Bureau of Statistics (2008a).

*Figure 1.3   Number of immigrants and rates of immigration per 1000
                population – Israeli 1947–2008**

that these peaks were in 1949 (and still the highest on record) with about
240 000 arrivals and 1990 when almost 200 000 arrived. The burden on
the receiving society created by the first peak was much greater than that
created by the second given that, at the time of the first peak, the receiving
resident population was considerably smaller and economic conditions
were far more challenging (Bachi 1977).

Conventional wisdom has it that *aliyah* (the ascent to Zion) can be
explained primarily in ideological terms where the State of Israel, as the
main focus of global Jewish aspirations, was an ideal destination. The
broad periodic fluctuations in the number of immigrants to Israel were,
from this perspective, primarily due to varying ideological and socio-
economic pull factors. Israel's role as a major country of Jewish immigration, however, requires a more pragmatic interpretation of global Jewish
population movements.

Detailed analysis of the intensity of *aliyah* country by country reveals
the dependence of immigration on the varying incidence of negative (push)
factors in the countries of origin (DellaPergola et al. 2005; DellaPergola
2009a). Thus, an analysis of the frequency per 1000 Jews of migration
to Israel in 2001 from 73 countries with a range of political regimes
and economic standards of living revealed a strong negative correlation

(−0.66) between *aliyah* frequencies and a country's Human Development Index (HDI) in 2000. (In that year, data availability permitted the HDI ranking of 180.) Countries whose *aliyah* propensities were above the expected average were especially negative socio-economic, political and physical environments. These included all the FSU republics and, in the past, Islamic countries. Countries with lower than expected *aliyah* propensities included the leading English-speaking countries (USA, Canada, Australia) whose high standards of living deterred emigration. Most countries in Latin America also displayed migration frequencies lower than expected on the basis of societal development and HDI levels. The likely reason was the prevalence among most Jewish communities in Latin America of personal standards of living far above the average standards of the population at large.

Emigration

While a great deal of research has been devoted to immigration, much less research exists on emigration, and the measurement of the phenomenon usually relies on partial and indirect evidence. Israel's sophisticated information systems do not provide direct data on emigration, partly because such data, in the past, were based on the self-assessment of Israelis departing abroad and proved to be unreliable.

Therefore, two indirect techniques were used to assess the number of emigrants: one is the follow-up of people who left but did not return after several years, while the other deducts the number of emigrants from the balance of incoming and outgoing residents after factoring in the number of new immigrants. The latter estimate accurately captures trends over time (Figure 1.4).

Like Australia, Israel experienced significant emigration either back to the country of origin or to a third country. While emigration closely trailed Israel's immigration cycles, the ratio of emigrants to immigrants was proportionately smaller in comparison with Australia and other major immigrant-receiving countries.

The main factor explaining emigration is economic downturn. While the number of emigrants has fluctuated, it remained between 5000 and 20000 per year for most of the last 60 years. Given the rapidly expanding population, this meant a general decline in the rate of emigration per 1000 residents (DellaPergola 2009a).

It is of interest to note that in contemporary Israeli society emigrants are much less devalued than in the past. The popular Hebrew term for emigration is *yerida* or going down/descending. It used to be a term with strong negative connotations, however, emigration is now much more accepted as 'normal', just as it is in Australia and many other liberal democracies.

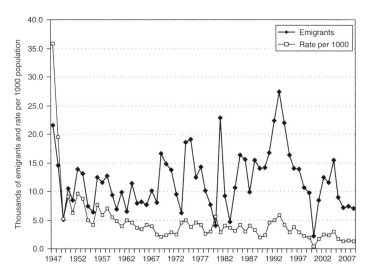

Note: *Computed as the difference between total migration balance and total immigrants.

Source: Israel Central Bureau of Statistics (2008a).

Figure 1.4 *Number of emigrants and rates of emigration per 1000 population – Israel 1947–2008**

CATEGORIES OF IMMIGRANTS

Australia

The Commonwealth of Australia was created in 1901 with a constitution that conferred powers to control immigration, citizenship and 'races other than Aborigines' on the national government. Thus, from its very outset, the new Commonwealth had clear views about what constitutes the 'preferred immigrant'. In common with other immigrant-receiving countries, these views changed over time and involved preferred categories of immigrants based on such factors, for example, as race (until the 1970s), country of origin/ethnicity and skill. Among the most significant changes that took place over the course of the last decade or so has been a widening in these views to include people who, on the face of it at least, had no intention of permanently settling in Australia. Another has been the emergence of a very marked preference for skilled migration over family reunion. The expression of these various and changing preferences over the history of Australia's migration program resulted in a 'population that has been planned and engineered to a greater extent than is true for almost anywhere else' in the world (Jupp 2007: 16).

Australia's program of immigration is comprised of the 'Migration Program' and the 'Humanitarian Program'. The Migration Program is comprised of three streams – the Family Stream, the Skill Stream and Special Eligibility migrants. The Family Stream consists of a number of visa categories under which a potential migrant (for example, spouse, fiancé/fiancée, child, parent meeting the 'balance of family' test, and so on) can be sponsored by a relative who is either an Australian citizen or a permanent resident. The Skill Stream, which is designed to contribute to Australia's economic growth, consists of a number of visa categories for skilled workers (and their dependants) where there is a demand for particular occupational skills, outstanding talents or business skills. The small Special Eligibility category caters for other types of visaed settler arrivals within the Migration Program that are not included in the Family or Skill Streams.

The considerably smaller Humanitarian Program comprises an off-shore component for the resettlement of people who are overseas, and an onshore component for people who are already in Australia and who seek Australia's protection. The majority of those who enter Australia under the Humanitarian Program are refugees referred by the UN High Commissioner for Refugees. However, the offshore component also pro-vides for people outside their home country who are subject to substantial discrimination amounting to gross violation of their human rights in their home country and who are proposed or sponsored by an Australian citizen or organization (the Special Humanitarian Program).

In addition to the Migration and Humanitarian Programs, New Zealand citizens can enter Australia under the Trans-Tasman Travel Agreement. Persons can also be approved for entry on temporary basis as a student, a temporary resident (including as a skilled sponsored employee for between three months and four years under the 457 visa scheme) and visitors (Department of Immigration and Citizenship 2008c).

As noted above, one of the most significant developments in the migra-tion program since 1998 was the shift in the balance between immigrants entering Australia under the Family Stream and those entering under the Skill Stream. The Liberal–National Party Coalition Government under Prime Minister John Howard took power in March 1996 after 14 years of Labor Party rule. In that year, nearly 69 per cent of admissions were in the Family Stream and only 29 per cent in the Skill Stream. By 2001–02, the proportions were 57 per cent in the Skill Stream and only 41 per cent in the Family Stream (Jupp 2007: 156). Today the balance between the major migration categories is the complete reverse of the situation when the Howard Government took office. Thus, the planning levels for 2008–09 Migration Program allocated 70 per cent of places to skilled migrants, which is the highest on record (Department of Immigration and Citizenship 2008d). This shift was driven by a boom in job creation for skilled workers and the inability to fill these skilled occupations within Australia.

International students
Educating overseas students is worth about AUS$15.5 billion to the Australian economy. It is Australia's third largest export behind coal and iron ore (Healy 2009). In the year ending September 2008, there were 494 507 enrolments by full-fee international students in Australia on a student visa, an increase of 20 per cent over the same period in 2007. These students were enrolled across vocational education and training, higher education, schools and ELICOS (English Language Intensive Courses for Overseas Students) sectors (Australian Education International 2008).

International students are an important source of migration under the Skill Stream. In 2005–06, for example, 13 698 Skill Stream visas were issued to former international students who had completed their professional studies at an Australian university. Indeed, since 1999 applications from such students have been privileged through being granted an additional five points in the points-tested Skill Stream visa category and, since 2001, being permitted to apply for permanent residence onshore provided they did so no later than six months after graduation (Birrell and Healy 2008: 2).

Temporary skilled labour migration
Discussion of Australia's immigration program would also be incomplete without reference to temporary labour migration. Not only is temporary migration of *skilled* workers a relatively recent phenomenon reflecting a seismic shift, historically speaking, in the views of what constitutes a preferred immigrant but these migrants are also sizable in number and a significant source, like international students, of onshore changes in visa status to permanent residency.

During the 1990s a shortage of health professionals, engineers, accountants and IT experts emerged. The 457 visa – an employer-sponsored visa category for temporary skilled workers – served as the vehicle for admitting these professionals to Australia for up to four years. Over time, however, as labour shortages became more acute, this same regime was used to accommodate a dramatic growth in the number of foreign workers across an increasingly diverse range of occupations, including quite moderately skilled ones.

The development of a 'guest worker' system had long been rejected in Australia. Thus, the growth in temporary labour migration represents a major policy change in the history of the Australian immigration program.

Large numbers of foreign workers have been admitted as temporary labour migrants. According to Hart (2007), by the end of 2006, 390000 temporary skilled migrants had been brought to Australia under the 457 scheme. Like the immigration program overall, the number of temporary labour migrants entering Australia has increased rapidly over the last few years. Thus, in 2005–06 and 2006–07 the numbers of principal applicants (that is, exclusive of dependants) visaed under the temporary entry 457 visa program were 39530 and 46680 respectively. In 2007–08 this figure was 58050. The 'stock' of 457 visa workers in Australia in December 2008 was 82500 (Birrell et al. 2009). These large inflows were facilitated by the less stringent English proficiency requirements for 457 visa-holders and the absence of labour market testing (the requirement for an employer to demonstrate that a job vacancy could not be filled locally at market wage rates and conditions).

In common with the experience of many other countries that have introduced temporary labour migration programs, temporary labour migration to Australia has served as a pathway to permanent settlement. Thus, about 90 per cent of the 17760 permanent migrants (principal applicant and accompanying visas) who were sponsored by an employer onshore during 2007–08 were 457 visa holders at the time of application (Birrell et al. 2009: 5).

Recent government initiatives will serve to reduce the temporary labour migrant intake through tightening the temporary skilled labour migration program. Changes announced in April 2009 by the Minister for Immigration and Citizenship provided for 457 visa-holders to earn the same wage as local workers (a market-based minimum of at least AUS $45221 from 1 July 2009), a lift in the standard of English to that required of applicants under the permanent skilled migration program and tougher requirements for employers seeking to bring in foreign workers to prove they are committed to training and hiring local workers (Berkovic 2009). These changes were ostensibly designed to protect foreign workers from exploitation and to ensure that local wages and conditions were not undercut, although reducing competition for jobs in a deteriorating labour market was, most likely, also a salient consideration.

Illegal migration

In some countries, such as the USA, illegal immigrant numbers are substantial and a great source of concern to policy-makers and the public alike. While Australia also has illegal immigrants, the number is relatively small. Thus, at 30 June 2008 there were an estimated 48 500 people who were unlawfully in Australia by virtue of having either overstayed their visas or breached their visa conditions. (Department of Immigration and Citizenship 2008e).

But it is not these illegal immigrants that arouse the greatest public concern in Australia. Rather, it is the unannounced arrival by boat into Australia's northern waters of relatively small numbers of asylum seekers that generates the greatest concern. During the first ten months of 2009 36 boats with 1828 people arrived (Grattan and Murdoch 2009). While seeking asylum is not illegal, the political debate that is stirred up by such arrivals, arrivals which are typically facilitated by Indonesian people smugglers, often conflates illegal immigrants with asylum seekers. The number of asylum seekers who arrive by boat is only a small fraction (4 per cent in 2008) of the total number of onshore asylum seekers. (Steketee 2009).

Israel

Israel does not have an immigration program comprised of different categories of immigrants who need to meet multiple selection criteria with target numbers set by the government. However, like Australia, Israel has clear notions about what it regards as the preferred immigrant. While in the 1990s both countries introduced temporary labour migration programs, Israel's focus has been on unskilled temporary labour migrants while Australia's has been on skilled ones.

In contrast to migration to Australia and, indeed, the migration of Jews to other parts of the world, the migration of Jews to Israel can be characterized as a returning Diaspora, a peculiar albeit not entirely unique feature within the general framework of international population movements.

Although Israel served for more than 2000 years as the religious–cultural homeland for the Jewish people, very few Jews lived in the land of Israel prior to the twentieth century. At the turn of the twentieth century when the Zionist movement was established, less than 1 per cent of the Jewish people lived in Israel. In 2009, 61 years after the establishment of the state of Israel, about 42 per cent of the world Jewish population lived in Israel, about 40 per cent in the USA, and 18 per cent in other countries (DellaPergola 2008).

Israel as a home for the Jewish people was and remains a central tenet of her Declaration of Independence and social ethos (Borowski and Yanay 1997: 496). As a centre for a returning Diaspora, Israel encourages immigration of Jews. There is no limit to the numbers that may be admitted.

Immigration of non-Jews is not formally discouraged but is dealt with under separate legislation. According to the 1950 Law of Return and 1952 Law of Nationality, every Jew has a right to settle in Israel and can claim and obtain citizenship upon arrival, including children and grandchildren of Jews and their respective spouses, regardless of religious identity. Only minor and mostly nominal limitations are specified on health and security grounds. In consequence, immigrants to Israel, apart from being overwhelmingly Jewish, have often been much more heterogeneous than those who settle in countries which, like Australia, employ such selection criteria as educational attainment, skill, language proficiency and age.

Newcomers to Israel are not referred to as immigrants but as *olim* – a term with a strong positive connotation meaning, as noted earlier in this chapter, people who have *gone up* or *ascended*. A government ministry is responsible for immigrant issues and settlement. It seeks to facilitate the successful integration of new immigrants into Israeli society. Furthermore, as the homeland of the Jewish people, the government of Israel, together with the Jewish Agency for Israel, sees itself as responsible for rescuing Jewish communities at risk. Entire Jewish communities were thus transferred to Israel, for example, the Jews of Yemen and Iraq soon after Israel's independence and, more recently, the Ethiopian Jewish community.

Temporary and illegal labour migration

Israel's experience of temporary labour migration is about a decade longer than Australia's and its negative social 'fallout' has been much greater. Until the Six Day War of June 1967, Israel remained self-sufficient in her labour requirements, a situation that accorded with one of the major precepts of modern Zionism. And from then until late 1987 when the first Palestinian Intifada (uprising) began, unskilled labour shortages were substantially met by Palestinians who commuted on a daily basis from the Gaza Strip and the West Bank to Israel proper. However, the wave of murderous terrorist attacks on Israeli civilians unleashed by the Intifada resulted in periodic border closures. In pursuit of more 'reliable' sources of unskilled labour, attention turned to importing foreign workers from outside the Middle East. For the first time in Israel's modern history, alongside the flows of Jewish immigrants from the FSU and Ethiopia, an increasing number of non-Jewish (and non-Palestinian) immigrants (albeit supposedly temporary) began, for the first time, to arrive in significant numbers (Raijman and Kemp 2010). This process accelerated in the wake of the spate of Palestinian terrorist attacks that followed the signing of the Oslo Peace Accords in September 1993.

Documented labour migrants came to Israel from various source countries. At the beginning of the 1990s about 60 per cent were from Eastern Europe (Romania and Turkey) and 30 per cent were from Asia (China, Philippines and Thailand). However, by 2004 only 20 per cent of the labour migrants came from Eastern Europe, with the majority coming from Asia.

Three main sectors employ the majority of documented labour migrants: 28 per cent work in construction (mainly from Romania, China, Turkey and the FSU), 27 per cent work in agriculture (mainly from Thailand), and 45 per cent are employed in the nursing service sector (mainly from the Philippines). Other documented labour migrants work in other industries and in restaurants and hotels (mainly from Africa) (Raijman 2009). The shifts in both the sending counties and sectors of employment are related to governmental decisions on foreign worker quotas for the different sectors.

According to the Israel Central Bureau of Statistics (2008a), there were 186 000 labour migrants in Israel in 2006 and, in contrast to Australia's temporary labour migrants, they are a significant part (9 per cent) of the total Israeli workforce. While they have helped to meet the unskilled labour shortages, they have also raised a number of challenges for Israel. For example, students of immigration have long known that illegal immigration is a natural by-product of legal immigration, whether permanent or temporary. Since only half of the 186 000 labour migrants have work permits, Israel's labour migrants are seen by many as undermining the rule of law. The Israeli-born children of undocumented workers have also presented new legal challenges to Israeli society, including the issue of citizenship. Some Israeli commentators also see labour migrants as threatening the character of Israeli society. And many labour migrants have come to view their supposedly temporary sojourn in Israel as, not unexpectedly, permanent. There are well-established communities of African, Latin-American and Filipino communities of mostly undocumented labour migrants in Tel Aviv. This led the Israeli government to establish an Immigration Police Unit in 2002 charged with apprehending and deporting undocumented labour migrants.

Refugees and asylum seekers
Israel, like Australia, has become a safe-haven destination for refugees and asylum seekers. Most are escaping from man-made disasters – wars and political uprisings – in Africa. Non-Jewish refugees seeking asylum in Israel is a new phenomenon. Whereas Australia's asylum seekers mainly arrive by air and some by boat via Indonesia, those seeking asylum in Israel cross the porous Sinai border with Egypt into Israel. The exact numbers are unknown but the estimates range from between 13 000 and

17000 people, most of whom are from Southern Sudan and Eritrea. The Israeli government allows some to remain temporarily but restricts them to living in select parts of the country. They may only live in the Northern and Southern parts of Israel. However, most of the refugees find their way to the centre of Israel (mainly Tel Aviv) and obtain support from NGOs.

EFFECTS OF IMMIGRATION ON POPULATION COMPOSITION

Australia

Prior to 1945 Australia prided itself on being 90 per cent British and 98 per cent white. Since that time Australia has moved from being a British-oriented society to a highly diverse, multicultural one that selects citizens from all over the world (Jupp 2008: 21). In the course of this transition Australia, like other immigrant-receiving countries, has had to face the challenge of developing a stable political community amidst growing ethnic, linguistic, religious and regional diversity (Kymlicka 2003). Managing this diversity has required conscious state policies. Since the beginning of the post-war immigration program these policies have shifted from policies of assimilation, to policies of integration, to policies of multiculturalism (Borowski 2000) and, in the last years of the Howard Government, back to a semblance of integration policies.

These policies and their shifts are explored elsewhere in this volume. Here we seek to trace the evolution of the diversity of the Australian population, with a focus on the period since the 1940s, and to describe some select dimensions of difference in Australian society, namely, immigrants' country/region of origin, country of birth and language, and religion.

Country/region of origin

Since 1945 6.8 million people came to Australia with a view to permanent residence (Department of Immigration and Citizenship 2008e). A distinguishing characteristic of Australia's immigration program (and Israel's) was that immigrant inflows came in waves from particular countries and regions. These waves of movement occurred in response to changes in Australia's immigration policy and changing economic and political conditions in immigrants' countries of origin.

The UK and Ireland had always been the major source of immigrants to Australia both in absolute numbers and as a proportion of all immigrant settlers. The active encouragement of non-British European immigrants began under Labor Immigration Minister Arthur Calwell in 1947

(Richards 2008). Thus, in the immediate post-war period, large numbers of displaced persons from Poland, Yugoslavia and the Baltic States came to Australia. Large numbers of Dutch, German, Greek and Italian immigrants were also admitted, with a preference for Northern Europeans. By the 1950s and 1960s, the proportion of immigrants contributed by the UK had declined to around half of all immigrants. Europe remained the major source of immigrants until the abandonment of the White Australia Policy in the 1970s, after which the proportion of immigrants from Asia began to grow steadily.

Immigrants from Asia compromised about 10 per cent of the immigrant intake in 1972, over 40 per cent in 1984, 51 per cent in 1991 and averaged around 39 per cent during the time of the Howard Government (1996–2007) (Jupp 2007: 31). Immigrants from Asia accounted for 42 per cent of all immigrants in 2007–08 while those from Europe, sub-Saharan Africa and North Africa and the Middle East accounted for 20.6 per cent, 7.1 per cent and 5.5 per cent respectively. While the UK and Ireland continue their historic role as major source countries of immigrants, the proportion of immigrants contributed by these countries is considerably lower than in past decades. Thus, in 2007–08 the major source countries were New Zealand (18.5 per cent), the UK (15.6 per cent), India (10.3 per cent), China (8.7 per cent) and the Philippines (4.1 per cent) (Department of Immigration and Citizenship 2008e).

Country of birth and language
At federation in 1901, 23 per cent of the Australian population was overseas-born, mainly in the UK and Ireland. By 1947 this proportion of overseas-born had declined to 10 per cent. At the 2006 Census, however, this proportion was again almost one in four (24 per cent); 26 per cent of people born in Australia had at least one overseas-born parent; 16 per cent of the population spoke a language other than English at home with the top five 'other' languages being, in descending order, Italian, Greek, Cantonese, Arabic and Mandarin (Roth 2007).

Religion
Religion is another important dimension of difference in immigrant-receiving societies. Unlike the USA (where the collection of such data is prohibited) and UK, for example, Australia has collected census data on religion for well over 150 years, although the religion question is optional and about a quarter of all Australians either do not answer it or answer 'No Religion'.

At the beginning of the twentieth century, Christianity was the predominant religion, peaking at 96.9 per cent in 1921 (Australian Human

Rights Commission 2008). Until as recently as the 1970s, most Australians claimed to subscribe to Christian denominations. With the abolition of the White Australia policy and the consequent changes in the mix of immigrants, the variety and numbers of non-Christian religions rapidly increased. Non-British varieties of Christianity increased due to European migration, strengthening in particular the various national Orthodox churches (for example, Greek, Russian). The number of Catholics also increased by non-British migration. The previous numerical domination of the Anglicans, Methodists and Presbyterians has declined while the Irish-descent element among Catholics has become less important.

The most dramatic changes that have taken place in religious identification are for non-European, non-Christian religions. Census data indicates that in 2006 the top four non-Christian religions were Buddhism (419 000 adherents or 2.1 per cent of Australia's population), Islam (340 000, 1.7 per cent), Hinduism (148 000, 0.7 per cent) and Judaism (88 000, 0.4 per cent). These four non-Christian religions combined represented 5 per cent of the population; 63.9 per cent of the population identified as Christians – 25.8 per cent as Catholics, 18.7 per cent as Anglicans and 19 per cent as adherents of other Christian denominations. Despite the continued dominance of Christianity, there is no doubt that Australia has become religiously multicultural (Jupp 2003; Roth 2007).

Geographic distribution
The Australian population is concentrated in two coastal regions, the larger of which lies in the south-east and east of the country. The smaller is in south-west Australia. The population is especially concentrated in the State and Territory capital cities where 64 per cent of the population resides. Indeed, between 1996 and 2006 when Australia's population grew at an average rate of 1.2 per cent, the population of the major cities grew at an annual rate of 1.6 per cent, mainly at the expense of outer regional areas (Australian Bureau of Statistics 2008d).

In Australia, international migrants settle disproportionately in certain states and locations within those states, notably the capital cities. New South Wales has always been the preferred state for settlement. In 2005–06 one-third of immigrants (35.8 per cent) intended to settle in that state. Victoria has been the next most popular destination followed by either Queensland or Western Australia.

The preferred settlement destinations also vary by the type of visa category under which immigrants enter Australia. Thus, while New South Wales and Victoria were the preferred destination for most Family Stream visa-holders, these two states also take the majority of Humanitarian Program and Special Eligibility entrants. In contrast, immigrants entering

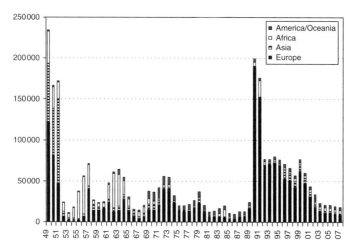

Source: Israel Central Bureau of Statistics (2008a).

Figure 1.5 *Immigration to Israel by year and continent of origin, 1948–2007*

under the Skills Stream's Employer Nomination Scheme were more evenly spread with Victoria ranked as the fifth most popular intended destination after New South Wales, Western Australia, Queensland and South Australia (Walmsley et al. 2007).

Israel

Countries of origin

Yearly migration flows by continent of origin since the establishment of the Israeli state are presented in Figure 1.5. The shifts in immigrants' continents of origin yielded changes in the social and ethnic composition of Israeli society.

 In Israel a distinction is often made between Jews who originated from African or Asian (AA) countries (mostly *Sephardim*) and Jews from European or American (EA) countries (mostly *Ashkenazim*). This dichotomy is clearly an oversimplification given the origins of many of Israel's Jews in tens of different countries. Empirically, however, the latter group was characterized by higher socio-economic status than the former group in almost every aspect of social stratification including education, occupational status, income, wealth and standard of living. As will become evident below, these socio-economic differences were rooted, at least in part, in the national contexts from which the flows of a *returning Diaspora* originated. The following discussion employs the five-period classification of Semyonov and Lewin-Epstein (2003), discussed at the beginning of the chapter.

The first wave of migration to Palestine before the establishment of the State of Israel came mostly from Central and East European countries at the turn of the twentieth century and during the inter-war period. These migrants included a Zionist ideological segment whose motivation was to establish a homeland for the Jewish people. These early immigrants, to a large extent, established the political, economic and civil institutions of the state-to-be and occupied a large share of the upper echelons of the social, cultural and economic institutions and constituted the elite of the newly founded state.

The second wave of immigration included immigrants who arrived immediately after the establishment of the State. This wave was characterized by a massive inflow of refugees from Muslim countries in the Middle East and North Africa, along with European survivors of the *Shoah* (Holocaust). During the first five years after independence, the Jewish population of Israel more than doubled, from 600000 to over 1.5 million people (Hacohen 2003). The combination of mass heterogeneous immigration with a scarcity of resources had a significant effect on the socio-economic achievements of these immigrants.

The consequences of this period are still evident today, even among the second and third immigrant generations. Research shows that the integration of European immigrants and their sons and daughters was much more successful, or at least more rapid, than the integration of Asian and North African immigrants and their offspring (for example, Ben-Rafael 1982; Semyonov 1996; Cohen and Haberfeld 2003; Amit 2005; DellaPergola 2007).

Immigration during the third period, the years 1953 to 1989, was quite intermittent and mostly a result of political, economic and social events in the immigrants' countries of origin. For example, the decolonization process in North Africa generated a massive departure of Jews from the Maghreb, Egypt and Libya. Periods of political unrest in Eastern European countries also opened the way to significant Jewish emigration from Poland, Hungary, Romania and Czechoslovakia. The Iranian revolution and political unrest in South Africa and Argentina were followed by waves of Jewish immigrants from these countries. Likewise, changes in emigration restrictions led to a significant increase in the number of immigrants from the FSU. In this period the rate of integration of immigrants into Israeli society was high.

A major turning point in immigration to Israel came at the end of 1989. Following the fall of the Berlin Wall and the beginning of the break-up of the Soviet Union, a sudden liberalization occurred in formerly restrictive emigration policies and a massive wave of emigrants began from the FSU. Israel was the primary viable destination for these Jewish emigrants. As a result, Israel – a country of 4.5 million in 1989 – was faced with about one million immigrants during the subsequent years, 400 000 of whom arrived in 1990 and 1991.

The overwhelming majority of these immigrants were of Jewish ancestry but increasing proportions of non-Jewish family members also arrived as immigrants. Most of the these immigrants had academic and professional degrees; most experienced downward occupational mobility upon arrival but considerable upward occupational and economic mobility with the passage of time (Raijman and Semyonov 1998).

At the same time, immigrants from Ethiopia also arrived, many of whom were rescued in two major airlifts. In 2008, about 115 000 Ethiopian immigrants and their offspring lived in Israel. Their socio-economic attainment was still very low and they faced severe difficulties in adjusting and integrating into Israeli society (Semyonov et al. 2007).

After 1995, when the massive stream of immigrants from the FSU substantially weakened, immigrants to Israel arrived from Western and economically developed countries, mostly from the USA, France and Argentina. About 85 000 immigrants came between 1990 and 2007 (Israel Central Bureau of Statistics 2007). They were, for the most part, highly educated and skilled. The immigrants from North America and France were mostly ideologically and religiously motivated (Amit and Riss 2007). In the case of France, a strong push factor was the rising anti-Semitism related to the growing Islamization of the country. For immigrants from Argentina, the push factor was the political and economic crisis of 1999–2002 (Schenkolewski-Kroll 2004; Dgani and Dgani 2004).

Data from the latest *Labour Force Survey* (2007) conducted by the Israeli Central Bureau of Statistics (2008b) and using a representative sample of the Israeli population aged 15 years and over permit further exploration of the demographic characteristics of Jewish immigrants in Israel. We first looked at the distribution of surviving immigrants according to the five-period classification of Semyonov and Lewin-Epstein (2003), by seven main origin groups: Jews from Arab countries, North Africa, Ethiopia, FSU, East Europe, Western Europe and USA. We used a more elaborated classification of origin groups than the common continent classification.

In the first period (up until 1947), most of the immigrants (about 84 per cent) came from Europe (East and West). In the second period (1948–1952), just after the establishment of the Israeli State, immigrants came from Arab countries and from Europe (East and West) in portions that are more similar. The majority (about 76 per cent) of North African

immigrants came to Israel in the third period (1953–88) as well as a significant portion of immigrants from the FSU (about 14 per cent of the FSU
immigrants) and Western countries (about 46 per cent of the Westerners).
In the fourth period (1989–95), most of the immigrants came from the
FSU (about 71 per cent of the immigrants in that period) but a relatively
high number of immigrants came from Ethiopia; about 45 per cent of
Ethiopian immigrants arrived at that time. In the fifth period (1996–2007),
the immigration from the FSU continued and comprised about 74 per
cent of all immigrants in that period, but the second significant immigrant
group was those coming from Western countries (about 16 per cent).

Demographic and socio-economic characteristics
What were the demographic characteristics of the immigrants coming in
the different periods? This question can be answered by examining Table
1.1 which presents the major demographic characteristics of immigrants
who came in each period, and survived and remained in Israel up to 2007.
This table also provides comparable information for the Israeli-born (Jews
and Arabs). Comparing the immigrant sample to the Israeli-born, on
average the surviving immigrants were older than Israeli-born (54 versus
35 per cent), had a lower percentage of males (45 versus 51), had a higher
percentage of married couples (56 versus 50), lived more often in development towns (13 versus 7) and were more likely to have an academic degree
(24 versus 17).

However, there were differences between immigrants arriving in different periods. The sample of immigrants for the first period (up to 1947) is
less representative, given the impact of mortality on an aged group. As
to be expected, the sample includes a lower percentage of males; 99 per
cent of them were Jewish, 39 per cent were married, 11 per cent had an
academic degree and only 1 per cent lived in a development town. These
immigrants came to Israel very young, on average at the age of 15.

Immigrants who came in the second period, after Statehood, resembled
the immigrants in the previous period in the average age at migration and
in the proportion Jewish. However, these immigrants were less educated
and about 6 per cent of them lived in development towns. Immigrants
arriving in the third period were older upon arrival (21) and were significantly more educated (21 per cent with an academic degree). Nearly
14 per cent of them lived in a development town. Immigrants arriving in
the fourth period came, on average, at the age of 32, a significantly older
age than in the former periods. These immigrants were better educated (33
per cent with an academic degree) and the percentage of non-Jews was significantly higher (about 10 per cent). Nearly 17 per cent of them lived in a
development town. In the last period, the age at migration was higher still

Table 1.1 Demographic characteristics of surviving immigrants, by period of immigration – 2007*

Periods of immigration	N	Average age	% male	% Jews	% married	% in development towns	Age at migration	Years of schooling	% with academic degree
1. Up to 1947	2222	79.1 (6.6)	38.1	98.7	39.4	1.4	15.4 (8.6)	10.6 (4.4)	11.1
2. 1948–52	5834	69.6 (9.3)	46.9	99.2	61.6	6.2	14.8 (10.3)	9.5 (4.9)	8.9
3. 1953–88	11577	56.76 (16.0)	44.9	97.1	65.2	13.9	20.9 (15.6)	11.9 (4.9)	21.2
4. 1989–95	11134	44.3 (7.20)	46.6	91.1	48.2	16.8	31.8 (20.1)	13.1 (3.7)	32.6
5. 1996–07	6067	43.2 (18.5)	41.2	78.8	52.3	14.6	36.4 (18.4)	13.0 (3.9)	30.5
Total immigrants	36834	54.1 (20.1)	44.7	92.7	55.8	12.9	25.4 (18.4)	12.0 (4.6)	23.6
Israeli-born	59745	34.9 (15.5)	50.9	74.8	50.0	7.4	–	12.1 (4.1)	16.5

Note: * Numbers in parenthesis are standard deviations.

Source: Israel Central Bureau of Statistics (2008b).

Table 1.2   Demographic characteristics of surviving immigrants, by origin groups – 2007*

Characteristics	Country of origin						
	Arab countries[a]	North Africa	Ethiopia	Former Soviet Union	East Europe	Western Europe, America	Israeli-born
Average age	63.7	60.7	34.6	48.6	69.9	49.9	34.9
	(14.5)	(11.6)	(17.6)	(20.0)	(14.1)	(20.7)	(15.5)
% male	47.9	47.1	45.8	43.8	40.7	46.2	50.9
% Jews	94.2	99.8	95.6	88.2	97.6	95.4	74.8
% married	64.4	71.6	37.8	54.4	53.5	57.7	50.0
% in development towns	6.1	23.1	19.6	15.6	5.5	8.6	7.4
Age at migration	15.7	15.7	21.6	33.2	22.8	22.7	–
	(12.6)	(12.5)	(16.9)	(19.6)	(15.8)	(16.7)	
Years of schooling	9.2	9.9	7.3	13.2	11.5	14.2	12.1
	(5.1)	(4.8)	(5.4)	(3.4)	(4.5)	(3.9)	(4.1)
% with academic degree	8.4	7.7	2.4	33.7	18.0	33.6	16.5
N	3 722	4 210	1 163	15 350	5 102	4 719	59 745

Notes:

* Numbers in parenthesis are standard deviations.
[a] Not including North Africa.

Source: Israel Central Bureau of Statistics (2008b).

(36) and the level of education was high. These more recent immigrants also included a higher proportion of non-Jews (over 21 per cent).

Table 1.2 presents the demographic characteristics of surviving immigrants from different origin groups. The youngest immigrant group was Ethiopian whose average age was quite similar to the average age of the Israeli-born (35). The older immigrants came from East Europe (70), Arab countries (64) and North Africa (60). But the immigrants from the FSU were older than all other groups upon arrival (33 in comparison to 15–22 in the other groups). The percentage of males was a little lower than 50 per cent for all immigrant groups. Immigrants from the FSU had a higher percentage of non-Jews (12 per cent in comparison to less than 5 per cent for the other immigrant groups). The group with the highest proportion in development towns was the North African (23 per cent), followed by Ethiopian (20 per cent) and FSU (16 per cent).

After 1953, as part of a policy of population dispersion, immigrants were directed to development towns in the north and south of Israel. Most North African immigrants came during the third period (1953–88) and were directed to these towns. In addition, immigrants from Ethiopia and the FSU who came after 1989 were also located in these towns due to the lower cost of housing.

Geographical distribution

Data drawn from the 1995 Census provides evidence on the process of immigrant distribution. Different experiences of the various immigrant groups reflected both Israel's initial settlement policies and subsequent patterns of mobility. Both of these factors operated very differently over the course of the various periods of Israel's immigration history. Census data disaggregated into secondary administrative regions called *Nafot* (or sub-districts) makes it possible to establish detailed patterns of concentration for immigrants from each country of origin.

The strongest tendencies to concentrate in a given sub-district – indicated by ratios of three or more times the national average for a given group – appeared among immigrants from India, Pakistan, Uzbekistan, Georgia in the central sub-district of Ramle (the latter also in Ashkelon); from Libya in the Sharon sub-district (including the city of Netanya); from Iraq in Ramat Gan; from Bulgaria and Greece in Holon; from North America, Australia and New Zealand in Judea, Samaria and Gaza as well as in the Golan Heights (the areas occupied by Israel during the 1967 Six Day War) and in Jerusalem; and from France in Judea, Samaria and Gaza.

CONCLUSION

As two among only a handful of liberal democracies which have long sought immigrants for permanent settlement, immigration to Australia and Israel has been very substantial over the course of the last six decades. Figure 1.6 compares the numbers of immigrants to the two countries between 1947 and 2008 and finds interesting similarities and differences. In both cases, the inflow of immigrants has been subject to significant annual variation. In both cases, the post-World War II period and the late 1980s– early 1990s were times of major immigration intake. But with the exception of these two peak periods Australia has received more immigrants than Israel and has experienced two further peaks, one around 1970 and one still developing in 2008. The latter increase is in contrast with the more recent decrease in immigration to Israel.

Immigration has deeply marked the demographic growth, economic development and social history of both countries and its direct impact

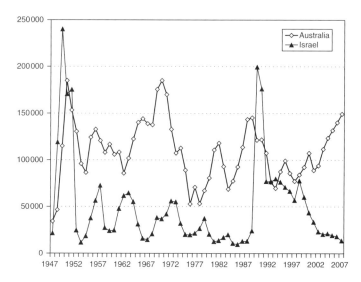

Figure 1.6   Immigrants to Australia and Israel, 1947–2008

is evident in the current population composition. Emigration from both countries has in part been a lagged response to previous immigration, but Israel has had a higher retention rate. Both countries have shared a concern over the loss of highly educated workers.

However, the imperatives driving immigration 'programs', conceptions of the preferred immigrant and, related to both, the scope (relative to the size of their resident populations) of immigration have been quite different. In consequence, although immigrants have played a major role in shaping the societies of both countries, their influence on Israel has been much more profound. As far as the immigrants themselves are concerned, pull factors have played a more salient role among Australia's immigrants than push factors while the reverse has been true for Israel, despite widely held assumptions about the special place of Israel in the hearts and minds of Jews as the Jewish homeland. The 'strength' of the push factors has been such that a very high proportion of immigrants to Israel have been refugees – Holocaust survivors, those fleeing from Arab countries following the establishment of the State, from Poland in the 1950s and from the FSU from the late 1980s onwards. Some of the more recent arrivals from countries like France, the UK and Argentina have also been prompted by uneasiness about anti-Semitism or years of economic crisis.

Despite these many differences, the immigration experience of the two countries share many common elements. For example, net migration has contributed to rapid population growth in both countries. It has also yielded highly diverse populations, even while allowing for the fact that the overwhelming majority of immigrants to Israel have been Jews. Immigrants to both countries have produced ethnic concentrations in specific regions.

There also appear to be some nascent elements of convergence in the immigration policies and experiences of Australia and Israel. Both countries have relatively recently adopted temporary labour migration programs (unskilled labour migration in Israel's case and skilled labour migration in Australia's) which, like other such population movements to other countries, have served as a pathway for many to achieve permanent residence, whether de facto or *de jure*. And both countries are now experiencing 'unauthorized' arrivals of asylum seekers – via Indonesia in Australia and from Africa across the Egyptian border in Israel. These developments suggest that, like Australia, Israel may have to move towards a more articulated program of migration categories and selection criteria and targets, following the established policies of Australia.

2. Immigration laws

Na'ama Carmi and Susan Kneebone

For those who've come across the seas
We've boundless plains to share (McCormick 1878: 2nd verse)

The State of Israel will be open for Jewish immigration and for the Ingathering
of the Exiles. (Declaration of Independence 1948)

One central way to look at the focus and effect of immigration laws and
policy is in terms of inclusion and exclusion; that is, as determining whom
we admit as 'one of us' and whom we reject and so cannot join us as a
member. If we look at the Israeli immigration laws and practices from
this perspective, the answer to the above question is clear: as the above
statement recognizes, Jews and family members of Jews are welcome to
join the Israeli collective, a policy embodied first and foremost in the Law
of Return. Non-Jews are, generally speaking, 'persona non grata' in terms
of joining the collective as full members, precluded by de facto practices
even without an explicit immigration policy. As we will explain, Israel has
shaped its laws, which are based on ethnicity, to fit contemporary patterns
of international migration.

In the case of Australia, although it may appear to be a 'classical' welcoming country of immigration, a colonial heritage as part of the British
Empire and its geographical position in the Asia-Pacific region have
shaped its laws and underlying policy. The welcoming words of Australia's
national anthem exaggerate the inclusiveness of Australia's immigration
policy and laws. From the pre-Federation period up to World War II,
the broad aim of immigration policy was to fill the arable empty spaces
of Australia with persons of 'British' (including English, Scots, Irish and
Welsh people) and white stock (Langfield 1999: 11–13), and in particular
to exclude the 'coloured races' from the neighbouring region. This policy
was seen to be an imperative for security reasons as much as cultural ones.
Between the two world wars, Australia's immigration policy included
restrictions on European migration and a very chary approach to refugees,
many of whom were Jewish.

Since World War II, external factors, combined with the continuing need to increase Australia's population to sustain economic growth, meant that admission policies had to be less exclusive. Since the mid-1970s a new focus has been the need for 'securing the border' by deterring 'spontaneous' arrivals. The largest number of immigrants over the last 60 years under the planned migration scheme have still been from the UK.

Clearly the vision of an exiled nation reclaiming its land that underlies Israel's Law of Return has no equivalent in Australia, where the British came to colonize a land with which they claimed no prior connection. Unlike other immigrant nations such as Canada and the USA, Australia with its convict origins has not accorded central place in its dominant narratives about itself as a 'settler' nation, or as the embodiment of the beliefs of the Founding Fathers. Today Australia has plural ethnic identities which exist together under an official policy of multiculturalism.

Two issues in particular demonstrate Australia's attempt to fashion a national identity and sense of community. These are the experiment with multicultural policy in Australia from the 1970s, and its replacement with the notion of citizenship in the last decade of the twentieth century. In particular, issues about refugees demonstrate the limits of immigration policies which since World War II have focused strongly on the contribution that migrants can make to the economy, as well as upon border control.

In terms of the laws however, one difference lies in the fact that Australia has a mono legal system (albeit that it is a federated nation, immigration is a federal matter), whereas Israel has a plural legal system which includes jurisdiction over aspects of immigration law. Australia's laws and policies are shaped around the notion of planned migration, with two main programs – the migration stream which includes skilled and family reunion components and the Humanitarian Program. By contrast, Israel has maintained an ad hoc response to non-Jewish immigration, including humanitarian entrants other than through changes to the Law of Return, as discussed below. Yet ultimately as we will explain through an examination of the laws and policy in relation to immigration and citizenship of each country, the differences in the two legal systems collapse around points of inclusion and exclusion; about who can join the community of the nation.

AUSTRALIA'S LEGAL FRAMEWORK AND POLICY

The Commonwealth of Australia Constitution Act (the Constitution) contains two heads of power dealing with immigration, namely the 'Immigration and emigration' power, section 51(xxvii) – the 'immigration power' – and the 'Naturalisation and aliens' power, section 51(xix) – the 'aliens power'. While both powers appear to be inclusive, under this framework the government and the courts have been able to frame exclusive policies. Importantly there is no express power for citizenship. Indeed until the first Citizenship Act of 1948, the categories of 'belonging' were British subject or Australian national. A person could become a 'belonger' either by birth, descent or naturalization. Those who did not belong were known as 'aliens'.

Subjects, Aliens and Nationals

The existence of the 'aliens power' in the Constitution reflects the legacy of Australia's background in the English common law distinction between 'subject' and 'alien'. Under that law an alien is a person who does not owe permanent allegiance to the Crown. However, the common law accepted that a person could become a 'subject of the Crown' by birth ('*jus soli*') in the territory of a sovereign.[1] But the concept of 'subject' also incorporated the notion of '*jus sanguinis*' (descent by blood) for those born to another subject, who acquired the allegiance of their parents. As Justice McHugh explained, the *jus soli* principle was 'a rule as central to the unwritten constitution of the United Kingdom and its colonies as could be found'.[2] Under this principle: '[U]pon birth in any part of the Crown's dominions, the new born child immediately owed permanent allegiance to the Crown and was entitled to claim a reciprocal duty of protection on the part of the Crown'.[3] However, as we explain below, this principle now has modified application in Australia.

Importantly, until roughly World War II, the courts relied largely upon the 'immigration' power, and sometimes applied an inclusive understanding of 'subject'. For example, in some cases it was decided that the immigration power could not extend to anyone who had become part of the Australian community by 'assimilation' or being 'absorbed' into the community.[4] Thus such a person could not be removed or deported from Australia under the 'immigration' power. However the notion that a person might become absorbed into the community by their own action was contested by some judges, particularly in the context of restrictive legislation that denied some classes of aliens the right to enter Australia.

The Immigration Restriction Acts 1901–1905 (Cth) and the Pacific Islanders Labourers Act 1901 (Cth) were examples of such legislation that had overtly racist overtones. The Immigration Restriction Act 1901 contained the infamous 'dictation test',[5] which defined a 'prohibited immigrant' as including 'any person who fails to pass the dictation test: that is to say, who, when an officer dictates to him in not less than 50 words in any prescribed language, fails to write them out in that language'. There is ample evidence that this test was applied to exclude Asians. For example in *Potter v Minahan*[6] it was administered to a young man who had been born in Australia to an Irish mother and a Chinese father, but who had lived in China for most of his life. Archival records establish that the Collectors of Customs were directed to apply the dictation test 'in such a manner as to ensure its efficiency' (Langfield 1999: 33; Yarwood 1967), that is, to exclude persons of Asian race. The Pacific Islanders Labourers Act 1901, as the title suggests was intended to ensure that labourers from the Pacific Islands remained in Australia only so long as the period of their licence or contract permitted. Upon completion of that they were required to return home.[7]

The racial-exclusion policy underlying these pieces of legislation, and which were held to be valid exercises of constitutional power by the High Court, contained the so-called White Australia Policy. This policy, which was never acknowledged in those explicit terms, was officially abandoned only in 1973 (Tavan 2005). Although in Australia the concept of *jus sanguinis* (descent by blood) applies, it exists alongside policies of controlled entry, which at periods has been based on ethnicity.

In keeping with the Immigration Restriction Acts 1901–1905, the naturalization (or nationality) legislation was also restrictive. The Naturalisation Act 1903 (Cth) and the Nationality Act 1920 (Cth) expressly excluded certain categories of persons such as the indigenous populations ('aboriginal natives') of Asia, Africa and the Pacific.[8] But the Australian indigenous people were not classified as aliens; instead, they were 'British subjects' born on British soil (another example of the *jus soli* principle). However they were not eligible for Australian citizenship until 1976.

The current Migration Act 1958 (Cth) relies on the aliens power and the 'aliens' concept as shown by its preamble which describes it as 'An Act relating to the entry into, and presence in, Australia of aliens, and the departure or deportation from Australia of aliens and certain other persons'.

From Nationality to Citizenship: the Link to the Visa Regime

The Migration Act 1958 also makes it clear that the status of citizen is all-important. For example, section 4(4) of the Migration Act elaborates on its purposes: 'To advance its object, this Act provides for the removal or deportation from Australia of *non-citizens* whose presence in Australia is not permitted by this Act' (emphasis added). The difference between a 'lawful non-citizen' (a non-citizen who has a valid visa) and an 'unlawful non-citizen' (one who does not hold a visa) is all-important under Australian law.[9]

The visa regime evolved after the dictation test was abolished when the Immigration Restriction Acts 1901–1905 were replaced in 1958 with a new Migration Act and a system of entry permits and exemptions. After several decades, this was replaced in 1989 with a system of visas for all immigrants. Today all non-citizens of Australia are required to obtain an entry visa to enter Australia.[10] This linking of citizenship and the visa regime demonstrates that citizenship is used as an instrument for migration control and exclusion, as the development of the concept in Australia illustrates.

It is unclear why no constitutional head of power for citizenship was included in the Constitution in 1901. Some have suggested that it arose from the fact that many persons of other races (for example Indians and Chinese from Hong Kong) were British subjects under the Empire. Others by contrast have suggested that because all born on Australian territory were British subjects, there was no need for a specific power. However, the awkwardness of being obliged to accept races from other colonies was evident in the debates on the Constitution (K. Rubenstein 2000: 576). Importantly, the word 'citizen' only appears in one section of the Constitution.[11] Other provisions refer to 'subject of the Queen'[12] or 'people of the Commonwealth'.[13]

Before World War II an alien could become a 'subject' or Australian national through naturalization. It was accepted that the process of naturalization could effect a change in allegiance. But the underlying concept was 'nationality' rather than citizenship (which reflected the British rather than the American Republican tradition which was influential in debates on the Constitution). The term 'citizenship' was first used in the 1948 Australian Citizenship and Nationality Act (Cth) (which in 1973 was retitled the Australian Citizenship Act). Under this legislation, citizenship could be acquired through grant (in place of naturalization), birth (as consistent with the *jus soli* principle), or descent (*jus sanguinis*).

The 1948 Act required new citizens to swear an oath of allegiance to the Crown. There are two points to note about this legislation (and its successors). First, it appears to embody a 'formal' or legal notion of community membership, as opposed to a substantive or 'normative' one. As there is no constitutional head of power dealing with citizenship (as in the USA), but its scope is defined by legislation, it is often described as a 'statutory' concept. As Kim Rubenstein (2000: 588) states, the legislation: '[O]ffers a definition of citizenship stripped bare. While the Act tells us who is a citizen and who can lose their citizenship, it tells us nothing about the legal consequences of citizenship'.

The preamble to the Australian Citizenship Act 1973 sets out the meaning of citizenship as involving:

- full and formal membership of the community;
- a common bond involving reciprocal rights and obligations;
- unification of all Australians while respecting their diversity.

Indeed the concept of citizenship is used in Australian law as a 'device of exclusion' (K. Rubenstein 2000: 584, 589) as the object of the Migration Act 1958 and its link with the visa regime suggest. 'It is not about including everyone born in Australia as a member of the community, but rather determining first and foremost whom we want and whom we do not want to be a part of the Australian community' (K. Rubenstein 2000: 589).

The second point to note is that a notion of Australian citizenship was slow to develop. Until 1984, the conferral of citizenship was accompanied by status as a British subject. Moreover, Australian passports could be issued to British subjects who were not Australian citizens.

After this period there were two important amendments that demonstrated the Australian concept of citizenship being adjusted because of external pressures. The first was in 1986, when the Citizenship Act was amended to deprive some children born in Australia of their 'natural' or common law right to citizenship (on the basis of *jus soli*). From that time on only children born to at least one Australian citizen (*jus sanguinis*), or who had been resident in Australia for ten years could claim that they were not 'aliens'. This was a deliberate measure intended to deter failed asylum seekers from remaining in Australia to contest their status under the legal system. 'Asylum seekers' are people seeking asylum from persecution who have yet to be recognized as a 'refugee' as defined in the Convention Relating to the Status of Refugees ('Refugee Convention') and the Protocol Relating to the Status of Refugees ('Refugee Protocol').[14]

The 1986 amendment was challenged in the High Court of Australia in a test case involving a little girl born in Australia to Indian citizen parents, *Singh v Commonwealth of Australia*.[15] Opponents of the legislation were heartened by the suggestion of Justice Kirby (High Court of Australia 2003) in argument who said that 'the central issue' is: 'Whether there is a constitutional status of nationality quite apart from the statutory status of citizenship and whether implied in that constitutional notion of nationality being a subject of the Queen of Australia are certain irreducible minimum protections'.

But the High Court decided that despite birth in Australia, Tania Singh was an 'alien'. The minority thought that the common law meaning of 'alien' had become a constitutional concept which could not be altered by mere legislation. However, the majority were prepared to interpret the constitutional power more broadly and said that although 'alienage' is a constitutional status, Parliament could legislate to alter it. Justice Kirby for example, said: '[A]lienage is a status that must respond to forced migration [including] birth arranged in the receiving country'.[16] This decision thus confirmed there is no constitutional concept of citizenship and that 'citizenship' could be used as an exclusive concept, particularly in the context (broadly) of international migration.

The second important amendment was in 2002,[17] to permit Australian citizens to hold dual citizenship. This amendment was part of the push at that time to raise the profile of the notion of citizenship. It was part of the government's response to the Australian Citizenship Council's report (2000), 'Australian Citizenship for a New Century'. One purpose of this Act was to recapture the 'brain drain' of mobile Australian professional workers, to encourage them to return home to contribute to the national economy. Another was to resolve the position of persons with dual nationality who sought election to the federal Parliament. Under section 44 of Australia's Constitution, persons who are citizens of a 'foreign power' are prohibited from standing for office. The new amendment enabled such persons who take out Australian citizenship to qualify to stand for office.

AUSTRALIA'S DEVELOPMENT OF IMMIGRATION CONTROL SINCE WORLD WAR II: REFUGEES AND MULTICULTURALISM

Displaced Persons and Refugees

In the aftermath of World War II, migration policy was dominated by three objectives:

- to increase the population;
- to boost national development; and
- to strengthen security.

In this period, the slogan 'populate or perish' was much in use. In the immediate post-war period, 170 000 displaced persons from camps in Europe and southern Europe were selected to come to Australia as bonded labourers on the great projects that were to build the new post-war Australian nation (Jupp 2002b: 12). A high proportion of these displaced persons were refugees[18] – in everyday parlance, a person in flight or seeking refuge, rather than coming under the definition contained in the Refugee Convention – although they were not acknowledged as such at the time. These immigrants included Jewish refugees who would add greatly to cultural and intellectual life in post-war Australia. In this period Australia also signed up to and actively supported the drafting of the 1951 Refugee Convention.[19]

This post-war experience was to establish a pattern of offshore selection of European immigrants and provision of assisted passages, which lasted until 1982. As discussed, Australia's current controlled system of entry through visas (which dates from 1989) has its origins in the system of permits introduced in 1958. This policy is embodied in the current Act which requires all non-citizens of Australia to obtain an entry visa to enter Australia (there are some exceptions for New Zealand citizens who can apply for a Special Category Visa on arrival in Australia). The Act clarifies that the object is 'to regulate, in the national interest, the coming into, and presence in, Australia of non-citizens'.[20]

Unfortunately, the attempt to translate this policy of offshore selection to asylum seekers and refugees has not been as successful as the discussion below illustrates. It has failed to stem the tide of 'spontaneous' or uninvited asylum seekers (or 'boat people' as they are called more widely) arriving in Australian territory.

Refugees and Deterrent Measures

In the Cold War period between World War II and 1982, Australia accepted 400 000 refugees and displaced persons, selected mainly from European communist countries, as permanent settlers. This policy of selecting refugees existed in the context of a managed program of migration, based on assisted passages. However with the fall of South Vietnam in 1975, Australia was confronted with its first spontaneous refugee crisis, and was forced to act as a country of first asylum.

Initially Australia tried to manage and prevent the arrival of further asylum seekers by boat by signing bilateral agreements with Hong Kong, Indonesia and Malaysia under which Australia took refugees it selected from camps in these countries on the condition that these nations took steps to prevent the 'boat-people' from travelling to Australia. In 1982, in line with its resettlement/selection-oriented approach, the Australian government reached an agreement with the government of Vietnam for an Orderly Departure Program (ODP) based on family reunification and established a system of individual assessment of refugee claims.

By 1986, 100 000 Indo-Chinese refugees had been admitted to Australia, most under the ODP directly from Vietnam, under which the government gave priority to those with family already settled in Australia. Then in 1989, along with 50 other countries, Australia endorsed the Comprehensive Plan of Action for Indo-Chinese Refugees (CPA).[21]

Arguably, the CPA had an important role in the development of

Australian policy towards 'spontaneous' refugee arrivals (the term used in government policy documents to distinguish visa holders from non-visa holders) or 'boat people'. Under the CPA more than 18 000 Vietnamese were resettled in Australia from camps in South-east Asia. Thus the CPA reinforced the trend to selective resettlement and the distinction between onshore asylum seekers and offshore refugees which persists in Australian refugee policy today. Subsequently the Australian government linked the existence of its offshore processing (described below) to the 'problem' of 'boat people'. It has used the availability of offshore processing to discriminate against such spontaneous arrivals. Thus the CPA was the catalyst for the development of policies of deterrence, including mandatory detention for refugees.

After the CPA, the next significant wave of 'boat people' coincided with the end of the Cold War and the 1989 Tiananmen Square incident. In reaction to the world events of 1989 and consequent leap in onshore claims for asylum in Australia, the Australian Government commenced a program of reform which included the introduction of restrictive policies. To begin with, the Migration Act 1958 was rewritten. The Act now provides (as noted above) for a system of entry by visas and a distinction between 'citizens' and 'non-citizens' (and arising from that, between 'lawful' and 'unlawful' non-citizens). Under this legislation, spontaneous asylum seekers who arrive without visas are 'unlawful non-citizens', but asylum seekers who arrive with a visa, such as a tourist or student visa, and who subsequently claim asylum are 'lawful non-citizens'. Importantly, at all times, this latter category of lawful non-citizen asylum seeker has constituted the highest proportion of persons seeking asylum in Australia.

In 1992 the Government introduced the mandatory deterrence regime, in Division 4C ('Detention of unlawful non-citizens') of the Migration Act. This legislation, which was upheld in *Lim v Minister for Immigration* (*Lim*)[22] arose from a class action by 36 Cambodians who had fled Cambodia and arrived in Australia in 1989 or 1990 during the operation of the CPA.

In 1989 the Migration Act had been amended to provide a discretionary power for detention of persons arriving by boat suspected of not holding an entry permit. However, in practice, many Cambodian asylum seekers were detained for several years after their vessels had been burnt. The detention system was attended by long delays and many unsuccessful asylum seekers were deported. The plaintiffs in Lim had been detained for two years after the rejection of their claims for asylum. They had then successfully sought judicial review and their applications for asylum had been remitted to the minister. At the same time they also sought orders that they be released from custody. It was two days before the release applications were to be heard, that the government brought in legislation to legalize their detention and to prevent their release. This 1992 legislation made the detention scheme mandatory (obligatory) rather than discretionary.

The legislation, the Migration Reform Act 1992, was challenged on the basis that it usurped the role of the judiciary. The argument was upheld in part in the High Court but the court accepted that authority to detain aliens in custody for the purpose of processing, expulsion or deportation was a valid exercise of the aliens power. The effect of Lim was to sanction a regime of detention which is mandatory and non-reviewable. This arises from the provisions in the Migration Act 1992 that create the powers to support this system.[23] Since Lim, in a number of challenges it has been argued that the consequences of detention took the exercise of powers outside the limits of the 'aliens' power. In one line of cases it was held that the fact that the applicants and their children had suffered psychological damage as a result of their detention did not make the exercise of power a 'punitive administrative detention'. Other decisions confirmed that neither the harsh conditions of detention nor the fact that the children are detained in contravention of international human rights standards affects the legality of the detention regime.[24]

However, the limits of the power were tested by the situation of stateless people who were theoretically subject to indefinite detention as they were ineligible for a visa and had no country to which they could be removed under the Migration Act. In a significant shift from the original basis of Lim, in 2004 the High Court upheld the legality of the detention of this category of persons in a decision that appears to ignore breaches of human rights.[25]

The Creation of the Humanitarian Program and TPVs

A second way in which 'spontaneous' (that is, undocumented or visa-less) asylum seekers or 'boat people' were singled out in Australia's refugee policy was under the Humanitarian Program. This program is one part of Australia's planned Migration Program, which also includes special pro-visions for skilled immigrants and family reunions.

The Humanitarian Program is an offshore resettlement program directed at two categories of persons:

- the refugee component for those who meet the Refugees Convention defi-nition of a 'refugee';
- the special humanitarian (SHP) component is for people subject to 'sub-stantial discrimination' or human rights abuse.

Very roughly, in most years until the late 1990s, the offshore program was shared almost equally between these two components and it was mostly filled by people from Europe. Initially the program was set at 12 000 places and was increased to 13 750 by 2003. Initially a linked 'quota' of 2000 places was also reserved under the program for boat arrivals, but this was absorbed into the overall program and disappeared in the early part of the twenty-first century.

Although the Liberal–National Party Coalition government (in office from 1996 to 2007) held out the Humanitarian Program as evidence of an 'orderly queue' for refugees, the evidence showed that this was a myth. The Humanitarian Program operates as part of the United Nations High Commissioner for Refugees' (UNHCR) resettlement program and access to it is dependent upon being near an Australian Embassy that processes refugees, or to an UNHCR office. For many refugees this is not realistic. Further, there is a perception that the processes themselves are not always fair and transparent.

Additional deterrent measures, which are arguably in contravention of Australia's obligations under the Refugee Convention, were introduced in 1999. This was through the visa regime and in particular the Temporary Protection Visa (TPV) regime which involved the grant of three-year visas. From 1999 until mid-2008, asylum seekers who arrived without a visa could only obtain temporary protection. The TPV regime carried limited rights, and was thus arguably in breach of Australia's obligations under the Refugee Convention. For example, it permitted only limited resettlement services and denied the right to re-enter Australia (Kneebone 2006).

In summary, there were three policies introduced in the period leading up to 2001 that were specifically intended to deter 'boat people'. They were the mandatory detention policy, the linking of the onshore and the offshore 'quotas' under the Humanitarian Program, and the introduction of the TPV regime. Although the Labor government, elected in late 2007, modified these policies to a certain extent (the TPV has been abolished, along with remote detention centres in Australia), asylum seeker 'boat people' who arrive in excised territory (in Australia's northern waters) without a visa continue to be processed offshore under administrative arrangements on the remote Christmas Island. Further, Australia has entered into arrangements with Indonesia to facilitate the detention and processing of asylum seekers intending to sail to Australia on Indonesian territory.

The Rise and Death of Multiculturalism: the 'One Nation' Phenomenon

While these restrictive policies to refugees were being formulated, successive Australian governments from the mid-1970s were experimenting with multiculturalism as a more inclusive policy. This was intended to replace the racially charged concept of integration or 'assimilation', which had been espoused in the first 25 years after World War II (Jabukowicz 2009: 27). Its rising influence coincided with the official end of the unofficial White Australia Policy in 1973. Institutions to support the policy were established.

But in the 1980s, several damning reports revealed fissures in the policy which was seen as divisive, and as leading to the creation of elites. In particular in 1988 the FitzGerald Report (Fitzgerald 1988) critiqued the policy as sentimental, elitist and promoting cultural relativism. The debate over the merits of multiculturalism and its usefulness as a concept for immigration policy continued for two decades. Although the word 'multi-cultural' has largely disappeared from the official Australian lexicon, it is seen as policy that is 'dead but cannot be buried' (Jabukowicz 2009: 30).

To a large extent the death knell of multiculturalism was sounded by the success in the polls of the exclusive anti-immigration policies of Pauline Hanson's One Nation Party in the late 1990s. Paradoxically, after a decade, official multicultural policy was replaced by a stronger focus on citizenship and upon the integration of migrant populations. In part this is a response to the arrival of more immigrants from non-traditional sources such as the Middle East and Africa, perceived as a threat to social cohesion (Klapdor et al. 2009: 2).

Australian Citizenship Testing and the Citizenship Act

As asylum seekers started to make their presence increasingly felt, and as interest in multicultural policy waned in the 1990s, attention turned to citizenship and Australian 'values'. The year 1989 was declared the Year of Citizenship. In 1993 the Australian Citizenship Act was amended to incorporate a pledge to replace the old oath of allegiance. The Preamble to the Act recognized Australian citizenship as a 'common bond uniting all Australians involving reciprocal rights and obligations'. In 1994 the idea of Australian citizenship was scrutinized in a report, 'Australians All – Enhancing Australian Citizenship' (Australia Joint Standing Committee on Migration 1994). But concern was raised by public attention to the reality that nearly one million eligible immigrants had not taken out citizenship.

In the early part of the twenty-first century, with debate over multi-culturalism fuelled by fears over terrorism and the racially motivated Cronulla riots in 2005, public debate stressed the need for immigrants to integrate and to learn English. A new Citizenship Act in 2007 increased the qualifying residence period from two to four years, and introduced a controversial citizenship test.

The explanatory memorandum of the Australian Citizenship

Amendment (Citizenship Testing) Bill 2007 stated that 'the introduction of a citizenship test is a key part of the Government's ongoing commitment to help migrants successfully integrate into the Australian community'. Upon introducing the Bill to Parliament, Minister Kevin Andrews suggested that 'the material which will form the basis of the citizenship test will highlight the common values we share'. The test was reviewed in 2009 by the Australian Citizenship Test Review Committee as there was concern that it was discriminating against those already disadvantaged. For example, there is evidence that there is a much lower pass rate amongst entrants under the Humanitarian Program as distinct from the skilled entrants under the general migrant program. The review committee made a number of recommendations for assisting these persons that ultimately were not accepted by the government. It has been suggested that the new citizenship policy represents a backward step in encouraging migrants to take out citizenship (Klapdor et al. 2009: 1).

ISRAEL'S LEGAL FRAMEWORK AND POLICY

Israel's basic immigration law, the 1950 Law of Return, does not enjoy formal constitutional status. Because of its express link to Zionism, it is an overt instrument of inclusion/exclusion. The term 'Law of Return' refers to the idea in traditional Jewish sources of returning to Zion; to the historical return, by right, to the land of the forefathers. The other main Israeli law is the Nationality Law, which was enacted by the Knesset exactly two years after the Law of Return. This law specifies the terms by which Israeli nationality may be acquired: return, birth, residence and naturalization.[26] The law grants automatic nationality to every *oleh*[27] (emigrating Jew) under the Law of Return. Technically, Jews 'ascend' to Israel (make *aliyah*), while other immigrants must naturalize. Thus a distinction was created between the law of *aliyah* and immigration (for a comprehensive discussion of the historical background, see Carmi 2003: 21–2).

In addition to these two laws, the religious laws are also relevant. Through this combination of laws, Israel has attempted to meet the competing demands of sections of the Jewish community and international migration. Although the Law of Return is based upon *jus sanguinis*, it does not include all Jews, but paradoxically the 1970 amendment includes non-Jews. Since the 1950s, when the Law of Return and the Nationality Law were enacted, Israel has become a favoured place of immigration not only for Jews. Non-Jewish immigration to Israel occurs also independently of the Law of Return, as part of the pattern of immigration from the Third World into developed countries. This phenomenon has led to the government attempting to formulate immigration policy for the first time in Israel's short history.

Laws: The Law of Return

The Law of Return is the central immigration law of Israel. Although it does not have the formal status of a Basic Law (which enjoys constitutional status), many people view it as the country's most important law, its very constituent law as a Jewish state. The Supreme Court recognized this when it declared: 'The Law of Return is one of the most basic laws of the State. It may even be said that it is its first Basic Law'.[28] Enacted in 1950, the Law of Return recognizes the right of every Jew to make *aliyah* to Israel and to settle there. Restrictions on this right are:

- engagement in an activity directed against the Jewish people; or
- endangering public health or the security of the State; or
- a criminal past, likely to endanger public welfare.

The Law of Return is intended to serve not only as an 'immigration' law, but also as an instrument to keep and maintain the unique character of the state as a Jewish state. This is done by ensuring a Jewish majority and 'balancing' the Arab population by control on immigration. As such, one can view it as a law that deals with the very core of Israel's collective identity. In order to understand the Law's importance and meaning, it is necessary to review its historical background and the amendments enacted subsequent to 1950.

The Law of Return was enacted by unanimous vote of the Knesset in 1950, on the anniversary of the death of Theodor Herzl, the founder of political Zionism. Its objective was to implement the principle expressed in the Declaration of Independence that 'The State of Israel will be open for Jewish immigration and for the Ingathering of the Exiles'. It was designed to realize the aim of Zionism, the return of the Jewish people to their homeland in order to exercise political sovereignty and gain 'the status of a fully privileged member of the comity of nations'. The Law of Return is based on the recognition that Jews are returning to their homeland, not immigrating to a foreign country. Thus, the Law of Return is not regarded as an ordinary immigration law. The term 'return' refers to the Jews' historical return, by right, to the land of their forefathers. This is viewed as the inherent right of every Jew. The Law of Return is the instrument that recognizes, rather than creates, this right. The law expresses the idea that Israel is the state of the Jews, and its consequent duty is to allow every Jew who so desires to immigrate and to settle there.[29]

When the state was established the majority of the Jewish people lived outside its borders, in the Diaspora. In the light of the persecution that the Jews experienced in the Diaspora, which reached its extreme in the Holocaust, the Law of Return was seen as an essential historical correction, which enabled every Jew to obtain asylum from persecution and the Jewish collective to implement its right to self-determination and to national sovereignty. Still, most Jews regard the Law of Return as expressing Israel's unique character.

Somewhat paradoxically the Law of Return is also responsible for the immigration of non-Jews, leading to deep controversy concerning the impact of such immigrants on the character of the 'Jewish state'. The key to this riddle lies in the 1970 amendment that extended the Law's application to the non-Jewish family members of Jews.

'Who is a Jew?'

There have been few amendments to the Law of Return, an indication of its central, constitutional-like, status. The most significant amendment was in 1970, and is connected to a major controversy in Israel over the question 'Who is a Jew?' If Israel is the nation state of the Jewish people, which opens its doors to every Jew, what is the definition, in this context, of the term 'Jew'? The approaches to this question differ widely. On the one hand, there is the view that the religious-Orthodox component is the sole component of Jewish identity. According to this understanding, a Jew is a person who was born to a Jewish mother, or who has undergone an Orthodox religious conversion. On the other hand, there is the view that Jewishness is something much wider than religion, encompassing ethnic and cultural aspects. Jewish identity, according to this view, is determined not solely by *halakha* (Jewish religious law), but also by personal identity and a sense of belonging to the Jewish people. This debate has clear implications for immigration issues, since it relates to eligibility criteria for immigration: religious, ethnic or national.

For 20 years after its enactment the Law of Return lacked a definition of 'Jew'. During the mass immigration of the 1950s Israel accepted all persons who considered themselves as Jews and no legal definition seemed to be needed. Two cases decided in the 1960s led to the 1970 amendment. In the Rufeisen (Brother Daniel) case, the Supreme Court held that a Jew who had converted to Catholicism was not entitled to the right of return, even though he still regarded himself as a member of the Jewish people.[30] The Shalit case did not deal directly with the Law of Return, but with inclusion in the Population Registry. The majority on the court held that the registration officer had to register the children of a Jewish father and non-Jewish mother as Jews in the national sense, as the parents had requested.[31] This case caused a political storm that led to amendment both of the Law of Return and the Population Registry Law.

After the Rufeizen and the Shalit cases, a double-edged amendment was introduced into the Law of Return in 1970. On the one hand, the term 'Jew' was defined, and thereby narrowed; on the other, application of the Law itself was extended. The term 'Jew' was defined in article 4B, as 'a person who was born of a Jewish mother or has become converted to Judaism, and who is not a member of another religion'. This matriarchal definition adopts the approach of religious law, except in one respect: while under religious law a person born a Jew remains a Jew even if he/she converts to another religion, following the Rufeisen precedent the amended Law of Return provides that a person who belongs to another religion is not to be regarded as a Jew.

Had the amendment been confined to definition of the term 'Jew', the Law's application would have been narrowed by defining a 'Jew' in matriarchal terms. Anyone not covered by the definition would not have been entitled to the right of return. However, while narrowing the meaning of 'Jew' the amendment also applied the Law not only to Jews, but also to their family members. Article 4A provides:

> (a) The rights of a Jew under this Law and the rights of an *oleh* under the Nationality Law, 5712-1952, as well as the rights of an *oleh* under any other enactment, are also vested in a child and a grandchild of a Jew, the spouse of a Jew, the spouse of a child of a Jew and the spouse of a grandchild of a Jew, except for a person who has been a Jew and has voluntarily changed his religion.
> (b) It shall be immaterial whether or not a Jew by whose right a right under subsection (a) is claimed is still alive and whether or not he has immigrated to Israel.
> (c) The restrictions and conditions prescribed in respect of a Jew or an *oleh* by or under this Law or by the enactments referred to in subsection (a) shall also apply to a person who claims a right under subsection (a).

The overall application of the *Law of Return* after 1970 thus became 'broader' than the strict Orthodox (religious) definition of a Jew, including persons who are not Jews according to religious law (*halakha*). In order to be eligible to return and enjoy adjunct rights, notably Israeli citizenship, an applicant has only to be a person of Jewish descent or such a person's spouse. The Law of Return's basis became a wide definition of *jus sanguinis*, as opposed to *jus soli*. Since the law was amended the right of *aliyah* is given not only to Jews but also to their descendants and spouses. One prominent consequence is that non-Jews can now make *aliyah* to Israel as if they were Jews. It has been argued that this extension was adopted to protect family union and to facilitate *aliyah* of 'mixed families' (in which a Jew has married a non-Jew).[32]

Controversy Concerning the Law of Return

The 1970 amendment reflected a political and principled compromise. It also led to an ongoing controversy. One criticism relates to the dual tendency of the amendment, which leads to it being both over-inclusive and under-inclusive.

'Over-inclusiveness' of the Law of Return is reflected in the definition of those entitled to return. It grants this right to persons who are not required to establish their identification with the Jewish people and who may regard themselves as Christian. There are demands to revoke article 4A (referred to in public discussion as the 'grandchild clause') in whole or part, to remove the entitlement to make *aliyah* solely on the basis of Jewish ancestry. Advocates of this change argue that article 4A is incompatible with the original intent of the Law.

A second criticism relates to the fact that in Israel personal matters are covered by religious law.[33] One consequence is that people from different religions cannot marry each other, and persons who do not belong to one of the recognized religious communities cannot marry at all. Thus there is a contradiction between the effect of the Law of Return and the religious law. The 'family clause' of the Law of Return has led to the entry of some 200 000 persons who are not considered Jews according to religious law and thus (in most cases) cannot marry in Israel.

'Under-inclusiveness' of the Law of Return is reflected in the fact that a person who is not Jewish under religious law but is regarded as a Jew (and may even be persecuted as a Jew) does not acquire rights on his or her own accord, but only by virtue of being a family member, such as the son or daughter of a Jewish father.[34]

A further criticism is not connected to the 1970 amendment but to the Law of Return per se, and is based on a liberal approach to immigration. As understood in international law, granting 'preference' to members of a certain national group in issues of nationality and naturalization is not regarded as unlawful discrimination.[35] But from a liberal perspective which holds that immigration criteria should be based on principles of universality and non-discrimination (see Carmi 2003: 96–106), the Law of Return raises special problems (see Carmi 2003: 25–9). It also bears implications for 'citizens' of the state. According to this criticism, the needed amendment lies in 'liberalizing' immigration law (Carmi 2003: 51–5).

The Entry into Israel Law

In matters of entry to the country, *de jure* Israel follows international standards.[36] Israeli law recognizes the right of every citizen to enter the state,[37] but entry and residence are at the discretion of the Minister of Interior. The Entry into Israel Law regulates, first, the entrance to Israel of non-citizens and people without an *oleh* visa, and, second, the stay and residence in Israel of these people. This law is part of the legal framework that provides for two different routes to entry and residence: the Law of Return provides the route for Jews and their family members, the Entry Law for persons who are neither Jews nor family members of Jews ('people without an *oleh* certificate').

Israeli Citizenship: the Nationality Law

The Nationality Law of 1952 specifies that nationality may be acquired by return, birth, residence and naturalization.[38] The law grants automatic nationality to 'every *oleh* under the Law of Return'. Return is the first basis specified; acquiring nationality by return complements the Law of Return in a way that makes the immigration policy of Israel descent-based. Being a Jew or a family member of a Jew is the main route for inclusion in Israel.

Until 1980, Israeli-born Jews also acquired nationality by return, as if they had immigrated under the Law of Return (for discussion of the consequences and problems see Carmi 2006).[39] Section 4 of the Law of Return specified that: 'every Jew who was born in this country, whether before or after the coming into force of this Law, shall be deemed to be a person who has come to this country as an *oleh* under this Law'.

Acquisition of nationality by birth or by residence was acquired only by non-Jews, mainly Arabs. The difference was symbolic, though, and the way Israeli nationality was acquired had no practical consequences in terms of status, rights or entitlements. However, the version of the statute before 1980 made it difficult for some Arabs who resided in Israel to acquire its nationality, because it required them to have registered in Israel by a certain date; to have been resident in Israel since the date on which the law came into force; and to have remained in Israel or in a territory that became part of it from the day of the establishment of the state until the law came into force, or to have gained legal entrance to the state during this period. These cumulative terms were hard to meet by many Arabs who fled from Israel during the 1948 war, and were afterwards forbidden from returning legally (Kretzmer 1990: 39–40). These terms were eased by the 1980 amendment. At the same time, the amendment provided that

Israeli-born Jews, one of whose parents is a citizen, would acquire nationality by birth as well.

The *de jure* basis of Israeli nationality is not exclusively ethnic, with provision for naturalization on other grounds. But as in every state, naturalization is a privilege, dependent on administrative discretion. In Israel, the Minister of Interior has the discretion to grant nationality to applicants who meet the conditions specified in law, but the minister is not obliged to do so. Article 5 of the Nationality Law specifies that an applicant must meet six conditions (unless exempted from specific requirements by the Minister):

- residence in Israel at the time of the application;
- residence for three of the preceding five years;
- entitlement to reside in Israel permanently (an entitlement which is also subject to the ministerial discretion);
- settlement or intended settlement in Israel;
- some knowledge of the Hebrew language;
- renunciation of prior nationality.

Prior to the grant of nationality, the applicant must declare loyalty to the State of Israel. The main criticism that is made of the Nationality Law is not its specific terms but the practice Israel employs: that is, the broad way the ministerial discretion is used, which in effect excludes those who are not covered by the Law of Return from becoming part of Israeli society.

Enemy Aliens: The Nationality and Entry to Israel Law (Temporary Provision) 2003

Under a temporary provision both the Entry Law and the Nationality Law were restricted in 2003 (in the context of terrorist acts originating in the Occupied Territories) so as to deny entry and residence permits to enemy aliens. This Act prevents Palestinian inhabitants of the Occupied Territories particularly, and enemy aliens generally, from gaining any residence status within Israel. It applies also to spouses of Israeli citizens, thus limiting the authority of the Minister of Interior under the Nationality Law[40] to enable the naturalization of spouses of Israeli citizens[41] and to grant a visa to reside in Israel under the Entry into Israel Law.[42] In effect, this law has had a significant impact on Israel's Palestinian population as it prevented the naturalization of Palestinians who had married Israeli citizens (Barak-Erez 2008).

Enacted in 2003 as a temporary provision, the law recognizes some exceptions (extended in its 2005 amendment) to this sweeping prohibition on the minister's discretion: temporary permits of up to six months for work or medical purposes; permits in order to prevent separation of a child, aged up to 14, from his or her parent who resides in Israel legally; permits to the wife of an Israeli citizen if she is more than 25 years of age, and to the husband of an Israeli citizen if he is more than 35 years of age; and permits in order to promote state security or other state interests.

The government is authorized to extend the Act from time to time, with the Knesset's approval, for a period that shall not exceed one year on each occasion. A petition was submitted to the Supreme Court claiming that this law was unconstitutional as it violated the rights to family life and to equality.[43] By a majority of six to five, the court rejected the petition.[44] The law was subsequently amended further, so as to apply not only to residents of the Occupied Territories but to enemy aliens in general.

ISRAEL'S NEW CHALLENGES: ASYLUM SEEKERS AS A TEST CASE

The entry of non-Jewish immigrants, mainly migrant workers and asylum seekers, has created a new situation not foreseen in the 1950s when the Law of Return and the Nationality Law were enacted. As a developed nation, Israel has become a country of immigration for non-Jews. This has forced decision-makers to confront new issues.

Asylum seekers from Africa have entered Israel in significant numbers only since 2000, crossing the land border with Egypt. Most have come from Sudan and Eritrea, many to escape the conflict in Darfur. Currently there are close to 20 000 'persons of concern' to the UNHCR in Israel.[45]

Israel is a signatory to the Refugee Convention but has not incorporated the Convention into its national law. Israel is not obliged to admit people who are not entitled to refugee status, but the *non-refoulement principle* prohibits their return to a country where there is a danger to their life or liberty so their individual standing must be checked.[46] Until recently it relied upon the UNHCR to meet the requirement to determine who is entitled to refugee status. Today refugee status determination (RSD) is undertaken by a local unit of the Ministry of Interior, but still not in a satisfactory manner.

To 2010 there has been no developed and consistent policy towards asylum seekers in Israel. In part this reflects public controversy over the genuineness of the refugees, with some arguing that they are economic immigrants, and Israel's unresolved problems with Palestinians. The fact that the increase in the number of asylum seekers in Israel raises such an active public debate reveals the sensitivity that exists in regard to entrance and residence of non-Jews in Israel.

CONCLUSION

Immigration and nationality law in Israel is based primarily on ethnicity. This is expressed mainly in the Law of Return, which grants every Jew and family member of a Jew the right to immigrate to Israel. 'Nationality by return' (*oleh*) is the main route to acquire Israeli nationality under the Nationality Law, apart from being born in Israel to a citizen parent. Non-Jews who are not members of Jewish families have a *de jure* path to immigration and naturalization, but they are dependent on ministerial discretion. There is no explicit immigration policy for non-Jews, who are perceived as a threat to the Jewish character of the state; administrative policy makes clear that they are not wanted in Israel as immigrants.

However, the reality of the absorption of millions of immigrants establishes Israel as a country of immigration. But the law accommodates itself to the concept of 'return', Israel's self-determined status as an *aliyah* country. The legal framework coupled with administrative practice serves as a tool for ensuring the Jewish character of the state by maintaining a stable Jewish majority.

By contrast in Australia, which is an immigrant country and which embraced a limited diversity through its multicultural policies, there is a planned migration program and a non-discriminatory selection process. Whereas in Israel the Law of Return leads automatically to nationality, in Australia citizenship follows from access to the visa regime. These measures are designed to ensure optimal selection of those who will have the right to seek citizenship.

In Israel, Jewishness controls the application of the law as it did in 1950. Australian policy was traditionally based on *jus sanguinis* as the preferred method of entry but has moved to favour selection based on skill in occupations of economic demand, although this selection takes place in a culturally determined context. The issue of uninvited asylum seeker 'boat people' has raised a high level of concern in Australia because, while the numbers are small, their entry challenges the right of selection, the principle that it is the Australian government that will determine who gains the right of residence and the path to citizenship.

Ultimately, as our discussion illustrates, while there are important differences at a formal level, the underlying objectives of the laws and policies on immigration and nationality/citizenship determine the composition of both Israel and Australia according to the perception of who are the 'right' people. That perception in both countries is shaped by history, culture and geography.

NOTES

1. *Calvin's Case* (1608) 77 ER 377.
2. *Singh v Commonwealth* (2004) 209 ALR 355 at 375.
3. Ibid. Note Justice McHugh was dissenting in this case (discussed below), but arguably these general propositions are uncontestable as a matter of historical principle. Justice McHugh acknowledged some exceptions re children born to ambassadors and children of 'enemy aliens'.
4. For example *Ex parte Walsh and Johnson ex p Yates* (1925) 37 CLR 36. In that case the applicant had been naturalized. But in *Potter v Minahan* (1908) 7 CLR 277 it was held that a person born in Australia to an Irish mother and Chinese father was 'coming home' when he returned from China after a long absence.
5. This test could be administered in any 'European' language at the discretion of the immigration officer, and could be used to exclude certain unwanted people. For example in *R v Wilson; Ex parte Kisch* (1934) 52 CLR 234 Mr Kisch who was considered to be a political activist was administered the test in the Gaelic language. The High Court 4:1 said that Scottish Gaelic was not a European language.
6. *Potter v Minahan* (1908) 7 CLR 277.
7. *Robtelmes v Brenan* (1906) 4 CLR 395.
8. Naturalisation Act 1903 (Cth), s. 5.
9. Migration Act 1958, ss. 13, 14. As are the consequences of becoming an 'unlawful non-citizen' – the Act ss. 198, 189 and 196 contain the powers to remove and detain such persons. See discussion of the mandatory detention policy below.
10. Migration Act 1958, s. 4(1). Citizens of New Zealand only need a valid New Zealand passport; when presenting their passports for immigration clearance they are considered to have applied for a visa and, subject to health and character considerations, automatically receive a Special Category Visa which entitles them to reside and work in Australia.
11. Citizens of foreign powers ineligible to stand for Parliament – Constitution s. 44.
12. Constitution ss. 34 and 117.
13. Ibid., ss. 7 and 24.
14. As defined in Art. 1A(2) of the Refugee Convention, Geneva, 28 July 1951, in force 22 April 1954, 1989 UNTS 137 and the Refugee Protocol, New York, 31 January 1967, in force 4 October 1967, 19 UST 6223, 6257.
15. (2004) 209 ALR 355.
16. Ibid., para 255.
17. The Australian Citizenship Legislation Amendment Act 2002 (Cth).
18. It has been estimated that between 1945 and 1985 roughly half of the immigrants coming to Australia were 'refugees' from Nazi Germany or the Soviet Union. See Doulman and Lee (2008), p. 176.
19. Australia acceded to the Refugee Convention in 1954 and to the Protocol relating to the Status of Refugees, New York, 31 January 1967, in force 4 October 1967, 19 UST 6223, 6257 in 1973.
20. Migration Act 1958 (Cth) s. 4(1).
21. International Conference on Indo-Chinese Refugees, Geneva, 13–14 June 1989: Declaration and Comprehensive Plan of Action, UN Doc A/CONF. 148/2, 13 June 1989.
22. (1992) 176 CLR 1.
23. The critical provisions are ss. 189, 196 and 198 which are contained in Part 2 of the Migration Act 1992 dealing with 'Control of arrival and presence of non-citizens'. Division 7 of Part 2, which contains sections 189 and 196, deals with 'Detention of unlawful non-citizens' – those without visas. Division 8 of Part 2, which contains s. 198, deals with 'Removal of unlawful non-citizens'.
24. *Re Woolley and Another; ex parte* M276/2003 (2004) 80 ALD 1, confirmed (2004) 225 CLR 1 (High Court).
25. *Al-Kateb v Godwin* (2004) 219 CLR 562.

26. The Nationality Law 1952, article 1.
27. The Law of Return, s. 1 defines the right of *aliyah* (immigration) as 'Every Jew has the right to come to this country as an *oleh'*.
28. HCJ 265/87. *Beresford v Minister of Interior*, 43 PD (4) 793 (1989). In another decision the Court listed the right of every Jew to make *aliyah* as one of 'the core characteristics which forge the minimum definition of the State of Israel as a Jewish State'. EA 11280/02, *Central Elections Committee for Sixteenth Knesset v MK Tibi*, 57 PD (4) 1, para. 12 (2003).
29. 6 Knesset Records, 1950, pp. 2036–37
30. Rejecting both the view of Jewish religious law according to which 'once a Jew always a Jew', and a subjective definition, the Court held that the term 'Jew' in the secular Law of Return had to be interpreted as it was understood by popular opinion. HCJ 72/62. *Oswald Rufeisen v Minister of Interior*, 16 PD 2428 (1962).
31. HCJ 58/68, *Shalit v Minister of Interior*, 23 PD (2) 477 (1969). Under the Population Registry Law details of each resident are registered. These details include 'religion' and 'nation' (*l'eom*). A person registering himself or herself or minor children for the first time may choose to leave these details blank. Benjamin Shalit requested that his son will be registered as having no religion and as a Jew by nation.
32. See, for example, HCJ 3648/97, *Stamka v Minister of Interior*, 53 PD (2) 728, para. 21 (1999)
33. Following the Millet system instituted when Palestine was part of the Ottoman Empire, in matters of marriage and divorce residents of Israel are subject to the law of the religious community to which they belong. With respect to Jews, the monopoly of religious law was strengthened by the Rabbinical Court Jurisdiction (Marriage and Divorce) Law 1953.
34. See, for example, Artsieli (2004).
35. The International Convention on the Elimination of All Forms of Racial Discrimination (ICERD) excludes from the definition of such discrimination provisions of law 'concerning nationality, citizenship or naturalisation, provided that such provisions do not discriminate against any particular nationality'. ICERD article 1.3
36. International Covenant on Civil and Political Rights 1966, article 12.4.
37. Basic Law: Human Liberty and Dignity, article 6b.
38. The Nationality Law 1952, article 1.
39. See article 4 of the Law of Return.
40. The Nationality Law, article 5b
41. Ibid., article 7.
42. The Entry into Israel Law, article 2.
43. The vast majority of Israeli citizens who marry residents of the territories belong to the Arab minority. While neither of these rights appear explicitly in the Basic Law: Human Dignity and Liberty, they fall under the protection of the right to human dignity, protected in Articles 2 and 4 of the law.
44. Although a majority of the Justices did find that the right to family life is constitutional and that it was violated by the Act. HCJ 7052/03, *Adala v The Minister of Interior and others*.
45. See UNHCR (2010).
46. Article 33 to the Convention Relating the Status of Refugees.

3. Labour market integration

Yitchak Haberfeld and Anne Daly

This chapter compares the economic assimilation of post-World War II immigrants in Australia and Israel. As discussed in earlier sections of the book, almost one-third of the Israeli Jewish population and one-quarter of the Australian population were born abroad, the highest proportions within the industrialized world. However, the immigration policies adopted by the two countries are quite different and can be expected to result in different levels of economic assimilation of immigrants.

While Australia selects from a large pool of applicants and requires a period of residence before eligibility for citizenship, Israel provides open access to Jews and specific categories of their family members, who receive citizenship upon arrival. Australia has a record of generous assistance to immigrants, particularly those in preferred categories, but the level of assistance has been progressively reduced. Israel actively recruits Jewish immigrants and provides a wide range of benefits during the initial settlement period.

There are two possible ways that the differences between the two countries could affect immigrants' economic assimilation. On the one hand, Australian immigration policy has the potential to attract more qualified immigrants. Consequently, the economic assimilation of immigrants can be expected to be more successful in Australia. On the other hand, the higher level of support provided by the Israeli government may offset, at least in part, the Australian advantage.

There are various dimensions of immigrants' economic assimilation, including labour force participation rates and occupational distribution. However, the single most important dimension of economic integration is earnings assimilation. Typically immigrants earn less than their native-born counterparts upon their arrival. However, as they accumulate more experience, they improve their relative earnings position. Full earnings assimilation occurs when the immigrant and native-born earnings converge for those of similar levels of qualification and other earning-enhancing attributes.

The level of earnings assimilation is related to two main factors. First, immigrants' country of origin has been found to be directly related to earnings assimilation (Semyonov and Lerenthal 1991). Immigrants who arrive from less developed countries find it more difficult to reach full earnings assimilation than immigrants who arrive from developed countries. Second, patterns of immigrants' self-selection from their countries of origin are found to be the key determinant of earnings assimilation (Chiswick 1978; Borjas 1990). The main determinant is the level of earnings-enhancing attributes, considered in relative terms, above or below the levels of the host society. Immigrants with above-average attributes more readily achieve earnings assimilation.[1] The destination country's immigration policy (and the country's attractiveness to immigrants) determines both the countries from which immigrants arrive and their self-selection patterns.

As discussed, in the post-war period Australian policy recruited immigrants from the UK and continental Europe, with preference to the English-speaking and northern Europeans. There was a large measure of success in absorption of immigrants into the labour market (Withers and Pope 1993). There were two major changes to the initial migration program beginning in the early 1970s with potential implications for immigrants' assimilation. First, while immigrants from the UK remained the largest group of new arrivals, there was a shift from other European sources to Asia. In 1981, 40 per cent of new permanent arrivals came from the UK, New Zealand (NZ), the USA and South Africa (SA) but in 2004 the share arriving from these countries had almost halved to 21 per cent. In 2004 the second largest country of origin for Australian immigrants was China, with India, Malaysia, Hong Kong, Indonesia, Japan and South Korea also in the top ten (Productivity Commission 2006).

The second change followed the introduction of the points system in the early 1970s, with shifts in the proportion of places allocated to the 'skill' and 'family' categories and the marked shift, beginning in the 1980s, in favour of skilled immigrants. In 1988–89, 38 per cent of visas were issued in the Skill category, increased to a record 70 per cent in 2005 (Productivity Commission 2006). There was also beginning in the mid-1990s the introduction and then expansion of a temporary visa to enable employers to bring in skilled workers to meet the growing skill shortage.

Israeli policy has been entirely different. Since 1948 Israeli governments have sought actively to attract Jewish immigrants by offering reimbursement of travel expenses, subsidized housing and mortgages, exemptions from a range of taxes, free Hebrew language classes, and free job training and retraining. Israel has succeeded in attracting a large inflow of population. Of the approximately 5.4 million Jews who lived in Israel at the end of 2007, 30 per cent were foreign-born (first-generation immigrants) 34 per cent born to an immigrant father (second-generation immigrants) (Israel Central Bureau of Statistics 2008a, Table 2.22). In other words, more than two-thirds of the Jewish population in Israel comprises immigrants and their children.

IMMIGRANTS' SELECTIVITY AND THEIR PARTICIPATION IN THE LABOUR FORCE

Australia

James Jupp has observed that 'for 150 years Australian immigration policy has been dominated by economic considerations' (Jupp 2007: 137). The level of immigration has been controlled and closely reflected the state of the business cycle. In the period following World War II, Australia experienced sustained economic growth, and until the 1973 oil price shock unemployment remained below 2 per cent. After 1973 unemployment rose and a period of structural readjustment began with a shift away from the manufacturing sector in favour of service industries. The 1980s began a period of significant microeconomic reform, including the floating of the Australian dollar and the privatization of government-owned enterprises. Unemployment remained well above the pre-1973 levels. The recession of the early 1990s saw unemployment reach in excess of 10 per cent, the highest level since the Great Depression. When economic growth was restored in the mid-1990s the Australian economy performed well, becoming a leading economy in terms of growth and declining unemployment in the OECD.

At the time of the 2001 Census, almost three-quarters of the prime working age population (aged 25–64 years) were born in Australia, 10 per cent in the UK and New Zealand, and 18 per cent in other mainly non-English speaking countries.

Australian studies of the immigrant workforce integration have followed international migration literature. Key factors considered are the role of human capital investment both before and after entry to Australia, English language competence, the process of transition into a new labour market, including the role of job search and recognition of existing skills and credentials, and the effects of barriers to integration such as discrimination. The results emphasize the importance of fluency in English and duration of residence in Australia in promoting immigrant integration.

Studies of immigrant unemployment in Australia show that after holding educational attainment, age and marital status constant, immigrants have higher unemployment rates but that they decline with duration of residence and increased English language proficiency (Chapman and Miller 1985; Miller 1986; Miller and Neo (n.d.)). The Productivity Commission (2006) decomposed the difference in unemployment rates between immigrants and the Australian-born for the four census years, 1986, 1991, 1996 and 2001. They found that English ability, gender, education, location and age did not explain the differences in the unemployment rate of immigrants and the Australian-born in 1986. These factors accounted for about a third of the difference in 1991 and 1996 but less than 10 per cent of the difference in 2001. It is interesting to note, however, that the size of the gap in unemployment rates declined between 1991 and 2001.

Cobb-Clark (2000) analysed employment data from the Longitudinal Survey of Immigrants to Australia over an 18-month period between 1993 and 1995. She found that immigrants arriving on skill-based visas were more likely to be in employment six months after arrival than those arriving on other visas, for example humanitarian visas. However, after 18 months this gap was reduced for both males and females. Also, those who had visited Australia before they migrated found employment more quickly than those with no direct knowledge of the country. Cobb-Clark (2000) and Miller (1999) also argue that visa category is not an important determinant of unemployment once the labour market characteristics of immigrants are taken into account. It is perhaps not surprising to find that the evidence does show that those entering the Australian labour market with English proficiency, education and working experience valued by employers are most likely to be in employment.

Israel: Pre-1967 Immigrants

The economic assimilation of immigrants in Israel has been studied extensively for a number of years. The first two immigrant waves – those that arrived between 1948–51 and 1952–67 – have characteristics entirely different from post-1967 immigrants. While the pre-1967 immigrants are characterized by the preponderant number of refugees, the immigrants that arrived in later years were mainly motivated by economic factors, and in a relatively small numbers by ideology. Consequently, the self-selection patterns of the early immigrants are quite distinctive.

Most empirical studies that examined economic assimilation of pre-1967 immigrants have used an ethnic dichotomy of the Jewish population in Israel based on continent rather than country of origin – a differentiation of those born in Asia and Africa (*Mizrahim*) and Europe and America (*Ashkenazim*). The classification of the second generation, the offspring of immigrants, was also based on the father's continent of origin. In contrast, studies of post-1967 immigrants focus more on specific country of origin, particularly the studies of immigrants from the Former Soviet Union (FSU).

Upon its establishment, Israel was faced with an extremely difficult economic situation, particularly in the period 1948–51. It had to finance a war fought against Arab neighbours, immediately absorb a very large number of Jewish immigrants, and provide for the basic needs of its new and existing population. These challenges were met by a rigorous economic policy that included price control, rationing of basic commodities, and a high level of central planning. The most difficult problems during these years were to provide housing and employment to the newly arrived.

The situation changed gradually during the early 1950s. Large capital inflows came from the USA through transfers and loans; from the German government in the form of compensation to both the Israeli government and individuals; from the sale of government bonds abroad, and from individual transfers by Jews in Western countries to the Jewish Agency, which was responsible for the absorption of immigrants. This incoming capital was used for both consumption and investment. Consequently, the Israeli economy experienced very rapid growth (Halevi and Klinov-Malul 1968).

1948–51

Approximately 690 000 Jewish immigrants arrived in Israel during the three and a half years between May 1948 and December of 1951, doubling the Jewish population in less than four years. Two groups of roughly equal size, the European Holocaust survivors and those from under-developed regions of Asia and Africa, arrived in this period.

Most immigrants in these two groups were refugees, including survivors of the Holocaust and those escaping from hostile Muslim and East European countries. These characteristics explain the relatively low levels of human capital levels. The European immigrants had, on average, 8.7 years of schooling, the Asian-African 4.2 years; 4.1 per cent of European immigrants had a tertiary qualification, 1.1 per cent Asian-African counterparts. By contrast, in 1950 the native-born Israelis in the age range 25–45 years had 9.4 years of schooling and 4.5 per cent had a tertiary qualification, marginally higher than the European immigrants.[2]

In 1972 (approximately 20 years after arrival), 89 per cent of the European immigrant men and 85 of the Asian-African immigrant men were actively engaged in the labour market, compared with 89 per cent of native-born Israelis. These figures indicate a high level of economic integration for men. The figures for European, Asian-African and native-born women were 28, 19 and 27 per cent respectively.

Contrary to the relatively small group-based gaps in labour force participation rates, the occupational distribution of those who participated in the labour force in 1972 show an entirely different picture. The proportion of European and Asian-African immigrant men who had a professional, managerial or technical job in 1972 was 14 and 8 per cent respectively, compared with 27 per cent of native-born men.

1952–67

During the second major wave of migration, approximately 590000 immigrants arrived in Israel. Of those, about 65000 immigrants arrived from Asia, 280000 from Africa, 205000 from Europe, and approximately 32000 from America and Australia (Israel Central Bureau of Statistics 2008a, Tables 4.2, 4.4). The largest group of immigrants in this wave was from Morocco, followed by Romania. Those from Asian-African countries constituted about 60 per cent of the immigrants.

The European-American immigrants in this second wave were better educated (both compared with the first wave and the native-born), with 9.8 years of schooling and 11.5 per cent with a tertiary qualification; the Asian-African had 4.7 years of schooling and 1.2 per cent had a tertiary qualification. The low educational level of the Asian-African was similar to the first wave.

In accordance with their relatively high levels of education, European-American immigrants of the second wave had the highest labour force participation rate in 1972 – 96 per cent for men and 46 per cent for women, as compared with 91 and 23 per cent among Asian-African immigrant men and women, and 89 and 27 per cent among native-born men and women. In addition, of those in the workforce in 1972, 25 per cent of the European-American men and 6 per cent of the Asian-African immigrant men had a professional, managerial or technical job as compared with 27 per cent of native-born men. The equivalent figures for European-American, Asian-African, and native-born women were 27, 7 and 22 per cent respectively.

The higher educational levels of a minority of the European-American immigrants thus translated into a relatively high proportion with high-status jobs in 1972. The level of labour force participation of immigrants and native-born was similar, with the exception of Asian-African women.

Israel: Post-1967 Immigrants

The Israeli economy changed dramatically during the post-1967 period. Strict government controls were gradually removed (Ben-Bassat 2002). Economic growth during this period was much lower and ranged between 0 to 6 per cent of gross domestic product. The fluctuations in economic activity were influenced by the immigration intake: the absorption of large numbers of immigrants (mainly from the FSU during the 1970s and 1990s) led to economic downturn, followed by higher growth and lower levels of unemployment.

1968–89

Approximately 560 000 immigrants arrived between 1968 and 1989. The relatively small numbers from Ethiopia (about 55 000) were the only refugees. A relatively small fraction, mainly from North America and some from the FSU, were ideological immigrants. However, most of the other immigrants – from Eastern and Western Europe, as well as from Iran, Morocco and South Africa – were economic immigrants (Cohen 2002). The vast majority arrived from Europe (about 308 000), America (about 137 000), and South Africa (about 10 000). Asia and Africa contributed 56 000 and 46 000 immigrants respectively (Israel Central Bureau of Statistics 2008a, Table 4.2).

The post-1967 immigrants (with the exception of those arriving from Ethiopia) had, on average, high levels of education. Of the immigrants from the FSU, the largest single national group, close to 30 per cent held a tertiary qualification upon their arrival (as compared with 5 per cent and 26 per cent of second-generation Asian-African origin and European-American origin respectively in the year 1983). This advantage in education could indicate a pattern of positive self-selection of immigrants from the FSU to Israel, but there is indication that the first preference was the US; of those who gained entry into the US, more than half held a tertiary qualification (Cohen 2002; Cohen and Haberfeld 2007; Haberfeld 2010).

The other large national groups of economic immigrants in the period 1968–89 also show high educational levels, with educational levels rising over time, with the exception of immigrants from the US. The proportion of college-educated immigrants from the US was 77 per cent during the late 1960s and early 1970s and 64 per cent during the early 1990s. This decline is even more pronounced when considering the rise in college education of US Jews during this period (Cohen 2002). Immigrants from the FSU and the US both had higher levels of education than native-born Israelis.

1990–2007

In the most recent wave of immigrants to Israel, from 1990 to 2007, more than 950 000 arrived from the FSU, constituting 80 per cent of all immigrants arriving during the period (Israel Central Bureau of Statistics 2008a, Table 4.4). More than 400 000 arrived between December 1989 and December 1991, and 250000 between 1992 and 1995 (Cohen and Haberfeld 2007).

Almost half of the immigrants arriving in Israel from the FSU during the first two years of this wave held a college degree,[3] however the proportion among successive cohorts declined to about one-third (Cohen 2007; Cohen and Haberfeld 2007; Cohen and Kogan 2007). As was the case earlier, the most highly educated segment went to the US, with almost 70 per cent of those arriving during the early 1990s having a college degree (declining to 60 per cent at the end of the decade) (Cohen et al. 2008).

A high proportion of immigrants from the FSU found employment shortly after arrival, but they faced difficulty gaining high-status jobs commensurate with their qualifications (Semyonov 1997; Raijman and Semyonov 1997, 1998; Eckstein and Weiss 2002; Cohen and Kogan 2007; Gorodzeisky and Semyonov 2008; Raijman 2009).

Immigrant and Native-born: Statistical Overview

Tables 3.1 (for men) and 3.2 (for women) present summary measures for those who arrived in Australia and Israel as adults. For Australia, the tables present ratios for men and women born in the UK and New Zealand, and mainly non-English speaking countries. The top half of the table compares those immigrants who arrived before 1972 with the Australian-born and the second half of the table, those who arrived after 1971. For Israel, native-born of European-American origin serve as the base line of European-American immigrants, and native-born Asian-African origin serve as the base-line of Asian-African immigrants.

The characteristics of pre-1972 immigrants to Australia from the UK and New Zealand were similar to those of the Australian-born. There was, however, a lower rate of self-employment among both males and females and a higher proportion of immigrant males had a tertiary qualification. The differences between those born in non-English speaking countries and the Australian-born were much more pronounced. Although the average person born in a non-English speaking country worked similar hours to the native-born, the income of those in employment was lower, especially for males. This probably reflects the smaller proportion of males in professional, technical and managerial occupations and the smaller proportion with a tertiary qualification. The labour force participation rate was lower for those born in non-English speaking countries and a smaller proportion were self-employed.

The differences between pre-1967 immigrants to Israel and their native-born counterparts are wider than those found in Australia, mainly in earnings, education and employment in high-status occupations. However,

Table 3.1 Immigrant-to-native men (25–64 years of age) ratios – by country, period of migration, and place of origin

	Australia		Israel	
Immigrants' origin	UK and NZ	Other Countries	Europe-America	Asia-Africa
Pre-1972(Australia) Pre-1967(Israel)[a]				
Average earnings[c]	0.98	0.84	0.82	0.69
Average hours of work[c]	0.96	0.97	0.99	0.96
Labour force participation rate	1.03	0.94	1.03	0.99
Percent self-employed	0.71	0.92	1.85	0.85
Percent professional, technical and management[c]	0.94	0.62	0.40	0.29
Per cent with an academic degree[c]	1.17	0.63	0.38	0.23
Post-1972 (Australia)[b] Post-1967 (Israel)[a]				
Average earnings[c]	1.11	0.95	0.56	0.81
Average hours of work[c]	1.00	0.92	1.03	0.99
Labour force participation rate	0.99	0.92	1.00	0.95
Per cent self-employed	1.08	0.67	0.43	0.65
Per cent professional, technical and management[c]	0.96	0.78	0.63	0.84
Per cent with an academic degree[c]	0.97	1.72	1.30	1.97

Notes:
[a] Australia – the comparison group for pre-1971 immigrants is Australian-born males or females aged 45–64 years. The census does not include age on arrival so the sample of immigrants has been restricted to those who arrived before 1971 and were aged 45–64 years in 1991 to focus on those who arrived in the country as adults. Israel – Jews, 25–64 years of age; immigrants: arrived in Israel at the age of 25–45. Native-born of European-American origin serve as the base line of European-American immigrants, and native-born Asian-African origin who have native-born fathers serve as the base line of Asian-African immigrants.
[b] Immigrants who were 25 years of age or older when they arrived are compared with Australian-born males and females aged 25–64 years.
[c] The samples used to calculate these ratios: Australia – males and females in employment with positive annual income and hours of work; Israel – salaried who worked at least eight hours per week, and earned at least NIS 500 per month (in 1995 prices).

Sources: Australia – Australian Bureau of Statistics 1 per cent sample of the 1991 census. Israel – Israeli Population Census 1972 (for the pre-1967 immigrants) and Israeli Population Census 1995 (for the post-1967 immigrants).

European-American immigrants are much closer to their native-born counterparts than Asian-African immigrants to native-born of Asian-African origin.

With regard to the more recent immigrants in both countries, there was a marked improvement in the ratios for those immigrants arriving after 1971 as adults and the Australian-born population. As with the earlier immigrants, those from the UK and New Zealand had labour market characteristics that were similar to those of the Australian-born. One notable difference was that both male and female immigrants from the UK and New Zealand in employment had, on average, higher incomes than the Australian-born. The incomes of those in employment from non-English speaking countries remained below those of the Australian-born, although the gap had decreased. A larger proportion of the newer immigrants were employed in professional, technical and managerial occupations than the earlier arrivals. The most significant change is in the proportion of the more recent immigrants from non-English speaking countries with a university qualification. The proportion of highly educated immigrants arriving before 1971 was about two-thirds of that of the Australian-born but it was 72 per cent higher for males and 59 per cent higher for females arriving between 1971 and 1991. This illustrates the shift in the criteria used for approval of immigrants after the early 1970s.

Similar findings are found for the more recent immigrants who arrived in Israel. Recent immigrants had higher levels of education than native-born Israelis. Consequently, a much higher proportion of them held professional, technical or managerial jobs. At the same time however, and contrary to Australia, the earnings gap between European-American immigrants and those native born of European-American origin has grown dramatically. In contrast, recent Asian-African immigrants improved their earnings position relative to their earlier immigrant and native counterparts.

Table 3.3 uses data from the 2001 to update the data presented in Tables 3.1 and 3.2. It shows that among those arriving in the five years prior to the 2001 census, immigrants from the UK and New Zealand earned higher incomes and were better qualified than both their Australian and earlier-immigrant counterparts. They were, however, less likely to be self-employed. Recent immigrants from non-English speaking countries were much less likely to be self-employed, but much more likely to have a tertiary qualification. The labour force participation ratio of this group fell below that of the Australian-born, especially for women born in non-English speaking countries.

In sum, early immigrants to Australia were found to be a more select group than early immigrants to Israel. In both countries, early immigrants belonging to the ethnic background of the stronger native-born groups

Table 3.2 Immigrant-to-native women (25–64 years of age) ratios – by country, period of migration, and place of origin

	Australia		Israel	
Immigrants' origin	UK and NZ	Other countries	Europe-America	Asia-Africa
Pre-1972 (Australia)				
Pre-1967 (Israel).[a]				
Average earnings[c]	1.02	0.92	0.91	0.67
Average hours of work[c]	0.99	1.03	1.23	1.09
Labour force participation rate	1.04	0.82	0.60	0.52
Per cent self-employed	0.80	0.79	1.52	0.53
Per cent professional, technical and management[c]	0.91	0.74	0.47	0.18
Per cent with an academic degree[c]	0.94	0.64	0.61	0.20
Post-1972 (Australia)[b]				
Post-1967 (Israel)[a]				
Average earnings[c]	1.07	1.04	0.68	0.85
Average hours of work[c]	1.05	1.08	1.17	1.11
Labour force participation rate	1.00	0.89	0.96	0.63
Per cent self-employed	0.92	0.69	0.58	1.32
Per cent professional, technical and management[c]	0.99	0.79	0.63	0.62
Per cent with an academic degree[c]	0.99	1.59	1.36	1.54

Notes:
[a] Australia – the comparison group for pre-1971 immigrants is Australian born males or females aged 45–64 years. The census does not include age on arrival so the sample of immigrants has been restricted to those who arrived before 1971 and were aged 45–64 years in 1991 to focus on those who arrived in the country as adults. Israel – Jews, 25–64 years of age; immigrants: arrived in Israel at the age of 25–45. Native-born of European-American origin serve as the base line of European-America immigrants, and native-born of Asian-African origin who have native-born fathers serve as the base line of Asian-African immigrants.
[b] Immigrants who were 25 years of age or older when they arrived are compared with Australian-born males and females aged 25–64 years.
[c] The samples used to calculate these ratios: Australia – males and females in employment with positive annual income and hours of work; Israel – salaried workers who worked at least eight hours per week, and earned at least NIS 500 per month (in 1995 prices).

Sources: Australia – Australian Bureau of Statistics 1 per cent sample of the 1991 census. Israel – Israeli Population Census 1972 (for the pre-1967 immigrants) and Israeli Population Census 1995 (for the post-1967 immigrants).

Table 3.3   Ratios of immigrants arriving between 1996 and 2001 to
*   Australian-born[a] by gender, place of birth*

	Males		Females	
Country of birth	UK and NZ	Other countries	UK and NZ	Other countries
Average income [b]	1.18	0.95	1.28	0.94
Average hours worked [c]	0.99	0.87	1.14	1.00
Labour force participation rate	1.07	0.88	1.07	0.74
Per cent self-employed	0.61	0.45	0.52	0.48
Per cent occupied in professional, technical or managerial occupations [b]	1.16	1.07	1.17	0.96
Per cent with a bachelors degree[b]	1.76	2.72	1.40	1.90

Notes:
[a] The comparison group is Australian born males and females aged 25–64 years.
[b] The sample used to calculate these ratios were males and females in employment with positive annual income and hours of work.

Source: Australian Bureau of Statistics 1 per cent sample of the 2001 census.

(UK and New Zealand in Australia, European-American in Israel) had higher qualifications and higher earnings than other early immigrants ('other countries' in Australia, Asian-African origin in Israel). In addition, all groups of the more recent immigrants show higher qualifications and earnings relative to their native-born and earlier-immigrant counterparts.

EARNINGS ASSIMILATION OF IMMIGRANTS

Australia

Comparisons with Canada and the US (Antecol et al. 2003) and with the US alone (Miller and Neo 2003) show that Australian immigrants face a smaller initial income penalty on entering the new labour market. Miller and Neo (2003) however, argue that the wage growth of immigrants in Australia is slower than for those entering the US market. They attribute these differences to the relatively high minimum wages in the more regulated Australian labour market. The evidence suggests that the immigrant population in Australia is likely composed of those who prefer the lower risk to expected income levels provided by the Australian welfare system, the relatively high minimum wages and compressed income distribution compared with the US.

Other Australian studies considered the transition effects associated with arrival, cohort quality and the macroeconomic effects on immigrant income. Results have depended on the time period studied and the data source. The studies of Chiswick and Miller (1985) and Beggs and Chapman (1988) show an income penalty for immigrants compared with the Australian-born in the early 1980s. There is evidence that the incomes of immigrants after 1965 from non-English speaking backgrounds were slower to catch up with those of the Australian-born than earlier non-English speaking immigrants (see also Will, 1997). McDonald and Worswick (1999), using data from the Australian Bureau of Statistics (ABS) Income Distribution Surveys for 1982, 1986 and 1990 rather than the Population Census, found no evidence of a catch up in immigrant earnings or a negative cohort effect among more recent arrivals. They also found little evidence that macroeconomic conditions had a different effect on the earnings of immigrants than on the Australian-born.

The most recent study on immigrant incomes by Chiswick and Miller (2008), using 2001 Census data, emphasizes the role of occupation in explaining the lower incomes of recently arrived immigrants. They argue that as part of the transition to the new labour market, immigrants begin by working in lower status occupations than is appropriate given their education and work experience. Their results emphasize the importance of English language proficiency. They show a smaller income penalty for immigrants from non-English speaking countries as duration of residence increases.

Israel

Pre-1967 immigrants

A number of studies have examined the level of the pre-1967 immigrants' integration in the Israeli labour market (Spilerman and Habib 1976; Boyd et al. 1980; Semyonov and Tyree 1981; Semyonov and Kraus 1983; Ben-Porath 1986; Lewin-Epstein and Semyonov 1986; Yitzhaki 1987; Semyonov and Lerenthal 1991; Haberfeld 1993; Semyonov 1997; Yaish 2001).[4] All reached a similar conclusion: the European-American immigrants who arrived pre-1967 fully integrated into the Israeli labour market. These findings are in line with findings in other immigration countries, where immigrants were found to reach full economic assimilation with native-born workers of similar attributes (Chiswick 1978). Language competence (in Hebrew), as distinct from ethnicity, has not been treated as a significant variable in Israeli studies.

Unlike their European-American origin counterparts, the pre-1967 Asian-African immigrants failed to reach economic parity with native-born Israelis or with European-American immigrants (Cohen 1998; Cohen and Haberfeld 1998). Most of the gap in earnings (and in occupational distribution) between the Asian-African and the other Jews living in Israel can be attributed to the Asian-African's lower educational levels as compared with those of the other groups.

Post-1967 immigrants
Most studies of the economic assimilation of immigrants who arrived in Israel during 1968–89 concentrated on the largest group, those from the FSU. Their conclusion was that these immigrants fully assimilated into the Israeli labour market in terms of participation and earnings (Klinov 1991; Semyonov and Lerenthal 1991; Raijman and Semyonov 1998; Friedberg 2000). However, Cohen and Haberfeld (2007), using the 1995 Israeli Census and differentiating between those who arrived as adults from those who arrived as children (what is labelled as 1.5 generation), reached other conclusions.

First, FSU immigrants who arrived during 1967–89 did not reach earnings parity with native-born European-American Israelis. Rather, they did worse than immigrants arriving during the same period from Romania and the US. Second, the FSU immigrants who chose to migrate to the US were more educated than their immigrant counterparts who chose Israel, and reached full earnings assimilation with US-born white non-Hispanic natives.

The few studies on the earnings assimilation of immigrants arriving from the FSU during the 1990s concluded that they have not reached earnings assimilation with native Israelis, both European-American and Asian-African origin (Eckstein and Weiss 2002; Cohen and Haberfeld 2007; Gorodzeisky and Semyonov 2008).

In sum, studies indicate that immigrants arriving from the FSU (and the US) did not fully assimilate in the labour market due to their negative self-selection from their population of origin. Other immigrant groups were more successful in the Israeli labour market, including immigrants from Morocco. In contrast to their predecessors who performed poorly, they reached full earnings assimilation due to their positive self-selection.[5]

Finally, the group of immigrants arriving in Israel from Ethiopia requires separate discussion. Most were brought to Israel through two secret government operations – approximately 17 000 in 1984 and 40 000 in 1991. About 25 000 additional immigrants have arrived from Ethiopia since 2000 (Israel Central Bureau of Statistics 2008a, Table 4.4). The

Table 3.4   Income convergence rates of immigrants to Australia – by gender and country of birth, 1991a

Birthplace	Males		Females	
	UK and NZ	Other	UK and NZ	Other
Initial income gap[b]	No statistically significant gap	0.199	No statistically significant gap	0.085
Annual assimilation rate[a][c]	NA	0.005	NA	0.003
Years for convergence	NA	40	NA	28

Notes:
[a] The samples were composed on Australian-born 25- to 64-year-olds who were employees and reported working positive hours and had a positive income and immigrants either from the UK and NZ or from other mainly non-English speaking countries.
[b] Derived from income equations with (ln) weekly income as the dependent variable as a function of a dummy indicating migrant status, years since migration, (ln) hours worked, age, age squared, years of schooling, dummies for those with a tertiary qualification, married, self-identified with poor English and living in a major urban area.
[c] The 1 per cent census data includes year of arrival in categories. The variable 'years since arrived' has therefore been taken as the midpoint of each of these categories and the value of the open-ended category, 'before 1971' set at 25 years. Some sensitivity analysis of the choice of value for this category suggests that it does not greatly change the size of the estimated coefficients.

Source: Australian Bureau of Statistics 1 per cent sample of the 1991 census.

Ethiopian-born immigrants came from an underdeveloped country and their education levels and labour market skills were very low. Consequently, their chances of finding employment are low, they hold low-skill jobs, and earn, on average, as little as one half of average earnings (Offer 2004; Raijman 2009).

A key indicator of labour market integration is the degree to which earnings of immigrants match those of the native-born of similar characteristics. Table 3.4 presents summary estimates from earnings regressions for male and female immigrants to Australia from the UK and New Zealand on the one hand and other countries on the other.[6]

The results presented in Table 3.4 show that there was no statistically significant difference in income between the Australian-born and immigrants from the UK and New Zealand. This group can be thought of as integrated into the Australian labour market from the time of arrival. There were, however, significant differences in income between the Australian-born and those arriving from non-English speaking countries. It would take a male immigrant from a non-English speaking background

Table 3.5   *Earnings convergence rates of immigrants to Israel – by gender, place of origin, and period of immigration*[a]

	Men		Women	
Immigrants' origin	Europe-America	Asia-Africa	Europe-America	Asia-Africa
Pre-1972(Australia); Pre-1967(Israel)				
Initial earnings gap[b]	0.305	0.472	0.243	0.288
Annual assimilation rate[c]	0.010	0.010	0.008	0.009
Years for convergence	30	47	30	32
Post-1972 (Australia); post-1967(Israel)				
Initial earnings gap[b]	0.688	0.439	0.723	0.399
Annual assimilation rate[c]	0.026	0.007	0.034	0.007
Years for convergence	26	63	21	57

Notes:

[a] Derived from earnings equations in which (ln) earnings is a function of a dummy indicating immigrant status, years since migration, (ln) working hours, age and its squared term, years of schooling, and two dummy variables indicating an academic degree and being married. Samples are composed of salaried workers, 25–64 years of age, who worked at least eight hours per week and earned more than Euro 100 per month in real earnings. Immigrants included are those who arrived at the age of 25–45. The Israeli samples do not include Arabs.

[b] The coefficient of the 'immigrant status' variable (coded as 1 = an immigrant; 0 = a native-born).

[c] The coefficient of the interaction term of 'immigrant status' and 'years since migration'.

Source: Israeli Population Census 1972 (for the pre-1967 immigrants) and Israeli Population Census 1995 (for the post-1967 immigrants).

40 years to catch up with the incomes of Australian-born males of similar attributes and it would take females from these countries 28 years to catch up with their Australian counterparts.

Table 3.5 summarizes immigrants' earnings assimilation in Israel. All immigrant groups arriving in Israel suffered substantial earnings gaps upon arrival when compared with the native-born. This difference with Australia is probably the outcome of the more restrictive selection rules of the Australian immigration policy. However, as expected, the annual assimilation rates in Israel are much higher than those found in Australia. This result of a smaller initial gap but a slower catch up rate in Australia is similar to that reported by Miller and Neo (2003) and Antecol et al. (2003) in their comparisons between Australia and the US and Canada.

Australia: The Second Generation

Another indicator of the extent of labour market integration for immigrants is the economic status of second generation immigrants. Khoo and Birrell (2002) and Khoo et al. (2002) use indicators from the census to compare the educational and occupational outcomes for second-generation Australians with those who are third generation or more. They found that second-generation Australians had higher education and occupational status than third or more generation Australians. This was particularly true for those of Southern European, Eastern European and Asian origin while those from English speaking countries and Western Europe looked more like third or more generation Australians. More recent data from the 2006 Census confirm these results (Australian Bureau of Statistics 2009). The Australian Bureau of Statistics report also shows that second-generation Australians had higher individual incomes than third or more generation Australians even after differences in the age structures of the populations were taken into account.

The results reported in Table 3.6 compare incomes for second-generation migrants, here defined as those who had both parents born overseas, compared with the Australian-born who had either none or one parent born overseas. There was no statistically significant difference between the income levels of second-generation Australians compared with other males. This supports the hypothesis of labour market integration for the male children of immigrants. The results provide some evidence that the female children of immigrants faced a wage penalty of about 3 per cent (see Chapter 6 this volume for further discussion of research on the second generation).

Israel: The Second Generation

The Israeli-born children of the immigrants arriving during 1948–67 are 25–60 years of age today. Many studies of their education levels and economic fortunes have been conducted by researchers belonging to various disciplines using different research approaches and data sets (see for example: Amir 1987; Nahon 1987; Yitzhaki 1987; Mark 1994, 1996; Haberfeld 1993). Despite these differences of approach, there is a broad consensus that the economic gap between native-born European-American and Asian-African were not attenuated. Findings indicate that despite a narrowing gap in the education levels of Asian-African and European-American origin, the earnings gap among members of the second generation have been widening over the years (Cohen 1998; Cohen and Haberfeld 1998; Haberfeld and Cohen 2007; Haberfeld 2009). The main explanation for the widening earnings gap relates to the increased

Table 3.6 Determinants of income for second-generation Australians, 2001[a]

Dependent variable	Males		Females	
	Ln FT hourly income[b]	Ln hourly income, all employees	Ln FT hourly income[b]	Ln hourly income, all employees
2nd generation migrant	0.0087	0.0080	−0.0312	−0.0308
	(0.010)	(0.011)	(0.012)**	(0.0112)**
Age	0.0493	0.0378	0.0314	0.0307
	(0.003)**	(0.003)**	(0.004)**	(0.004)**
Age ^{2}	−0.0005	−0.0004	−0.0003	−0.0004
	(0.000)**	(0.000)**	(0.000)**	(0.000)**
Married	0.0936	0.0788	0.0159	−0.0177
	(0.007)**	(0.008)**	(0.008)**	(0.008)**
Poor English	−0.1613	−0.1100	0.1980	−0.0589
	(0.116)	(0.125)	(0.133)	(0.127)
Years of schooling	0.0723	0.0704	0.0640	0.0517
	(0.001)**	(0.001)**	(0.001)**	(0.001)**
Lives in major urban area	0.0842	0.0710	0.0919	0.0538
	(0.007)**	(0.007)**	(0.008)**	(0.008)**
Intercept	0.8358	1.1323	1.2900	1.6258
	(0.061)**	(0.064)**	(0.073)**	(0.074)**
R^2	0.216	0.168	0.213	0.088
N	14 836	16 672	8 490	14 789

Notes:
* Indicates the coefficient is significant at the 5 per cent level, ** at the 1 per cent level.
[a] Second generation Australians are those who have both parents born overseas. The samples were composed of Australian-born 25- to 64-year-olds who were employees and reported working positive hours and had a positive income.
[b] Hourly income of those working 35 or more hours per week.

Source: Australian Bureau of Statistics 1 per cent sample of the 2001 census.

earnings inequality in Israel, mainly due to increasing returns on higher education. Since more of the European-American than Asian-African origin acquire a tertiary qualification, the earnings gap between the two groups has been widening (Haberfeld and Cohen 2007).

Cohen and Haberfeld (2007) also analysed the 1.5 generation (those at the age of 6–14 upon arrival) who arrived in Israel during 1968–83 from the five main source countries – the FSU, the US, Romania, Argentina and Morocco. Their results present a clear country-based hierarchy of the economic assimilation (or lack of) of the young immigrant generation in this wave. The worst off are the (mostly ideological) immigrant men who arrived at a young age from the US. By 1995, men belonging to this group did not reach full earnings assimilation with both native-born of European-American and Asian-African origin of equal attributes. They are followed by those who arrived from the FSU. Both men and women reached earnings parity with Asian-African but not with European-American origin native-born Israelis. By 1995 the three remaining groups reached full earnings assimilation with equally qualified native Israelis of Asian-African and European-American origin.

Similar to processes in other immigration societies, the second generation do better than their parents (Borjas 1990; Carliner 1980). However, the earnings gap among second-generation Israelis is wider than those found among their parents, which, in turn, makes the second-generation Israelis of European-American origin the dominant group in the labour market. Within each ethnic group, men earn more than women (Haberfeld and Cohen 1998b, 2007; Kraus 2002; Yaish and Kraus 2003).

Cohen et al. (2007) studied the young cohort (25–34 years of age) of third-generation Israelis. They found that third-generation Israelis of Asian-African origin had a lower level of higher education than second-generation Israelis of Asian-African origin and of similar family background. Consequently, the earnings gap between the third-generation of Asian-African and European-American origin is expected to be wider than the gap among their parents.

Non-Jewish Immigrants in Israel

There are two groups of non-Jewish immigrants to Israel, both of whom began to arrive in significant numbers in the early 1990s. The first comprise the non-Jewish spouses of Jewish immigrants, most from the FSU, entitled to Israeli citizenship under the Law of Return. Their economic assimilation is similar to that of others who arrived with them and in similar circumstances (Cohen 2007).

The second group comprise temporary labor migrants. As noted in earlier chapters, their overall number is estimated to be 200000, half of whom lack residence status and are 'illegal immigrants'. While in 1990 they constituted less than 1 per cent of the Israeli labour force, they reached an all-time high of 13.5 per cent in 2002, and have stabilized at around 10 per cent in recent years (Raijman 2009). At the end of 2009, the average monthly earnings of the 77500 migrant workers whose employers paid their social security tax were estimated to be US$1100. This represents 53 per cent of average monthly earnings of Israelis. The highest paying sectors are in the hospitality industry (hotels and restaurants) and

construction. The lowest are in health, nursing and temporary help services (Israel Central Bureau of Statistics 2009, Tables 1.1, 1.16).

Summary

A key factor in integration into the Australian labour market is proficiency
in English. This has been found in comparisons of both unemployment and
income between immigrants and the Australian-born. The gap in unemployment rates between immigrants and the Australian-born however,
appears to decline fairly quickly. In contrast, there are marked differences
in the labour force participation rates between immigrant groups from
non-English speaking backgrounds on the one hand, and the Australian-
born and immigrants from English speaking countries on the other, and
these have persisted over time. Immigrants from non-English speaking
backgrounds are estimated to take longer to achieve income parity with the
Australian-born than those from English speaking backgrounds. In fact,
some estimates based on data from the 1980s, suggested that they would not
achieve parity with the Australian-born of similar measured characteristics
over their working lives. Estimates presented here support this conclusion.

The results presented here show that second-generation Australians
are successfully integrated into the labour market. It is however, important to note that most second-generation Australians of working age had
European parents, and it will be interesting to see if the children of more
recent immigrants who are more likely to come from non-European backgrounds, are as successfully integrated.

All immigrant groups that arrived in Israel have been actively involved
in the labour market and showed rates of labour force participation similar
to those of native-born persons. The main differences among immigrants
are found in their earnings assimilation. The degree to which immigrants
successfully achieve earnings assimilation with native-born Israelis varies
along two main dimensions. The first is the immigrants' place of origin. In
general, immigrants who came to Israel from the more developed countries of Europe, US, Australia and South Africa succeeded more than
those who arrived from the less developed Asian and African countries.
Furthermore, the gaps between the children of pre-1967 immigrants have
widened. After 55–60 years in Israel, Asian-African immigrants and their
offspring have not reached full earnings assimilation, and probably will
not reach it in the coming decades.

The second determinant of immigrants' earnings assimilation in Israel
is their patterns of self-selection. Such patterns seem to be associated with
immigrants' place of origin. Pre-1967 European-American immigrants,
and especially those who arrived since 1952, show a pattern of a more

intense positive self-selection than the pre-1967 Asian-African immigrants. However, patterns of self-selection have become more complicated among post-1967 immigrants to Israel. More than one million immigrants who arrived in Israel after 1967 from the FSU have failed in their attempt to reach full earnings assimilation despite their exceptionally high education levels. This failure is explained by the fact that a relatively high proportion of the best qualified and most able immigrants from the FSU migrated to countries other than Israel (mainly to the US).

The issue of the large number of immigrant workers who are not covered by the Law of Return needs to be addressed in future research. There is now a large community of non-citizen workers living in Israel. Many of them have been living in the country for many years and yet do not have civil and economic rights, many have no status because they lack work permits.

CONCLUSION

Australia and Israel are two leading immigrant societies with very different immigration policies. While the Law of Return gives all Jewish people the right to immigrate to Israel, the current Australian system is orientated towards skill-based immigration and administered under a points system. The Australian immigration target is set each year through a political process and reflects, among other things, the state of the Australian labour market. The Israeli system has a Zionist and religious basis while the Australian system has a strong economic focus.

In both countries integration into the host labour market in terms of employment appears to be easier than integration in terms of income parity. As expected, earnings assimilation has been more successful in Australia than in Israel. The evidence suggests that the difference in outcomes in the longer term may be less pronounced, although there is evidence of widening inequalities in Israel. If the measure of economic integration were the sole outcome measure for immigration policy, then a policy with an economic focus such as the Australian one appears likely to deliver benefits to the host country faster than one based on alternative criteria. Economic criteria, however, are only one way of assessing the success of immigration policy.

NOTES

1. The best way to evaluate immigrants' patterns of self-selection is to compare them to the source population from which they arrive. However, it is often impossible to obtain

information about the population of origin, and instead immigrants are compared to the population in the host country.

2. These statistics and those that follow are derived from analyses of the 1972 Israeli census by the Israeli author. Immigrants included are those who arrived in Israel aged 25–45.

3. The educational level of immigrants arriving from the Asian republics was, as expected, lower than that of their European counterparts (Haberfeld et al. 2000).

4. Semyonov and Tyree (1981), Semyonov and Kraus (1983), Lewin-Epstein and Semyonov (1986), Semyonov and Lerenthal (1991) and Yaish (2001) did not separate between first and second-generation immigrants in their ethnic dichotomy. Such a classification might lead to biased estimates of the gap within first-generation immigrants.

5. Two exceptions are studies conducted by Rebhun (2008; 2010). He examined all immigrants (focusing mainly on immigrant women) who arrived in Israel at the age of 15 and above and controlled for country of origin. The findings indicate that in general, immigrants in Israel do not suffer an employment or earnings disadvantage.

6. The Australian Census has some limitations for the purpose of this analysis. In the 1991 Census, respondents were asked to indicate their annual/weekly income from all sources in income categories so the dependent variable used here includes both earnings from employment and income from all other sources. The midpoint of each income category was assigned to individuals and income for respondents in the open-ended category was estimated at 1.5 times the lower limit of this category. A second limitation is that the hours of work variable is also in categories which are quite broad. The midpoint from each category has been included as a determinant of weekly income and the open-ended category set at 60 hours of work per week. Finally the Census data reports period of arrival in categories and the midpoint has been chosen for each of the categories. For those who arrived prior to 1971, it is assumed that they had been in Australia for 25 years at the time of the 1991 Census.

4. The civil society

Olena Bagno, Majid Al-Haj and Andrew Jakubowicz

The term 'civil society' refers to voluntary collective activity to advance shared interests and goals. In conceptual terms, the realm of 'civil society' is distinguished from the 'state' and the 'marketplace', although in practice boundaries are rarely clear-cut. The Centre for Civil Society at the London School of Economics (n.d.), while noting that there are a number of competing definitions, argued for definition in the following terms:

> Civil society refers to the arena of uncoerced collective action around shared interests, purposes and values. In theory, its institutional forms are distinct from those of the state, family and market, though in practice, the boundaries between state, civil society, family and market are often complex, blurred and negotiated. Civil society commonly embraces a diversity of spaces, actors and institutional forms, varying in their degree of formality, autonomy and power.

In this chapter civil society is considered in terms of non-profit organizations (NPOs) such as registered charities, development non-governmental organizations (NGOs), community groups, women's organizations, faith-based organizations, self-help groups, social movements, coalitions and advocacy groups. We consider a range of welfare, advocacy, educational, cultural and political organizations formed by and for immigrants. Business associations, trade unions, professional associations and other non-governmental organizations related to the business sphere are not included in our definition of civil society, contrary to the approach of some authors (for example, Fisher 1997; Sadowski 2009).

Civil society is a 'third sector', distinct from but linked to the state and the economy (Hasan and Onyx 2008: 376). It is the sphere where interest groups and associations exchange ideas and engage in activities that generate values, build social relations and allow people to come together to advance shared interests – in other words, it is the area in which social capital is augmented and created. Democracy is integral to civil society, participation provides the means for groups to reach agreement on socio-economic goals and practices, which are conveyed to government, enacted in communities and mobilized in the labour market. Civil society provides the fabric that supports people in their wider social and political participation.

In pluralist societies such as Israel or Australia, civil society institutions proliferate, providing one of the ways through which people can organize together outside government or the economy, to pursue their goals. Civil society plays an important role in the experience of immigrants, both during initial settlement and later when immigrants become more entangled with their host society. While a country's state legal regulations frame the immigrants' entry and the economy determines their employment opportunities, the institutions of civil society provide the means for their social, cultural and political integration and at times for physical survival.

One of the core similarities between Israel and Australia lies in the unresolved issues associated with the earlier populations – the Palestinians in the case of Israel and the indigenous peoples in the case of Australia (Kenny 2007; Mikhelidze and Pirozzi 2008). As colonial settler societies, Israel and Australia have developed political structures and civil society organizations that essentially justify the settlement and political control by the current nation states of the territories they rule and populations within them. Civil society organizations of indigenous groups exist in both contexts, both as agencies for cultural survival and as avenues for the delivery of services and articulation of culturally-relevant demands upon the state. More broadly, Australian civil society organizations have been actively concerned with the disenfranchisement of indigenous people, especially with measures which allow governments to take control of indigenous communities and their resources, as in a joint statement made by the national peak Australian Council of Social Service in 2007 (ACOSS 2007). In Israel, Palestinian NGOs have played a critical role in the survival and functioning of communities within the internationally recognized boundaries of the state, providing a focus for similar processes – cultural survival, relevant services and political participation.

Given the concern of this book with the immigrant experience, the emphasis in this chapter is given to the civil society organizations and the frameworks established by and for immigrant communities. We describe the extent of involvement of the third sector in immigrants' integration in Israel and Australia; explore the mediating role that civil society plays for immigrants in relation to the political and economic spheres. We then examine the distinguishing characteristics of the two countries and the effect of these distinctions on the operation of civil society. We describe political environments in Australia and Israel and exemplify complex relationships among associations dealing with migrants' issues, the state and interest groups in the two countries along the lines of inclusion and exclusion of immigrants in the non-migrant community.

WHAT IS A CIVIL SOCIETY AND WHAT PURPOSE DOES IT HAVE?

Civil society reflects the full gamut of pluralism (political, religious, ethnic, cultural and social), providing much of the 'social cement', the trust, that holds democratic societies together. In societies experiencing rapid immigration, civil society becomes the source of the government's stability and simultaneously the opposition force that acts against the state's arbitrariness in tackling the various interests of the plural, multicultural societies. Civil society is sometimes perceived as an autonomous web of networks and sometimes as an entity that depends on the government for recognition and financial support. Civil society draws upon its relationship with the authorities, but at times replaces the government, when the authorities fail to achieve their aims.

The impact of neo-liberal economic reality in Australia and Israel made the state seek to pass off some of the responsibilities for social services to civil society (or privatize them, as the practice is generally called); in Australia this has encompassed education, health, welfare and employment services, while in Israel the most popular spheres are religious education, culture and welfare. In both countries, NGOs have undertaken a varied range of activities, including providing civil advocacy, influencing policy-makers, acting as identity, religious and cultural associations, protecting animal rights, implementing grass-roots or sustainable development, promoting human rights and social justice, protesting environmental degradation and pursuing many other objectives formerly ignored or left to governmental agencies (Fisher 1997).

Overall, civil society organizations act in three distinct planes, international, national and local, also populated by the state and intergovernmental agencies. All levels are interrelated in terms of sources of financing and functions performed by civil society organizations. In both societies (more so in Israel and to some extent in Australia) state institutions support and utilize civil society organizations. For example an organization may be supported by the European Commission (EC), the United Nations (UN), the state, the municipalities and economic enterprises (for example, Volkswagen, Siemens, Microsoft and Shell all provide financial support for various projects initiated by civil society organizations).

The civil society organizations usually act on several levels simultaneously. The local level is usually characterized by the everyday activities with target groups. The national level is addressed while an NGO is acting on behalf of groups or lobby their interests in the official institutions usually in parliament and the courts. The international level also involves the lobbying of interests in international courts and organizations such as the UN or its agencies. The borders between the NGOs and official bodies on the local plane are blurred as organizations may fulfil similar, complementary or sometimes even identical functions while satisfying the needs of the target groups.

Overall, the function of the civil society is to facilitate individual empowerment in the social (related to social inequality), political (related to the operation of state institutions) and cultural (related to the development of appropriate norms) spheres. The role of NPOs in strengthening civil societies and their impact on the relationship between interest groups and the state are constantly re-evaluated (Frantz 1987; Bratton 1989; Fowler 1991; Chazan 1992; Fox and Hernandez 1992; Ng'ethe and Kanyinga 1992; Sethi 1993; Ndegwa 1993, 1996; Sanyal 1994). The role of civil society vis-à-vis the state has been elaborated in the literature in terms of inclusion and exclusion (Dryzek 1996). Those two processes can apply but are not limited to social, political, economic and cultural spheres. Inclusion is essential for the survival of the political system and society as a whole because it minimizes inequality, sustains legitimacy and cultivates stability. The meanings of exclusion and inclusion depend on the nature or the dominant model of the society from which exclusion occurs and they vary in meanings according to national and ideological contexts (Silver 1994).

In formal terms the processes have their roots in the functionalist social theory of Durkheim who was concerned with how order and stability could be maintained in a society where massive social dislocations accompanied the transitions from an agrarian to industrial society. In the modern world increasing plurality of the states conditioned by the rise of post-materialist values and global migration can be roughly equated to the problems of dislocation experienced by European countries at the beginning of the twentieth century. The concepts of inclusion and exclusion have been informed by the problems associated with maintaining order, sustaining legitimacy of the state and providing socio-political stability. Immigrants' inclusion or exclusion also depends on the functions attributed to them by the host state. In liberal democracies even asylum seekers and humanitarian refugees are given certain functions by the state because dealing with them reinforces liberal values upon which the regime is based. In contrast in non-liberal democracies this interest group lacks function and is thus perceived as a sheer burden as it does not contribute to regimes' legitimacy.

We turn now to examine how each society responds to the realities of immigrant incorporation taking into account the differences in the status of different groups of immigrants.

THE CIVIL SOCIETY IN AUSTRALIA

Australia's civil society has evolved as part of its modernization process, with the extent, role and robustness of this sphere lying at the heart of Australian political life. The early role of the colonial governments in the nineteenth century set up a general expectation in the new societies of governmental leadership and economic investment, which often created tensions between the burgeoning expectations held by free market enterprises, and the concern about social cohesion and equity exemplified by the charitable organizations in the fields of welfare and education (Smyth and Cass 1998: 369). As an immigrant society from the outset, the recruitment, settlement, integration and care of immigrants have been major responsibilities of Australia's social infrastructure (Jamrozik et al. 1995: 370).

World War II and its aftermath presented Australian governments with key challenges in population building. The fear of Asian invasion, heightened by the Japanese wartime raids on Australian towns and cities, the critical bottlenecks in supply versus demand from decades of under-investment in basic social amenities and the economic necessity of rapid industrialization, generated a ramping up of immigration which transformed the Anglo-Australian society of 1947, into the cosmopolitan and multicultural society of the twenty-first century (Davidson 1997: 368). Civil society organizations were either created or drafted into the project of assimilating the immigrants, the goal being to transform them into real Australians from their status as 'New Australians' (Shaw 1973: 371). Ever since that period, the degree of pluralism in identity and socio-cultural practices to be permitted to newcomers has been a matter of serious contention, especially most recently in relation to Islamic beliefs and African cultural origins (Jupp 2007: 219).

The Attitudes of the General Public

The concept of civil society has become widely accepted in discourses about public policy (Farrar and Inglis 1996: 372). The many millions of Australians who belong to civil society groups participate in organizations with concerns as diverse as environmental activism, charitable aid, foreign aid, both advocacy and direct service delivery for people with disabilities, self-help groups around well-being, cultural activities, emergency services, adult and community education, and sport and recreation (probably the largest sector). From early on immigrant groups created their own societies, religious groups and other organizations, from the *landsmanschaft* among German and Jewish communities, county or clan houses for the Chinese, to the commune-labelled organizations drawing together arrivals from the various parts of Italy.

In the post-World War II period the Commonwealth government stimulated the creation of one of the most widely spread civil society networks, the Good Neighbour Council, with hundreds of branches all over Australia. It was designed to 'meet and greet' new immigrants when they arrived at their first home, usually coming from the nearest immigration camp, and help them wend their way through the intricacies of Australian society (Jordens 1995: 367). The council volunteers were expected to create 'bridging social capital', as one of the fears of the Government was the formation of what later came to be known as 'ethnic ghettos'. It was envisaged that the council volunteers, and its sparsely spread employees, would help immigrants slip gently into the Australian mainstream and learn to adapt their traditional values and behaviours to Australian norms. The council served this purpose to some extent, especially for British Empire/Commonwealth immigrants, through the assimilationist hey-day of the 1950s and 1960s (Tavan 2004: 307). However as policy debates moved more towards 'integration' and the greater acceptability of immigrants retaining their heritage cultures, the council attracted criticism as a bastion of the former mono-cultural British/Australian values. In the 1970s the council was wound down and then abolished (though it continued in a different form for a while in Queensland and remains in Tasmania), to be replaced by the locality-based government-funded Migrant Resource Centres (MRC), run by voluntary committees, either appointed by government or elected by members. The MRCs would employ a new generation of young immigrant or Australian-born ethnic professionals, mainly graduates of community development and social work courses from Australian universities, imbued with new ideologies of participation and ethnic rights (Cope et al. 1991: 373).

By the 1970s the pattern of ethno-cultural civil society was becoming clear – immigrants would be described as members of communities, which would formalize themselves through organizations. These organizations would at the very least be focused on engaging with new arrivals, and perhaps with the whole array of ethno-cultural survival and adaptation. This might include the creation of ethnic language schools, either 'after hours' or Saturday, initially informal then licensed by government. It would soon encompass direct counselling and welfare aid and might extend to wider community development strategies, using government

'Grant in Aid' workers. Larger groups might also develop youth clubs and retirement and hospice accommodation (Foster and Stockley 1988: 374).

The framework for these developments took place through consultative national policy reviews, occurring approximately once a decade from the late 1970s through to 2009. Each of these reviews sought to describe and then define a role for civil society in the acceptance and settlement of immigrants, in the process weaving non-government not-for-profit organizations more tightly into the fabric of services and programs (Australia: Review of Post-Arrival Programs and Services to Migrants 1978: 69). The key groups to do this were the ethnic communities' councils, established by the coming together of ethnic civil society groups at regional and state levels, and their 'federation' in 1979 as the Federation of Ethnic Community Councils of Australia (FECCA). The FECCA secured core organizational funding from the government soon after and was placed as the most overarching conduit for the views of ethnic groups on policies relevant to them (Jakubowicz and Morrissey 1984: 375). This location both benefited groups during periods of government interest and active engagement, but also rendered them inert when government was uninterested and threatening to cut funds if provoked by FECCA criticism.

Attitude of the State

Conservatives have by and large argued in favour of volunteering and the emergence of NGOs, finding the capacity of charitable and community organizations a major resource for social inclusion and stability and as an alternative to government direct services. The Institute for Public Affairs, a conservative organization close to the Liberal Party argues that:

> Australian society is best served by a strong, diverse and vibrant civil society. Civil society organizations, including charities, constitute a vital part of Australia's civil society. A vibrant civil society assists in building social capital which is important for the prosperity of Australian communities. Individual voluntary participation in civil society organisations, whether through giving or volunteering, increases individual and collective freedom. (Fox 2006: 2)

They have also been adamant that such groups should not play a political role; indeed the conservative coalition government in Australia (1996–2007) proscribed any public advocacy by Commonwealth-funded NGOs, demanding a code of practice that disempowered clients, reduced advocacy and marginalized any functions other than direct service-delivery to 'deserving' clientele. Those from the social democratic side of politics have been more interested in advancing an empowerment agenda, holding to the view that there needs to be a 'compact' between government and civil society, in which civil society bodies both advocate for and respond to the needs of the more impoverished, marginalized and dispossessed.

The defining moment for state attitudes to civil society in relation to immigrants occurred in the mid to late 1970s, when the coalition government of Malcolm Fraser, established and then adopted the report of the Committee of Review of Post-Arrival Services for Migrants (known as the Galbally Report) (Australia: Review of Post-Arrival Programs and Services to Migrants 1978: 69). The report has a strong 'community' bent, incorporating but upgrading the material developed by the state-based Migrant Task Forces, an innovation of the previous (Whitlam) Labor government (1972–75), and taking on board but modifying for conservative tastes the ethnic community Welfare Rights scheme created at that time. The Galbally Report took the community development model and expanded it into the Migrant Resource Centres, took ethnic radio and turned it into the Special Broadcasting Service and Multicultural Television, and created a string of other services. The Labor government (1983–96) continued the programs but added an 'access and equity' dimension, incorporating the ethnic rights movement's call for a strategy to end discrimination and a form of affirmative action for government agencies (Jakubowicz et al. 1984; Jakubowicz 2009).

All these approaches reinforced the role of civil society organizations, building their capacities and their sense of status in the borderlands of public policy. Most importantly governments institutionalized the philosophy of 'multiculturalism', legitimizing the pluralism that community organizations had been seeking, and authorizing civil society to pursue claims based on cultural diversity as a positive value. Such a watershed separated the older White Australian discourses of assimilation from the post-modern relativities of globalization. Immigrants became members of diasporas, trans-nationalism opened up new ideas about impermanence and transience, and evolving cultural hybridity replaced cultural hierarchies and assumed traditional values (Jupp 2007).

By the mid-1990s some of these transformations were discovering opponents in civil society. While government policies had abandoned the older assimilationist rhetoric, and embraced more or less warmly the language of difference and the 'racial' diversity it permitted, popular culture was still resistant to change in some quarters. The return of the conservative Coalition under Prime Minister John Howard (1996–2007) also raised the profile of many right-of-centre, neo-conservative and neo-liberal groups that endeavoured to redirect the national agenda towards a celebration of the Australian development story (Borowski 2000).

The Howard ascendancy decimated civil society organizations, especially those with advocacy or change agendas, as funding was cut and new performance agreements limiting advocacy were introduced. In particular, many agencies (including migrant working women's agencies) with a feminist agenda found themselves frozen out of resources. Meanwhile many government services were truncated, closed down or tendered out to the private and community sector. The Migrant Resource Centres became businesses, contracting to develop projects and programs in competition with other service-delivery agencies. Government employment services were contracted to either private providers or to large church agencies. There was a huge shift of resources from government schools towards the religious, ethno-cultural and independent private schools, and government ideology reframed social justice and rights towards services, responsibilities and accountability. Immigrant rights were cut back, with access to settlement services made more limited and intakes through family reunion reduced (Jupp 2002a).

In effect the Howard Government aimed to demobilize the social movements of civil society that had been the currents that Labor had ridden through the 1970s, the 1980s and the 1990s (Howard 1999). It managed to do this through its own mobilization of a social movement built around conservative social values, conservative Christianity and neo-liberal economic reforms. While this grouping had its own internal tensions, the movement was able, through its broad base in communities of religious faith, express its gratitude for the benefits that came from apparently good management of a buoyant economic situation and thereby keep Labor sufficiently marginalized (Betts 2008).

By the high point of coalition power (the 2004 federal election) (Community Relations Commission for a Multicultural NSW 2005) the government parties had won the national support of a majority of almost every segment of the population except working class immigrants and the urban intelligentsia. With the economy faltering and its leadership in disarray, the coalition lost to a conservative and communal Labor leadership in 2007 (Betts 2008). In some constituencies, ethnic activists from Asian communities were crucial in mobilizing support for Labor.

The Political Sphere

Australia has engaged with the presence of immigrants. at least in the formal state sense, by making citizenship fairly easy to acquire and making voting in federal and state elections compulsory for all citizens. So joining Australia's national project requires active participation by immigrant citizens if only in the most minimal way (turning out on election days and considering how to cast their vote). When immigrants participate in this way, it is argued that they become increasingly integrated into Australia's political world.

By 2006 (National Census year) over 40 per cent of the Australian population were either immigrants or the children of immigrants and the overwhelming majority of eligible immigrants had become citizens – particularly those who had come as refugees. The refugee population reflected the crises of the world, originally from Europe in the immediate post-World War II period (though wartime refugees from Asia were expelled), then from Hungary, Czechoslovakia, Chile, Cambodia, Vietnam, Laos, Poland, the Soviet Union, Somalia, Ethiopia, Eritrea, Sudan, Iraq, Afghanistan, Democratic Republic of Congo, Burma and dozens of other source countries. While the waiting period for citizenship had been reduced by the Australian Labor Party (ALP) government in the 1970s to two years, the conservative Liberal National Party (LNP) coalition after 1996 began a process to extend it to four years and introduced conditions (in 2007) under which it could be forfeited.

In Australian politics the minor parties (from a range of perspectives including evangelical Christian to radical Green) can play an important role in the upper houses (in the national and all state parliaments except Queensland), often holding the balance of power. However, except for the appearance of the Unity Party primarily in New South Wales after 1996, there has not been a successful immigrant party. Most immigrant groups soon begin playing in their mainstream political party of choice, with newer immigrant and refugee communities being concentrated in lower income and therefore ALP held seats. Most Australian elections are decided in middle income seats, with shifts within the mid-range 30 per cent of voters providing the outcome; small changes can affect the results in these 'marginal seats' and thereby change governments. As immigrants become more established and prosperous, moving into more marginal seats, they play a more significant role as election determinants, though the issues they confront are no longer those of the first settlement period.

Immigration and multiculturalism have been broadly accepted by the political classes as necessary elements in Australia's success as a modern nation, the latter more grudgingly than the former (Guild and van Selm 2005). A critical moment surrounded the debates within the ALP and the Opposition in the late 1980s over the size of the immigration intake and its sources. The bi-partisan agreement on immigration and multiculturalism (and the broad perspective that they should not be politicized as a basis for partisan advantage) began to unwind by the mid-1980s, partly driven by historian Geoffrey Blainey who in 1984 called for a cessation of Asian immigration. A see-sawing struggle intensified within the conservative parties between neo-conservatives and liberals, in which immigration and Australian ethnic identity played an important role (Jupp 2007).

The consensus though was shaky, and the return of John Howard as Liberal leader in 1995 generated a more active anti-immigration and pro-traditional Australian discourse. Howard's victory in 1996, accompanied as it was by the election in a once-safe Labor seat of ex-Liberal Pauline Hanson on an anti-Asian (and later anti-African) immigration platform seriously shifted the terms of debate. As a result many of the institutions of former Labor Prime Minister Keating's multiculturalism, such as the Office of Multicultural Affairs (OMA), the Bureau of Immigration Multicultural and Population Research (BIMPR) and the Human Rights and Equal Opportunity Commission (HREOC) were closed down or had their activities curtailed.

The distinction between ethnic and non-ethnic immigrants (essentially Jewish/non-Jewish), which so critically affects Israeli civil society has no clear parallels in Australia. Once a person is identified as being within Australia, their status is determined by their visa class, or if they have no visa, by any claims they may have pending regarding protection. Civil society organizations are closely involved in these processes, often with government support.

The case of Sudanese (many from Darfur) refugees and humanitarian entrants reflects the role of civil society organizations, and state-related institutions (Brown et al. 2006). These institutions both engage on behalf of Sudanese, but also help build social capital through supporting interactions between Sudanese and the wider society (Thomson 2005). The Sudanese population of Australia grew rapidly from 2001 to 2006 (Census years), rising from 4900 to 19 000 (Australia Department of Immigration and Multicultural Affairs 2006). Beginning in the 1990s, Sudanese immigrants were encouraged by the Government and mainstream refugee NGOs to develop local community associations (Cassity and Gow 2005). By 2008 this process was well-advanced, with the main umbrella body being the Sudanese Community Association of Australia (SCAA) established in Melbourne in 1989. Another example is the Sudanese Lost Boys Association of Australia which specifically supports those young refugees who survived the wars in camps in Kenya, Ethiopia, Uganda and Egypt. The organization's website notes that its goal is 'to bring together the Sudanese and Australian communities and promote awareness and understanding of both cultures' (Sudanese Lost Boys Association n.d.). A bridge opening from the other side, the Sudanese Australian Integrated Learning (SAIL) Program Inc., involves White Australians supporting educational initiatives for Sudanese, in part through local churches. At a broader level the Refugee Council of Australia (a civil society organization supported in part by the Government) undertakes more strategic issues, ranging from refugee policy, the management of the asylum seeking process, through to the provision of resources.

In the course of Australian history, immigrant communities have been very active in the creation of social, cultural and welfare organizations. In part this was their response to the reluctance of mainstream Australia to open up its institutions to more culturally and sensitive modes of activity. Since the first major recognition of cultural diversity as an issue (the Galbally Report of 1978, was tabled by the Prime Minister in eight languages) governments have tended to seek out community organizations as conduits for funding to deliver culturally focused services. While public opinion varied over the acceptability of these organizations (variously seen as too inward-looking and ghettoizing on the one hand, or very valuable just because of their sensitivity on the other hand) in general the concept of a pluralist society requiring institutionalized representation of diverse stakeholder interests has held sway.

By 2009 a state like New South Wales centred on Sydney, the most populous and urbanized, counted over 140 ethnic community organizations registered with the government (NSW Community Relations Commission n.d.). These ranged from ethno-religious (for example, Sabian Mandaean, Vietnamese Buddhist, Muslim Women) to ethno-cultural (for example, Russian Ethnic Communities Council, Lebanese Community Council) to ethno-political (for example, State Zionist Council, Federation of Italian Migrant Workers and Families) to ethno-welfare (for example, Islamic Charity Projects Association, Co.As.It. – Italian Association of Assistance, Chinese Australian Services Society). Pan-ethnic bodies were also active, including a New South Wales Ethnic Communities' Council, regional ethnic community councils and an African Communities' Council; so too were the local multicultural service organizations, and organizations that tie together ethnic and mainstream bodies, such as the Refugee Council.

The Labor Government elected in 2007 moved towards a social compact with civil society organizations, through which it plans to advance its goal to improve 'social inclusion' (after the Howard years focused on 'social cohesion'). 'Social inclusion' has been the subject of some concern for ethnic organizations, as the government has shied away from including any priority in relation to immigrant groups (Messimeri 2008). 'Social inclusion' refers to a primary socio-economic goal associated with the reduction in poverty and the improvement in social well-being. The government vision is that 'all Australians feel valued and have the opportunity to participate fully in the life of our society' (Australian Government n.d.).

The government vision includes the right to work, to a home, to education, to participate and be heard. However there is no specific reference to the critical issues regarding social inclusion of cultural and ethnic minorities. It is as though cultural difference makes no difference when the core concerns for social inclusion advocates are being addressed, creating ongoing tension. The Social Inclusion Agenda focuses on geographical communities with entrenched disadvantage. Key indicators include crime, poverty, truancy, dependence on social payments, morbidity and mortality. 'Being a migrant' is not an indicator, though pockets of immigrants demonstrate many of these characteristics. The challenge for policy remains to understand the cultural dimensions involved in overcoming disadvantage, given the role accorded by the government to participation by communities in 'owning' the problems and solutions.

THE CIVIL SOCIETY IN ISRAEL

The Attitudes of the General Public

According to the 2008 Israeli Democracy Index (Israel Democracy Institute 2008) most Israelis hold the state rather than civil society responsible for setting policy in political, social and economic issues, and for providing the full range of services required by the society. On the other hand, the public perception of civil society is far more positive than that of the established political system. The public accepts NGOs' role in providing various services, has no reservations about accepting services from social organizations.

On the other hand the majority of Israelis consider civil society to be an interim measure – 'a magic stick' recalled by the state to diminish harmful effects of the failures of the political system and the deficient performance of the state particularly in the social and economic areas and in the protection of public order.

Israelis do not perceive civil society as a cornerstone of democracy, it still holds that, in an ideal situation the state rather than civil society is the default option in charge of securing the effective functioning of society and ensuring its citizens the full spectrum of services. The vast majority of Israelis readily support civil society organizations financially (about 80 per cent make donations). However, compared to Australia the proportion of those who volunteer is relatively low (37 per cent). This low participation can also be related to the fact that the majority of Israeli citizens (77 per cent) had never been given services by any civil society organization.

Among those who live on the outskirts of large towns or even more remote locations, access to the services provided by NGOs is lower than the national average. Thus, civil society organizations located in Tel

Aviv and its vicinity are unreachable for people who need them most, and among them recent immigrants, asylum seekers and foreign workers. Despite the fact that they are formally allowed to settle anywhere in the country, the majority of new immigrants from the Former Soviet Union (FSU) are concentrated in the periphery because of the affordable costs of living. The situation of non-ethnic immigrants is even more difficult. The state has launched a programme that settles most of them 'South of Gedera and North of Hadera', that is to the peripheral areas, thus decreasing their ability to get in touch with the centrally located NGOs.

Contacting NGOs and benefiting from their services is related to greater willingness to volunteer (50 per cent compared to 32 per cent among those who have never used the services of NGOs) and donate money to these organizations (87 per cent compared to 78 per cent of those who have never used the services of NGOs). On the other hand, 41 per cent of Israelis believe that social organizations are corrupt. This attitude is well grounded taking into account frequent scandals related to dishonest treatment of target groups. In an ethnic immigrant sector this is most often related to the mistreatment of the Holocaust survivors (now aged at least in their 70s, often unable to raise their concerns because of language problems or poor health). Non-ethnic labour migrants (both legal and illegal) and asylum seekers also suffer from the breach of trust by certain NGOs that misappropriate compensations designated for the labour migrants.

One such case has been made public. The NGO 'Excellent Caregiver' cooperated with the National Insurance Agency (NAI) which annually transferred NIS2.7 million (about US$700 000) to various NGOs that employed legal foreign workers providing services for the elderly. These funds should have been transferred to caregivers as wages, health insurance, paid leave and lay-off pay, but the funds were not provided to the foreign workers employed. The misappropriation was revealed by the NGO 'Worker's Hotline', which acts to protect the rights of disadvantaged workers, both ethnic and labour immigrants, employed in Israel and by Israelis. The 'Worker's Hotline' approached the NAI (a state agency) and made the story public. This example illustrates the complexity and dynamism of relationships among NGOs and the state agencies. It may also be viewed as a partial explanation of the reservations expressed by Israelis regarding the acceptance of civil society organizations as an alternative to the state agencies.

The Attitude of the State

In legal terms in Israel four major types of non-profit organizations (NPOs) constitute the institutional framework of civil society. Each type of NPO has different requirements for formation, membership and public purpose. These include: associations, governed by the Law of Associations, 1980; private companies for public benefit, governed by the Companies Act, 1999; cooperative societies, governed by the Cooperative Societies Ordinance, 1933; and endowments, governed by the Trust Law, 1979. Some of these organizations blur the line differentiating civil society and the business world.

Yishai (1998) suggests that the relationship between state and civil society in Israel went through three evolutionary stages: 'active inclusion' of civil society organizations by the state followed by the state of 'active exclusion', and, ultimately the current stage that started in the early 1980s is characterized by 'passive exclusion'. In the first stage (1940s–60s) the state actively promoted civil society institutes and the social organizations heavily relied on the political system. This period signified the development of organizations that had a clear political agenda and were established to answer the needs of the ethnic Jewish public. Despite the fact that many Israelis were also immigrants these organizations did not differentiate between them and other citizens. This happened because social organizations' functions were dictated by the needs of the state and the latter promoted homogeneity and inclusion. In the early years of Israel's existence as a state, there was a remarkable match between the state and civil society organizations, this also led to the situation that there were no clear boundaries between the state agencies and the major civil society organizations that were established in that period.

The next period started in the wake of the Six Day War (1967) and continued until the 1980s. The society underwent rapid economic development which led to the decline in the authority of political establishment. However, the new civil society organizations that emerged in that period were also the product of a mono-ethnic society. Thus, environmental organizations such as the Society for the Protection of Nature, or the Council for a Beautiful Israel were mainly concerned with the advancement of Zionist ideals and inculcation of patriotic values rather than environmental safety. The same can be said about women's movements of that period that can be presented as the state's alter ego.

A visible exception to that cause was the Black Panthers group – a product of distress and poverty of marginalized young immigrants of Moroccan origin. That was the first evident sign of plurality of the Israeli society that the state failed to downplay. From that time the state faced the need to deal with groups that signified the bankruptcy of the melting pot idea. New non-conformist feminist organizations, associations of young immigrants from Morocco, ultra-right-wing groups (for example, Kach), Arab militancy, the Progressive Movement which promoted the establishment of a Palestinian state, caused diversification of the Israeli society and this increasing plurality was actively rejected by the state. It adopted the Law of Associations according to which a request for registration could be denied if the objectives of the association are contrary to law, public morale or if they endanger the security of the state of public order. The state endeavoured to delegitimize associations that contributed to the increasing diversity of society. In that period, the majority if not all of civil society organizations had clear political agendas, however, there were no organizations that dealt exclusively with the socio-economic needs of non-citizens.

The third stage started in the late 1980s. As discussed in the first chapter of this book, Israel received more than a million immigrants mainly from the FSU and Ethiopia. Rapid economic growth also turned Israel into an attractive destination for labour migrants and relatively small numbers of asylum seekers from Darfur, Sudan, Eritrea and other conflict driven areas entered across the Egyptian border. The Israeli political system also went through the process of fractionalization, reflecting a new structuring of interest groups. Major parities lost broad electoral support and became more closely tied to specific interest groups. Non-ethnic immigrants who are not eligible for citizenship and hence the vote became a visible group whose legal status is badly defined and interests poorly protected by the state. This increasing diversity required a reaction from the state, which adopted a strategy of 'passive exclusion . . . which allowed opposition, challenge and legal confrontation' (Yishai 1998: 161). There has emerged an unstructured, mainly loyal civil society that acts to meet the demands of groups that are either completely and permanently or partially and temporarily excluded from the national collective.

The Political Sphere

Israel has a proportional representation system that allows various ideological political bodies to preserve their independence. It constitutes the basis of Israeli pluralism that was especially important in a period in which far-reaching and rapid changes were taking place in the Israeli population as a result of immigration. Since it was considered important to enable representation of a range of groupings, Israel developed an electoral system with the low qualifying threshold of 1 per cent, which was raised to 1.5 per cent in 1988 and a still very low 2 per cent in 2003.

The role of civil society organizations is paramount in the sphere of political incorporation of ethnic immigrants and Israeli Arabs, which are represented by a broad range of voluntary organizations (for example, Horowitz 2005).

In the 1990s, the emergence of immigrant parties was precipitated by the Zionist Forum – a non-governmental organization created in 1988 – and an Association of Immigrants that nurtured the Tali political movement that participated in 1992. The committee of the Forum comprised 105 members; among them were Yuri Shtern, Ida Nudel and Avigdor Lieberman. The forum led by Natan Sharansky stated that it was non-political but served as the basis for the creation of the first immigrant party Israel-be-Aliayh (IBA) that openly appealed to FSU immigrants and placed their interests at the centre of its electoral campaigns.

By 1995 the membership in the Zionist Forum comprised 42 immigrant organizations with 60 000 members; however, this umbrella organization and its satellite-NGOs did not survive long as a consequence of the withdrawal of state support. The initial purpose of the Forum was to help integrate immigrants in the Israeli labour market. At first, the IBA enjoyed broad support among migrants but was soon abandoned by its supporters as it failed to fulfil their expectations to further cultural and economic incorporation.

Israel Beiteinu headed by Lieberman and Democratic Choice led by Bronfman, are two parties with immigrant agendas that emerged from the Zionist Forum. Other political entities organized by immigrants were less successful in winning votes. Aliyah – For the Renewed Israel ceased to exist, and was followed by the IBA and Democratic Choice, leaving its leaders isolated in the Knesset.

As has been noted, Arab Israelis form about 20 per cent of the Israeli population and in 2009 12 of the 120 seats in the Knesset were held by representatives of Arab political parties. There is one joint Arab–Jewish party with a large Arab presence, Hadash, and two exclusively Arab parties, Balad and the United Arab List, which is a coalition of several political organizations including the Islamic Movement. The best known political organizations working in the Arab sector are Abnaa el-Balad, which calls for the return of all Palestinian refugees, the establishment of a democratic and secular Palestinian state in place of Israel; Ta'ayush, established in 2000 which 'works against the occupation and against the discrimination done by the state to Palestinian Israelis'; and the Regional Council of Unrecognised Villages (RCUV). The latter is a democratic representative body for more than 80 000 residents of the Bedouin unrecognized villages of the Negev Desert. The RCUV was established in 1997 by local inhabitants who sought to defend the housing rights of the Bedouin population.

Non-ethnic immigrants (labour migrants, illegal migrants, refugees, asylum seekers) are not represented by political parties. Their interests are raised on the public agenda solely by the agencies of the civil society. This asymmetry in political representation of ethnic and non-ethnic immigrants is one facet of, and contributes to, the inequalities in economic, social and cultural spheres. On the other hand, the mechanisms of pressure used by NGOs to influence state policies are frequently more effective than political pressures exercised by politicians on behalf of ethnic immigrants. NGOs do not have to comply with the rules of a political system that inevitably constrains members of the parliament and makes them less effective in advancing the interests of their constituents.

The state is aware that NGOs can have substantial influence on public opinion and eventually on policy even if they represent groups void of formal political rights. In response to this reality and in the context of the ongoing conflict over the land, in 2008 the Israeli Knesset adopted the 11th amendment to the Law of Associations. This amendment requires NGOs with an annual turnover above US$70 000 to report any gift or donation given to the organization by a foreign political entity.

The Socio-Economic Sphere

Jewish immigrants receive political rights on arrival. In the interests of national development the state has facilitated economic integration, although, as has been discussed, with significant differences amongst the various groups. Civil society organizations were thus almost excluded from dealing with ethnic migrants. On the other hand, the state neglects their cultural inclusion, which has created a need for NGOs to accommodate a range of needs; for example, World War II veteran organizations, literature associations and cultural centres.

The role of civil society in dealing with non-ethnic migrants, both legal and illegal, covers a range of urgent needs. While denying a direct political role, the state is interested in their socio-economic inclusion to maintain stability and the status quo. Since the non-ethnic migrant sector is diverse, the state allows an almost free hand to civil society bodies to provide services. On the other hand, the state is very reluctant to facilitate cultural inclusion of groups who are viewed as aliens – whose socio-economic needs have to be met while they are in Israel, but whose permanent stay is not to be encouraged.

The absence of a legal basis for regulating the relationship with non-ethnic migrants led the state to welcome the activities of NGOs assisting those who are impoverished and to support those whose rights have been violated. On the other hand, political pressure exercised by the NGOs (at the national, on occasion at the international level) on behalf of non-ethnic migrants is a cause of tension, although the state circumvents open confrontation with NGOs.

For example, a highly critical report 'Migrant workers in Israel: a contemporary form of slavery' was produced by the Euro-Mediterranean Human Rights Network and the International Federation for Human Rights, with contribution from the Physicians for Human Rights (PHR) (Ellman and Laacher 2003). Despite the critical report, the state continued to support the work of PHR to provide free medical services to poor immigrants. On the other hand, financial contribution by the Netherlands, Spain and the European Commission to the political NGO 'Breaking the Silence' that revealed the confessions of soldiers involved in the 2008 Gaza military operation 'Cast Lead', produced an immediate negative reaction.

The difference in reaction can be explained by the respective functions performed by these NGOs. The PHR acts in the socio-economic sphere and contributes to the effective functioning of the economy, 'Breaking the Silence' is seen to undermine national consensus and acts exclusively in the political plane.

NGOs that focus on the socio-economic sphere enjoy better relations with the state because of their role in upholding the status quo, even when they become highly critical of the state and bring their concerns to the international level. NGOs such as the PHR are in a more tenuous position. PHR performs a range of functions. On the municipal level it provides non-ethnic immigrants with services that are provided to citizens by the state. Thus, PHR runs a clinic that delivers initial medical services to immigrants without insurance cover. The organization also assumes an advocacy role on the national level, appealing cases to the High Court of Justice and making submission to the Israel Medical Association (IMA). During 2008–09, the NGO succeeded in obtaining national recognition of the issue of health care for non-ethnic migrants. One result was the establishment of a state-funded refugee health clinic. On the international level the PHR has acted to exert pressure on the Israeli government by contributing to reports submitted to international organizations (UN agencies such as United Nations International Children's Fund (UNICEF) and International Labor Organisation (ILO)) and foreign governments (for example, the European Commission).

This multifaceted activity on three levels is typical of the work of the NGOs working in the socio-economic sphere, while other types of NGOs that focus on political or cultural spheres, mainly deal with their clients and operate at the municipal level. Centres for migrant workers that rely heavily on the support of local municipal authorities constantly appeal to national and international levels to advance socio-economic interest of their interest groups. On the other hand, organizations for World War II veterans who served in the Red Army are supported by municipalities and rarely raise their concerns at the national level.

While providing a greater level of support, the state has not ended its exclusionary practices. State agencies have proclaimed that the stream of illegal migrants into Israel in recent years has led to a situation in which the proportion of foreign workers is among the highest in the world, relative to the local population and the number of employed persons. Justice Minister Yaakov Neeman was given the role of formulating draft legislation to increase enforcement and punitive measures against Israelis who employ illegal migrants. In addition, in 2009 a newly created task force to deal with illegal immigrants was created, in succession to the former Immigration Police. It detains both legal and illegal workers, as part of the 'Hadera-Gadera' law, which rules that foreign workers must reside north or south of the two coastal Israeli cities (Haaretz 2009).

Summing up, the state allows NGOs to carry out socio-economic inclusion of non-ethnic migrants but adamantly opposes the grant of permanent status.

COMPARING AUSTRALIA AND ISRAEL

Despite the fact that Australia and Israel are formal democracies, they differ substantially in the rules of the political game. According to the Freedom House estimates, Australian democracy is more stable and closer to the liberal ideal than the Israeli political regime. Australia received the highest rates (i.e. rank 1) for civil liberties and political rights both in 1990 and 2008, while Israel was given less for political liberties (rank 2) and civil liberties (rank 2) in 1990. The situation changed by 2005, when political liberties reached the Australian level (i.e. rank 1). In 2009 in both countries the level of political liberties remains the same (rank 1) as well as the situation with civil liberties (rank 2 in Israel and rank 1 in Australia).

The Israeli electoral system of proportional representation, compared to Australian full preferential voting and single member constituencies, results in a need for coalition governments. In other words, the Israeli electoral system provides better opportunity for small interest groups to have political impact.

Despite the politicization process and the increasing pragmatic orientation among the predominantly Arab parties, the Arabs have remained outside the borders of legitimacy in the Israeli political culture and have been denied all access to the national power centre. Since the establishment of Israel, no Arab party has ever been allowed to be a full partner in a government coalition, including those based on Labor and the left wing. A good example is the situation of the predominantly Arab parties during the period of the Rabin-Peres government (1992–96). Even though these parties' support for the government was a crucial component in its parliamentary majority, they were permitted only to support it 'from the outside' as part of the 'blocking majority' that made it impossible for the Likud to form a government. This situation actually turned the predominantly Arab parties into a 'blocked minority', permanently denied access to any share in the benefits of the power centre, which is exclusively Jewish.

The international comparative analysis of social capital undertaken for the Australian Social Attitudes study (Donovan et al. 2007) suggests that Australians generally have a high level of trust in government (fifth out of 29 countries in the International Social Science Project) and 'generally feel Australian democracy is working well' (64 per cent). On the other hand, Israelis do not show such a high level of trust (twentieth out of 29) and are far less supportive of the effectiveness of the democratic system (38 per cent). Despite very different levels of trust in government, Australians and Israelis share attitudes on the need for more opportunity for political participation (about 50 per cent). Similarly Australians and Israelis believe that government does not care much about what ordinary people think (about 60 per cent). Australians are unwilling to support civil disobedience when governments are perceived to be acting badly.

In the division of civil societies on (a) stable, (b) active, (c) withdrawing and (d) young scale, Sadowski (2009) classifies Australia as a country with active civil society, while Israel is included in the group of young states. The active category includes the most active societies. These are represented by clusters of the former British dominions (Australia, Canada, New Zealand) and several European countries (Norway, Denmark, France, Switzerland). In these states social trust is high and attitude toward the government is very positive. Although citizens are very loyal, they do not limit themselves to conventional ways of influencing politics. More than one adult citizen in three is a member of an association relating to his/her own interests and over 20 per cent are active in other NGOs. The third sector is extremely powerful while parties and religious associations attract less attention.

The civil society in Israel is considered 'young' because the state evolved through the migration and mixing of groups of various origins which brought them to a common 'ethno-national' denominator. The society is relatively tolerant towards both minorities and extremists and declares a high willingness to engage in civil disobedience. Party participation and activity are also high, as are participation and activity in religious organizations. In Israel citizens have little trust either for the government or for other people. They are active in conventional political actions (electoral politics) but their pattern of participation differs from the patterns found in post-industrial countries like Australia where unconventional socio-political participation is higher.

In both countries nearly 40 per cent of the population are immigrants (first generation) or their children (second generation). However, the countries vary in their approaches to immigration which is reflected in differences in the functions and strength of their civil societies. Differences in the role of their civil societies are rooted in different concepts of the state (nation state in Israel and immigrant state in Australia); different approaches to nation building (focus on ethnic cohesion in Israel and economic cohesion in Australia); and difference in the levels of liberalism and multiculturalism. Australia is an officially declared immigrant society which constitutes one of the most multicultural and diverse nations in the world. Over 200 languages are spoken. Australia's approach to the level of immigrant intake is largely determined by economic need. In Israel the official approach serves the purpose of building a coherent mono-ethnic nation. In Australia three sets of criteria have served as the bases for permanent residence: family migration for relatives, skill-based migration to meet economic need, and humanitarian and refugee admission. Some vital services are still channelled via the state agencies, but civil society plays a key role in socio-economic and cultural integration of new immigrants. In contrast, the Israeli state has multifaceted functions in facilitating the inclusion of ethnic but not other types of migrants. The state allows permanent settlement and provides services and protection to immigrants coming under the Law of Return, while labour and humanitarian migrants have fewer opportunities to receive state services and virtually no opportunity to become citizens. Thus, in Israel, civil society organizations adopt functions of the state in order to provide services to the most vulnerable groups of immigrants (refugees and illegal migrants).

Overall, civil society organizations enter the scene when the state is unable or unwilling to provide the services necessary for inclusion of certain groups. In case of non-ethnic immigrants in Israel this picture is further complicated by the functions attributed to immigrants by the state. In liberal democracies, such as Australia, asylum seekers and humanitarian refugees are attributed some rights by the state because in so doing the state reinforces liberal values upon which it is based. In contrast in non-liberal democracies this interest group lacks function and is thus perceived as a sheer burden as it does not contribute to regimes' legitimacy. Thus, asylum seekers do not contribute to the legitimacy of the Israeli state, though, in recent decades the society has undergone a very slow transformation toward becoming more inclusive and multicultural. The role of civil society organizations in the development of pluralism are paramount as they act on the national and international levels to bring policy changes and contribute to greater official inclusion of non-ethnic migrants into Israeli society. In contrast, the development of Australian civil society is stronger and the country has one of the most vibrant civil societies in the world. However, Australian society also went through stages of liberalization following conservative retreat with regard to inclusion of immigrants. During the periods of retreats civil society organizations, including the organizations of immigrants, continued to advance the agenda of multiculturalism and assisted their members during these times of difficulty.

CONCLUSION

Civil society has become the basis for analysing key problems in contemporary societies – especially those issues of social cohesion and social inclusion that are generated by significant levels of cultural diversity, and social and cultural inequality. This chapter has discussed the two types of civil society that developed in Israel and Australia. The two states vary in national and ideological contexts, which results in the differences in functions performed by their civil societies.

In Israel, civil society advances the socio-economic rights of non-ethnic immigrants and local ethnic groups (Bedouins, Druze) and political and cultural rights of ethnic migrants and minorities, mainly Israeli Palestinians. Non-ethnic immigrants are gradually receiving recognition while their social inclusion is facilitated by the civil society organizations with a passive acceptance of this situation by the state. On the other hand, their national exclusion is not effectively resisted by civil society organizations. The ethno-national character of the state and popular consensus does not provide the basis of legitimacy for national inclusion of non-ethnic migrants, and the state acts actively to reinforce its exclusionist policies. In contrast, ethnic-migrants in Israel are legally accepted into both national and socio-economic collectives. Their integration in the host society is accompanied by difficulties that stem from the high level of socio-economic inequalities and their often vulnerable economic position. However, state institutions have a well-developed mechanism for dealing with this situation. Thus the role of civil society organizations for this population is limited to preservation of their linguistic and cultural identities and in some periods it has facilitated immigrants' political mobilization.

In Australia, immigrants are not differentiated by the state on ethnic grounds, although the right of entry is controlled by a complex set of migration categories. Thus the right to be an immigrant (with the capacity to settle legally) as against a temporary resident (resident for purposes of employment or education) is policed by the state. Civil society organizations predominantly work with permanent settlers – including refugees; there are however some groups who address the problems of temporary residents, especially where their concerns have created domestic political issues (such as exploitation of temporary workers or attacks on international students). Multiculturalism, although broadly accepted by the state as a necessary element of Australia's successful society, has not been encouraged in the periods of conservative retreat when the emphasis is on cohesion rather than pluralism.

Thus, the liberal nature of the Australian state and ethno-national nature of the Israeli state attribute different functions to their civil societies. In Australia, civil society is stronger in social and cultural spheres and performs various functions that aim at social, economic, cultural and political inclusion of all types of immigrants. In Israel, state agencies are responsible for ethnic immigrants' economic and social inclusion while multiculturalism is tolerated but not supported. Political inclusion of ethnic immigrants in Israel was initially facilitated by short-lived civil society organizations which allowed immigrants to create political parties with clear immigrant agendas. In Australia, the nature of the electoral system does not allow immigrant parties to become established. Thus immigrants are incorporated in the existing political parties. On the one hand, this situation contributes to political cohesion while on the other hand, it reduces the chances to promote specific political issues on behalf of immigrant interest groups. Thus civil society organizations in Australia have to advance political agendas on behalf of immigrants. In Israel the situation is similar when NGOs work to protect the human and socio-economic rights of non-ethnic immigrants.

Diverse societies like Israel and Australia inevitably face ongoing tensions which result from the heterogeneous nature of their populations. The role of civil society is, thus, twofold: to alleviate existing pressures and to advance the agendas that will result in policies to lessen the risk to the state of future tensions. This immense task can only be accomplished with the effective cooperation between civil society organizations and political and economic agencies on the three levels: the municipal, national and international.

5. Immigration and public opinion

Andrew Markus and Rebeca Raijman

INTRODUCTION

In the modern era, especially since the middle of the twentieth century, the arrival of immigrants has become a widespread phenomenon characterizing advanced industrial countries. These countries have experienced a dramatic increase in the number of foreign-born citizens and the emergence of new ethnic communities that changed the ethnic character of their societies (Soysal 1994; Pettigrew 1998; Castles and Davidson 2000). The development of the new communities has been accompanied by tension and anti-immigrant sentiment, which has varied over time and according to place (see, for example, Quillian 1995; Pettigrew 1998; Scheepers et al. 2002; McLaren 2003; Coenders et al. 2004; Lahav 2004; Kunovich 2004; Semyonov et al. 2006). While opposition to ethnic and racial minorities may be entrenched over long historical periods, heightened conflict is activated or triggered in specific circumstances, particularly in periods of economic difficulty or uncertainty, shifts in the pattern of immigration, accelerated social change and times of military conflict.

There are two arguments that are used to justify discrimination against ethnic and racial groups: the first is one of economic threat; the second is threat to identity or national character. While conceptually different, the arguments are typically interlinked and overlapping (see, for example, Curthoys and Markus 1978; Markus 1995; Quillian 1995; Esses et al. 2001; Semyonov et al. 2002; Raijman et al. 2003; Raijman and Semyonov 2004; Kunovich 2004).

In regards to the first argument, citizens with low social and economic status may fear that increased immigration will result in fewer jobs, lower wage rates, fewer opportunities for improving their own situation, more competition for housing and social services, and deteriorating conditions in the neighbourhoods in which they live, including increased crime rates (Espenshade and Hempstead 1996; Esses et al. 2001). Such perceptions may rationalize discriminatory attitudes and prejudice towards recent arrivals and demands for policies of exclusion and denial of equal citizenship rights.[1] Yet it is not all immigrants who typically mobilize these fears, as discussed below. Rather, it is the members of specific ethnic groups, for example immigrants from Asian countries in 1980s Australia, or non-Jewish immigrants amongst the majority group in 1990s Israel, who raise heightened concerns.

The second argument used against immigration is that of a perceived threat to society's cultural and national character, understood as unified or homogeneous before the arrival of culturally diverse migrants. The feeling of cultural threat reflects fear of intrusion of values and practices that are perceived as alien and potentially destructive to the national culture (Schnapper 1994; Baumgartl and Favell 1995; Fetzer 2000; Stephan and Stephan 2000; Raijman and Semyonov 2004; Canetti-Nissim et al. 2008). These perceptions are found within all national groups: for example, the perceived threat of Muslim immigrants to European national identities and Koreans to Japanese identity (Ryang 2000; Hicks 1997).

Feelings of cultural or national threat assume special importance and meaning in national states where ethnicity is a prerequisite for full citizenship. Australia was founded on a form of discrimination, embodied in the White Australia Policy (in force from 1901 to 1966), which denied permanent residence and citizenship to non-European peoples, with minor exceptions; in Israel, ethno-religious identity is a prerequisite for substantial membership in the state (see, for example, Shafir and Peled 2002).

This chapter looks at how immigrants have been seen by Australians and Israelis, by analysing the results of opinion polls. We consider the opinions of Australians to immigation in general and specifically on the number of immigrants arriving (or the level of intake), and the related issues of multiculturalism and cultural diversity, as well as the factors that influence people as they develop particular opinions. While Israel has generally not surveyed its citizens on immigration, we look at Israeli opinions, as far as possible, on parallel issues. We also compare Australian and Israeli attitudes to immigration as revealed in 2003 as part of the International Social Survey Program or ISSP (the same survey was used in both countries) (ISSP 2003).

AUSTRALIA

Sustained Australian polling over more than 50 years provides understanding of the broad contours of attitudes with a large degree of certainty.

In a minority of countries, which includes Australia and Canada, public opinion is supportive of non-discriminatory immigration policy in times of economic prosperity; its citizens see their countries as countries which benefit from immigration.

Cross-national data is available on attitudes to immigration. The following discussion draws on the 2003 International Social Survey Program (ISSP) and compares attitudes in Australia, Canada, the UK and West Germany. In response to the question of whether the number of immigrants should be increased, remain the same or be reduced, a minority of Australians (39 per cent) and of Canadians (34 per cent) favoured reduction, compared with a majority in UK (77 per cent) and West Germany (70 per cent).

In response to the proposition that immigrants are good for a country's economy, 71 per cent of Australians and 61 per cent of Canadians were in agreement, compared to 22 per cent of Britons and 29 per cent of West Germans.

When presented with the proposition that immigrants improve the country by 'bringing in new ideas and cultures', 75 per cent of Australians and 68 per cent of Canadians were in agreement, compared to 34 per cent of Britons and 57 per cent of West Germans.

While Australia may thus be seen as a country in which there is broad support for immigration, attitudes are changeable and volatile. When poll results are tabulated over a 55-year period, three different periods are evidenced: years when opinion is strongly supportive of immigration; years when opinion is almost evenly divided between those favourable and those opposed; and years when opinion is strongly negative.

It is a feature of Australian opinion that while there is the possibility of high levels of support for immigration in times of economic prosperity, there is a very strong negative reaction in the context of mounting unemployment. There is also a consistently low level of tolerance for what is seen as unregulated immigration and threats to national sovereignty, activated by the arrival of asylum seekers on boats from the north – a reaction captured in the campaign message of John Howard's Liberal Party in the 2001 national election 'We will decide who comes to this country and the circumstances in which they come' (Markus et al. 2009).

The level of employment (and unemployment) is the key determinant of attitudes to immigration. Long-run survey findings indicate that attitudes to immigration are closely correlated with trends in unemployment; a secondary correlation is with the extent to which immigration issues are politicized, as indicated by the impact of the debate over the supposed 'Asianization' of Australia in the mid-1980s, the public controversies of 1988–89 and the rise to national prominence of Pauline Hanson and her One Nation Party in the period 1996–98. These patterns are indicated by Figure 5.1.

Given the economic concerns with the Global Financial Crisis and the

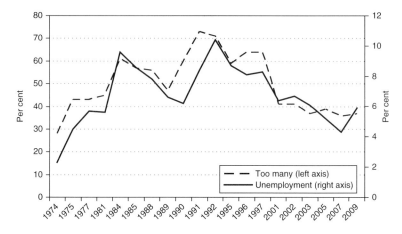

Note: Pearson Correlation = 0.83, *p* < 0.01.

Source: Markus et al. 2009; Markus 2009.

*Figure 5.1   Correlation between unemployment and those of the view that
the 'immigration intake is too high', 1974–2009*

rise in unemployment, increased negative attitude to immigration over the
last few years was expected. A major 2009 survey and other polling indicate that such a shift has not occurred. Belief in the value of immigration
continues to be widely held across the community; thus when asked for
their response to the proposition that 'accepting immigrants from many
different countries makes Australia stronger', 68 per cent (67 per cent in
2007) of respondents agreed while 27 per cent (26 per cent) disagreed. The
limited impact in Australia of the economic downturn is the likely explanation for the continuing high levels of support (Markus 2009).

While the issue of immigration is volatile and can lead to large majori-
ties expressing opposition to the level of intake, immigration is rarely
ranked as a major electoral issue, a finding in marked contrast with overseas polling. In the UK from 1997 to 2007, the period of the Blair government, concern about immigration and race relations increased twelve fold.
In the years 2005–07 immigration and race consistently ranked in the top
three British electoral issues (Ipsos MORI 2008).

In Australia the Newspoll organization regularly conducts a survey of
the ranking of electoral issues. In eight surveys conducted from 1993–98,
unemployment, health and education consistently ranked at the top of the
14 issues considered. Immigration was ranked last or second to last in six
of the eight polls; its highest ranking was 11th of 14 issues.

In recent polls conducted by researchers at the Australian National University, immigration and asylum issues have received similarly low ranking. Thus in 2005 the top issues were health care, taxes and an ageing population; asylum and refugee issues were ranked fifteenth. A 2008 poll found the economy and the environment were the top issues; immigration was amongst the lowest ranked, with 6 per cent of respondents considering immigration to be of major importance (ANU Poll various).

While Australian opinion is favourable to immigration in times of economic prosperity, there are limits to support, some of which have been indicated. There is strong evidence from polls that a majority of Australians expect their government to act to integrate immigrants into the national life, to unify rather than to accept, certainly not to support, cultural division.

Polls indicate acceptance of immigration from a broad range of countries, without support for overt discrimination on the basis of race or ethnicity and support for the ideal or abstract notion of multiculturalism (for Australian Polls, see Goot 1990). When in 1988–89 respondents were presented with the statement that 'multiculturalism is necessary if people from different cultures are to live in harmony', 77 per cent were in agreement. In 2005, when respondents were asked if they supported or opposed 'a policy of multiculturalism in Australia', 80 per cent were in support. But when multiculturalism is presented in concrete terms, the level of support falls away sharply. When four polls, conducted in 1995, 2003, 2007 and 2009, asked for response to the statement that 'ethnic minorities should be given government assistance to preserve their customs and traditions'; the first two polls found a small minority, 16 per cent, in support, and the third and fourth polls found about one-third of respondents (32 per cent) in support.

Majority opinion supports the desirability for immigrants to assimilate to Australian norms of behaviour. When in 1988 respondents were asked whether 'people who come to Australia should change their behaviour to be more like other Australians', two out of three respondents (66 per cent) were in agreement. The three national polls conducted in 1994, 1996 and 1997 elicited response to the forthright statement that 'Immigrants to Australia should adopt our way of life even if they have to put their own traditions and culture behind them'; the finding was consistent across the three polls, with 59–62 per cent in agreement.

A poll in 1994 made possible a clearer testing of opinion, providing respondents not with a statement but with options. Respondents were asked which of two statements came closer to their view: 'Migrants should learn to live and behave like the majority of Australians' or 'We should welcome and respect migrants who have different ways of living and behaving'; 61 per cent of respondents favoured the first proposition, that migrants should live like the majority, and 35 per cent were in agreement with the view that there should be a welcome and respect extended to those who have different ways.

In 2003 the ISSP survey posed two similarly differentiated options: 'some people say that it is better for a country if different racial or ethnic groups maintain their distinct customs and traditions; others say it is better if these groups adapt and blend into the larger society. Which of these views comes closest to your own?' This question, although framed in general terms, yielded an even sharper differentiation of opinion, with 82 per cent in support of adaptation and 18 per cent for maintenance of traditions.

There is thus a large measure of consistency in support of the view that immigrants should assimilate to Australian norms of behaviour at the cost of their own customs – depending on the wording of the question, around 60–80 per cent are in agreement, with a few poll findings above 85 per cent.

A number of leading researchers have considered attitudes towards settlement policy. Professor Ian Ang, one of the authors of the 2002 SBS sponsored study *Living Diversity* (Ang et al. 2002: 22), concluded that 'there is a high degree of ambivalence about cultural diversity in Australia'. A leading Melbourne pollster, Irving Saulwick, has commented on the strong desire for unity in Australia, with unity understood in terms of a common culture. Saulwick's findings indicated that 'the concept of multiculturalism raised in many minds an emphasis on separateness rather than togetherness' (Saulwick 1999: 91, 96).

Demographic and Socio-Economic Variables

To this point we have considered public attitudes at a general level, with attention to responses to different types of questions and to trends over time. Also of importance for understanding of attitudes is the extent of variation within sub-groups of the population (with reference to a range of socio-economic variables, including gender, age, level of education and income) and across regions of a country. Geographic and socio-economic variables are linked because these are unevenly distributed across major cities and across the regions of a country; for example, a person's occupation, income and even age change according to where a person lives.

With regard to the impact of population variables, there is a large measure of consistency in survey findings across the countries of the developed world. The Eurobarometer surveys conducted in the EU have found negative attitudes towards minority groups and support for exclusion in larger proportion amongst those with lower educational attainment; amongst those who are self-employed and those in manual occupations; those living on social security, including the unemployed, and amongst primary homemakers; those living in rural areas and country towns; those who attend religious services frequently; and people on the moderate-right and far-right of the political spectrum. These sub-groups of the population correlate with those more likely to perceive threat to economic well-being and to national identity from a large inflow of immigrants from cultures different to those of the host population (EU Agency for Fundamental Rights 2007).

The Australian researchers Murray Goot and Ian Watson collaborated in a detailed statistical analysis of the 2003 Australian Survey of Social Attitudes (Goot and Watson 2005). They found the strongest predictor of opposition to immigration amongst those who most strongly associated being 'truly Australian' with three attributes: being born in Australia, having lived in Australia for most of one's life, having an Australian ancestor. They term those with this outlook as the Australian 'nativists', those who most favour the native-born against outsiders. Goot and Watson developed a five point 'nativist' scale and found that those high on the scale were three and a half times more likely to favour reduced immigration than those low on the scale. They also found that even though there was this marked differentiation in attitudes to immigration in Australia even amongst the 'nativists' over 50 per cent of respondents agreed in seeing benefit to the country from immigration.

Goot and Watson's analysis highlights the significance of economic alienation, with those respondents suffering financial hardship and those without hope of improving living standards being most negative to immigration, with a similar finding for those indicating political conservatism. Pre-eminent in indicating support for immigration was completion of university education, an attribute related, as already noted, to occupation and place of residence. Those who spoke a language other than English in the home were likely to support immigration.

The 2009 Scanlon Foundation survey found the lowest level of support for the immigration program and the lowest level of recognition of the value of cultural diversity amongst respondents over the age of 54, those with trade level qualifications or no formal qualifications, those with the occupation of labourer, those who when asked concerning their financial circumstances responded that they were 'struggling to pay their bills' or were 'poor', and those resident outside capital cities. Conversely, the highest level of support was amongst those with university level qualifications, those under the age of 35, and those born in non-English speaking countries (Markus 2009b).

These response patterns varied only in the context of questions concerning asylum seekers, which elicited a high level of negative opinion across the demographic spectrum (Betts 2001). Thus, there was a high level of support for strict limitation on the entry of asylum seekers amongst those with high educational attainment and amongst the young.

A marked divergence occurs between those born in Australia, those born in English-speaking countries (ESB) and non-English-speaking countries (NESB). In 2007 twice as many of NESB as Australian-born respondents supported an increase in the immigration intake. When asked whether the government should provide assistance to ethnic minorities to maintain customs and traditions, less than 7 per cent of the Australian-born and ESB were in strong agreement, compared with 20 per cent of NESB. When those in strong agreement and agreement are combined, less than one in three Australian-born and ESB were in agreement, compared to two out of three NESB respondents (Markus and Dharmalingham 2008).

These differences are most marked among the recently arrived in the NESB group, an attitudinal differentiation which is attenuated with length of residence. Among the NESB who have lived in Australia for 25 years or more there is little difference from the responses of the Australian-born.

ISRAEL

As discussed in earlier chapters, the immigration context in Israel is distinctive in that Jewish immigration is not seen in terms of the entry of alien peoples, but as a return to the homeland. This return receives a large measure of public support.

Since statehood in 1948, immigration to Israel has been predominantly Jewish and encouraged by the Law of Return. Accordingly, most surveys on public opinion on migration have focused on Israelis' attitudes towards *aliyah* and *olim*. As has been noted, from the 1990s for the first time an increasing number of non-Jews began arriving in sizable numbers. Paradoxically, 60 per cent of them arrived under the Law of Return (as permitted under the 1970 amendment) and 40 per cent entered the country as temporary documented and undocumented labour immigrants (Raijman 2009). Hereafter, in keeping with the book's conventions: (i) Jewish immigrants arriving under the Law of Return will be labelled *olim*; (ii) non-Jewish immigrants arriving under the Law of Return will be labelled non-Jewish *olim*; and (iii) non-Jewish immigrant workers will be labelled labour migrants.

Attitudes to Jewish Immigration

A literature search yielded four surveys between 1970 and 1992 which polled opinion on *aliyah*, none before 1970. The following limited analysis of trends in attitudes to Jewish migration in Israel covers a period of moderate and low levels of immigration (1970s and 1980s respectively) and the years of massive immigration flows in the early 1990s (1990 and 1992).[2] Results are presented in Table 5.1. The early 1970s and 1980s were characterized by a low level of unemployment, but unemployment rose from 4.5 per cent in 1986 to 9.8 per cent in 1990 and 11 per cent in 1992. Economic estimates indicated that the massive inflows of the early 1990s led to a growth of 11.5 per cent in the annual labour force supply, compared with 0.05 per cent during the 1980s (Raijman and Semyonov 1998). Soaring demand for housing, for rent or purchase, led to a drastic increase in housing prices. Between 1989 and June 1990 the index of cost of housing rose by 50 per cent and the index of cost of renting rose by 33 per cent. In some places with high demand the index rose by 150 per cent.

Several conclusions may be drawn from the surveys between 1974 and 1992. First (and foremost), there is indication of overwhelming support for Jewish *aliyah*. In 1974, 85 per cent of respondents agreed that immigration was important for the country, in 1986, 82 per cent were in agreement. In 1974, 38 per cent agreed 'to a great extent' that the state should continue to assist immigrants even if there was an adverse impact on the standard of living, in the more optimistic times of 1986 the level of agreement reached 64 per cent.

The four polls posed the question of the importance of immigration for the country. Those indicating that it was 'very important' or 'important' were 85 per cent of respondents in 1974, 82 per cent in 1986, 77 per cent in 1990 and 71 per cent in 1992. Thus while there was a fall in support for immigration in the very difficult conditions of the early 1990s, seven out of ten respondents continued to endorse the importance for the country of Jewish immigration. This level of support was maintained despite the view of 61 per cent of respondents in 1992 that the existing population found difficulty finding work because of immigration and the view of 55 per cent that there were difficulties finding housing.

When respondents were questioned concerning the impact of immigration on their own lives the level of negative response was lower than in response to general questions concerning the social impact of immigration. Only 9 per cent of respondents reported feeling that migration affected them personally in 1990 and 26 per cent in 1992. The gap in the level of negative sentiment probably reflected the reality that a smaller number directly experience the impact of immigration than feared the impact of immigration on society (or on their future prospects) in times of difficult economic circumstances.

Heightened feeling of threat was reflected in declining support for state funding to assist absorption of new immigrants. The surveys indicate that

Table 5.1   Attitudes to immigration in Israel, 1974–92

	1974	1986	1990	1992
Number of immigrants	31 979	9 505	199 516	77 057
Total number of immigrants during the previous five years	221 433	70 757	250 070	489 757
Unemployment level	2.8	4.5	9.8	11.0
How important is immigration to the country ('extremely' and 'very important')	85%	82%	77%	71%
Existing Israeli population face difficulties finding work because of immigration (agree 'to a very great degree' and 'to a great degree')	–	18%	34%	61%
Existing Israeli population face difficulties finding housing because of immigration (agree 'to a very great degree' and 'to a great degree')	–	22%	33%	55%
Feel the economic impact of immigration in day-to-day life (agree 'to a very great degree' and 'to a great degree')	–	–	9%	26%
Immigrants should have first priority in getting state assistance (agree to giving 'first priority')	9%	5%	–	15%
The state should continue to assist immigrants even if this might affect individuals' standard of living (agree 'to a very great degree' and 'to a great degree')	38%	64%	40%	33%
Readiness to volunteer time to help absorb new immigrants (agree to devoting more than one hour a week)	–	–	53%	26%

Sources: Leshem (1998), Tables 1–7; Astman and Rozenbaum (1980); Damian and Rozenabum-Tamari (1992).

in 1986, 64 per cent of Israelis supported the view that the state should continue to assist immigrants even if this impacted on their own standard of living. By 1992 the level of support fell to 33 per cent. Likewise, while in 1990 53 per cent of respondents were ready to volunteer more than an hour a week of their time to help with the absorption of new migrants, by 1992 this readiness had decreased by almost half, to 26 per cent.

The 1990 and 1992 surveys establish continuing support for Jewish immigration, but in this atypical period of mass immigration a degree of negativity was evident. Once the peak of immigration had passed, a 1998 survey indicated that positive attitudes were again held by a large majority of Jewish Israelis.

Polled specifically for views on Russian immigration, 70 per cent of Jewish Israelis agreed that it was vital for Israel, 66 per cent that it contributed to the economy, 84 per cent that it made a cultural contribution. There were 75 per cent of Israeli Jews of European origin and a lower 60 per cent of Asian-African origin who indicated readiness to make an economic sacrifice to further the absorption of the Russian immigrants. These views were in marked contrast with the views of Arab Israelis, an issue discussed further below (Al-Haj 1998).

A 2009 poll undertaken by the Israeli Democracy Institute provides the most recent insight into attitudes to Russian immigration. A consistent two-thirds of respondents agreed that in the wake of this immigration intake crime escalated and that 'the Jewishness of most FSU [Former Soviet Union] immigrants is questionable'. But only one-third (35 per cent) agreed that 'it would have been better if FSU immigrants had not come at all' and a clear majority favoured continued attempts to encourage immigration from Russia (Arian 2009: 122).

Attitudes to Jewish and Non-Jewish Immigrants: 1999–2007

Survey data collected in 1999 and 2007 provides the basis for a study of attitudes to Jewish and non-Jewish immigrants and immigrants of different citizenship status. These surveys also provide for analysis of the views of Jews and Arabs and for a shift in attitudes between the dates of the two surveys.[3]

As discussed at the outset of this chapter, perceived threat or fear of competition has been advanced as one of the main factors that can affect the way citizens think about the presence of immigrants. Researchers distinguish different dimensions of threat, which can be broken down into socio-economic (or realistic) and cultural (or symbolic). Regardless of type of threat, it has been argued that fear of competition rationalizes exclusionary attitudes to others.

Table 5.2 Perceptions of threat by ethnic origin (mean, standard deviation and percentage 'strongly agree')

Perceptions of threat*	Arabs		Jews	
	1999	2007	1999	2007
Threat to employment opportunities:				
Olim	4.6 (2.5) 49.6	–	3.1 (2.4) 23.3	–
Jewish *olim*	–	4.5 (2.1) 35.7	–	2.3 (1.9) 10.6
Non-Jewish *olim*	–	4.4 (2.0) 32.7	–	3.4 (2.4) 25.6
Labour migrants	4.6 (2.6) 55.3	4.4 (2.3) 40.9	3.2 (2.6) 29.5	3.0 (2.3) 19.7
Threat to welfare benefits:				
Olim	3.4 (2.2) 25.0	–	2.7 (2.2) 16.6	–
Jewish *olim*	–	5.7 (1.4) 62.8	–	2.3 (1.9) 10.1
Non-Jewish *olim*	–	5.6 (1.5) 62.1	–	3.8 (2.4) 32.1
Labour migrants	3.5 (2.2) 25.4	5.5 (1.6) 60.4	3.1 (2.4) 23.5	3.2 (2.2) 21.0
Threat to wage level:				
Olim	4.7 (2.4) 53.1	–	3.0 (2.3) 21.4	–
Jewish *olim*	–	4.1 (2.0) 25.9	–	2.2 (1.9) 10.2
Non-Jewish *olim*	–	4.2 (2.0) 27.9	–	3.3 (2.4) 25.3
Labour migrants	4.7 (2.4) 53.0	4.0 (2.2) 30.6	3.4 (2.6) 30.8	3.0 (2.3) 18.6
Threat to personal safety (crime):				
Olim	–	–	–	–
Jewish *olim*	–	3.3 (1.8) 15.9	–	2.1 (1.8) 7.9
Non-Jewish *olim*	–	3.6 (1.8) 18.4	–	3.5 (2.3) 26.4
Labour migrants	4.3 (1.9) 30.0	2.9 (1.8) 33.0	3.3 (2.1) 19.8	2.7 (1.9) 10.8
Symbolic threat – Threat to the Jewish character of the state:				
Olim	–	–	–	–
Jewish *olim*	–	–	–	–
Non-Jewish *olim*	–	4.1 (3.1)	–	17.3 (6.9)
Labour migrants	5.3 (5.1)	3.9 (2.7)	16.4 (7.7)	14.6 (6.7)
N	316	358	670	667

Note: * 1–7 scale.

The data presented in Table 5.2 summarizes the ways different types of immigrants are perceived by Jews and Arabs in Israel, and gives some indication of change over the time interval of the two surveys.[4] Several findings illustrate the differences between majority and minority views on immigrants in Israel.

First, while Jews express fairly low to moderate feelings of socio-economic threat from migrants, Arab respondents indicate greater fear of competition. Second, among the Jewish respondents, feelings of threat are much higher in respect of non-Jewish *olim* and immigrant workers than towards Jewish *olim*. Arabs, the most disadvantaged group in Israeli society, display extremely high levels of fear of competition from both Jewish and non-Jewish immigrants. Third, perception of competition is most evident on the socio-economic level as Arabs tend to feel that the presence of all immigrants, Jewish and non-Jewish alike, has detrimental consequences for their welfare benefits, employment opportunities and wage levels.[5] Fourth, immigrants are less perceived as a threat to personal safety as both Jewish and Arab respondents tend to display lower levels of fear regarding the impact of immigrants' presence on crime rates. Feelings of threatened safety were substantially lower among Jews (about 15 per cent supported the claim that migrants – labour or Jewish – increased crime rates) than among Arabs (33 per cent and 40 per cent respectively). Jews and Arabs display similar attitudes to the impact of non-Jewish *olim* on crime rates.

With regard to the second major category of threat, cultural or symbolic, Israelis Jews perceive the presence of labour immigrants and of non-Jewish immigrants as a potential threat to the Jewish character of the state whereas Arabs do not agree. The difference between Jews and Arabs is clearly captured in the mean values of the term that measures symbolic or national threat which is very high for Jews (17.3 for non-Jewish *olim* and 14.6 for labour migrants) and very low for Arabs (4.0 average for the two immigrant groups).

The discussion proceeds to consider specific forms of exclusionary attitudes to Jewish and non-Jewish immigrants: opposition to their admission into the country, perceptions of social distance[6] and willingness to grant political and social rights.[7] Results are presented in Table 5.3.

Data in Table 5.3 reveal Arabs strongly oppose the admission of all types of immigrants (60 per cent). By contrast, the majority of Jews support the entry of Jewish *olim* but strongly oppose the admission of non-Jewish *olim* who are entitled to enter under the Law of Return. Opposition to entry of immigrant workers is markedly lower than to non-Jewish *olim*.[8]

One of the most commonly studied forms of prejudice and discrimination relates to peoples' intentions and dispositions to behave negatively to out-group members. This form of exclusion, labelled 'social distance' by Bogardus (1928), is typically measured by asking people about their willingness to have personal contact of various degrees of intimacy (as a neighbour, in close kinship by marriage, as a boss in the workplace) with members of particular social groups.[9]

Exclusionary attitudes to immigrants in Israel are manifested through

Table 5.3 *Exclusionary attitudes to immigrants in Israel by ethnic origin (Mean, standard deviation and percentage 'strongly oppose')*

Exclusionary attitudes	Arabs		Jews	
	1999	2007	1999	2007
% opposing entrance of:				
Olim	56.2	–	6.4	–
Jewish *olim*	–	59.3	–	8.6
Non-Jewish *olim*	–	60.5	–	50.6
Labour migrants	58.2	52.3	27.4	12.8
Social distance neighbour:				
Olim	5.8 (1.4) 64.1	–	3.0 (1.8) 8.8	–
Jewish *olim*	–	5.2 (1.6) 47.2	–	2.2 (1.6) 3.8
Non-Jewish *olim*	–	5.3 (1.6) 49.8	–	4.5 (2.1) 35.5
Labour migrants	5.7 (1.5) 61.6	5.3 (1.6) 52.2	4.8 (1.8) 38.2	4.5 (2.0) 35.6
Social distance family:				
Olim	6.2 (1.3) 78.4	–	3.6 (2.0) 18.9	–
Jewish *olim*	–	6.8 (0.7) 96.9	–	2.5 (1.9) 8.6
Non-Jewish *olim*	–	6.8 (0.6) 95.8	–	6.0 (1.6) 73.2
Labour migrants	6.2 (1.3) 79.0	6.8 (0.7) 94.3	6.1 (1.6) 76.3	6.2 (1.5) 79.1
Social distance child (in class):				
Olim	5.1 (1.8) 46.4	–	2.7 (1.7) 6.0	–
Jewish *olim*	–	4.4 (1.8) 34.5	–	2.2 (1.6) 4.2
Non-Jewish *olim*	–	4.5 (1.7) 35.0	–	4.5 (2.0) 33.7
Labour migrants	5.0 (1.7) 43.8	4.4 (1.8) 30.7	4.3 (2.0) 30.9	4.5 (2.0) 35.3
Social distance boss:				
Olim	5.5 (1.7) 57.0	–	3.7 (2.0) 20.0	–
Jewish *olim*	–	4.7 (1.7) 33.4	–	2.5 (1.8) 7.9
Non-Jewish *olim*	–	4.7 (1.6) 33.3	–	4.7 (2.1) 39.7
Labour migrants	5.5 (1.7) 55.0	5.3 (1.7) 47.4	5.4 (1.9) 58.7	5.1 (1.9) 48.1
Equal Rights:				
Olim	–	–	–	–
Jewish *olim*	–	4.9 (1.9) 47.0	–	1.8 (1.5) 4.1
Non-Jewish *olim*	–	5.1 (1.9) 52.6	–	3.7 (2.3) 28.1
Labour migrants	5.2 (1.7) 50.8	5.3 (2.0) 62.7	5.5 (2.0) 66.6	4.8 (2.0) 41.7

hightened feelings of social distance (especially in respect of close intrusion into private lives, for example, marrying a close relative).

In the 2007 survey Jewish respondents express very low feelings of social distance from Jewish immigrants (mean score of 2.3) but high levels in respect of non-Jewish *olim* and labour immigrants (4.5 for contact as neighbours; 6.0 for contact as family members; 4.5 for contact as their children's classmates; 4.7 and 5.5 respectively for contact as bosses in the workplace). In comparison with the 1999 levels, social distance from labour immigrants remained high and stable over the period.

Arab respondents consistently express higher levels of opposition to social contact with all immigrants as neighbours (mean score of 5.2 for all groups), as family members (6.8), as their children's classmates (4.4) and as bosses in the workplace (5.3). The data suggests some decline in Arab feelings of social distance from immigrants over time, except on the intimate level of family where feelings of social distance are close to the maximum level (6.8).

Overall, these findings indicate that for Arab Israelis all immigrants, and for Jewish Israelis non-Jewish immigrants, are considered as outsiders in the social sphere, manifest in the lower willingness to interact in everyday life.

Another form of discriminatory attitude is people's dispositions to share collective goods and services (for example, social, economic and political rights) with newcomers having the same or a different ethnic background. This is a crucial test for defining membership in contemporary societies. The 1999 and 2007 surveys indicate that a substantial proportion of Israelis support exclusion of immigrants from equal rights, although more among Arab Israelis than Jews. Overall, about 50 per cent of Arab respondents strongly support denial of equal rights to *olim* (whether Jewish or non-Jewish) and this opposition is stronger in respect of labour immigrants. As expected, there is a general consensus among Jews that ethnic immigrants deserve equal rights. Jewish levels of opposition to equal rights for non-Jewish immigrants is lower than the Arab levels, but is still substantial and more pronounced in respect of labour migrants.

Two main findings derive from the foregoing analysis. First, overall hostility to labour immigrants has apparently declined slightly over time. The slight decrease in the perceptions of socio-economic threat from, and exclusionary attitudes to, labour immigrants could be explained by Israel's strong exclusionary policy which denies the possibility for non-Jewish labour immigrants to become citizens. Although labour immigrants have become an integral part of the Israeli economy, they are excluded from state directed processes of integration. They hold the least desirable jobs, suffer the worst working conditions, and do not benefit from the welfare system and union protection accorded to Israeli citizens. The perception of securely 'closed doors' – hence lessened fear of competition – may lead to lower levels of hostility. Second, majority and minority groups differ in the way they perceive ethnic and non-ethnic migrants. Jews are hostile to non-Jewish *olim* but Arab Israelis are hostile to all immigrants.

Explaining Differences between Majority and Minority Attitudes

The previous findings elicit opinion regarding the way Arabs and Jews differ in their feelings of threat from, and their exclusionary attitudes to, Jewish and non-Jewish immigrants. Data collected through focus groups shed some light on these differences.[10]

Quantitative data analyses suggest that Jews mainly differentiate between Jewish and non-Jewish migrants. The qualitative data corroborate this finding by showing that for Jews there is no question about the legitimacy of Jewish migrants' presence in Israel. As one focus group participant stated:

> As long as they are Jewish I gladly welcome them. This is the only place for Jewish people and we have no other place to go. I accept them only if they are Jewish despite the fact that . . . it is at my expense in some way . . . . Having said that, I think that there should be a more strict control [of non-Jewish people entering through the Law of Return].

The main reason for displaying exclusionary attitudes to non-Jewish immigrants arriving under the Law of Return is based on the claim that most non-Jewish *olim* (especially those arriving from the FSU since the 1990s) were attracted to Israel by economic opportunities unavailable in their homelands, and falsified Jewish identity, which entitled them to immigrate to Israel. According to this view, non-Jewish *olim* entered the country on the 'Jewish ticket' (the terms of the Law of Return). They do not deserve, and they exploit and abuse, state benefits that only Jews are entitled to. In other words, non-Jewish *olim* are perceived as having no 'legitimate' right to equal rights upon arrival, in contrast to the Jewish *olim*.

Furthermore, some of the Jewish respondents think that non-Jewish immigrants are a real threat to the Jewish character of the state. Many complain about the rising number of shops that sell pork and condemn the proliferation of Christmas trees and celebration of Christmas. This pronounced feeling of threat to the national character and homogeneity motivates Israeli Jews to fear and oppose the presence of non-Jewish *olim*.

Jews also tend to agree that labour immigrants take jobs from Israeli workers, hence become a threat, especially to people who compete with them for the same kind of low-skilled jobs. However, the respondents do not condemn the immigrants themselves for this economic competition; instead they blame state policies, employers who want to benefit from cheap and unprotected labour and Israelis themselves who are unwilling to take these jobs. For some respondents the presence of non-Jews challenges the character of Israel as a Jewish state, and this aspect, coupled with concerns about economic competition, is crucial for understanding their perceptions of threat. As one participant commented:

> There is some level of risk [in allowing the presence of non-Jews]; I think this is why we have to be very careful in legislation. But there is a threat, of course there is, certainly, and it has to be considered, in my opinion. It is only a matter of definition: if you define Israel as a Jewish state then [the presence of non-Jews] threatens, it threatens its Jewish character. Is the Jewish character [of the state] that important? Again is it a question that I have long been asking myself and I still don't have a clear-cut answer. Like I said, I do feel that I'm here because of my being Jewish.

Unlike the Jews, Arab Israelis expressed strong feelings of competition from Jewish and non-Jewish *olim* and from labour migrants. Some argued that 'a high proportion of Russians are not Jewish and are taking advantage of the Law of Return . . . They are abusing state benefits'. At the same time Arab respondents expressed strong feelings of discrimination, as 'Russians are preferred', 'they always will get better treatment from Jews than we Arabs get'. Indicative of fears of threat and feelings of relative deprivation, one participant observed:

> I think first and foremost, they all brought with them all the bad things . . . prostitution . . . crime and theft . . .. We feel in a state of closure, . . . this large amount of new immigrants . . . that came and took our places [in the labour market]. Soon they will take over our lands. . . . They are considered to be Jews and when percentages [of the Israeli population] are measured they are considered Jews. . . . Our percentage [in the overall population] is getting small. All these things have important implications for us, mostly economic and social. They arrive and they have all the prerogatives. From the state's perspective they precede us. . . . They will always get better treatment than us just because they are Jewish.

As for the labour migrants, Arabs feel that their recruitment into the Israeli labour market has negatively affected their employment opportunities as employers prefer to hire cheap and flexible labour to replace native workers. This trend in labour force replacement was raised several times in the focus group discussions. For example, one participant explained:

> There was a time that in our village there were places [mainly in agriculture] where Arabs used to work. Now foreign workers have taken over these jobs and the natives remain unemployed without anywhere to work. . . . Labour migrants have taken over our jobs. . . . I can understand their economic needs . . . but they took my job.

To sum up, among Arabs, feelings of socio-economic competition, coupled with strong feelings of discrimination, explain their high levels of exclusionary attitudes to all immigrants in Israel. Among Jewish respondents, perceptions of competition over socio-economic resources together with expressions of threat to the character of the state are the underlying factors explaining exclusionary attitudes to non-Jewish immigrants.

In light of these findings it seems that the social climate surrounding newcomers to Israel is hostile to those who do not share the same ethno-background, and this is true for both majority and minority groups. As the number and proportion of non-Jewish immigrants (whether *olim* or immigrant workers) is likely to increase, questions about the rights of citizenship, the nature of nationality, and the viability of a multicultural society will become more crucial than ever before.

AUSTRALIA AND ISRAEL COMPARED: THE 2003 ISSP SURVEY

In this final section we compare attitudes towards immigrants in Australia and Israel drawing on International Social Survey Program (ISSP) module on national identity (ISSP 2003). In 2003 the ISSP administered a national identity survey in 42 countries, including Australia and Israel, with respective sample sizes of 2183 and 1218. It thus presents a unique opportunity to consider recent Australian and Israeli public views on a common set of questions related to immigration.

It is possible to disaggregate the ISSP data to a limited extent by ethnicity. For Australia one variable allows for disaggregation by citizenship of parents, a procedure which identifies respondents both of whose parents were citizens of Australia at the time of the respondent's birth, termed in the following analysis as 'long-time Australians' (1481 respondents), and respondents neither of whose parents was a citizen of Australia at time of birth (569 respondents). For Israel, it is possible to disaggregate those who identify as Jewish (1066 respondents) and Arab (152 respondents).

This procedure is far from ideal, highlighting both the value and limitation of cross-national surveying. The complexity of the meaning of 'immigrant' in Israel (the categories of Jewish *olim*, non-Jewish *olim* and labour immigrants) is not captured in the ISSP questionnaire; it is most likely that the responses of Jewish Israelis refer narrowly to those perceived to be non-Jewish *olim* and labour immigrants. The number of Arab respondents is low and can only be treated as indicative, not statistically significant – but where cross-validation with other surveys (discussed earlier in this chapter) is possible a large degree of consistency is found. With regard to Australia, a key variable that cannot be captured is the differentiation of those of English and non-English speaking background. It would also be of interest to have data on the views of Aboriginal Australians on immigration, but this is not available in the ISSP survey (or any other survey known to the authors). It may be that views of Aboriginal Australians and Arab Israelis are similar on the issue of immigration, but this cannot be established. There are thus a number of limitations in using the ISSP data, but it does lend further support to key findings presented in the previous discussion.

In Tables 5.4 and 5.5 we present a descriptive overview of the values for the indicators that compose the latent variables threat,[11] exclusion[12] from citizenship rights and support for reducing the number of immigrants coming to Australia and Israel by specific groups (disaggregated by birthplace of parent for Australia and Jews and Arabs for Israel).

The data in Table 5.4 reveal considerable cross-national variation in views of immigrants' impact on society. Overall, compared with Australians, there was a heightened tendency among Israelis to view immigrants (non-*olim*) as posing a threat to the social and economic order of society. Thus for example, negative views were most in evidence in Israel with regard to immigrants' impact on the increase of crime (34 per cent in Australia and 49 per cent in Israel) and immigrants' negative influence in the labour market (24 per cent and 52 per cent respectively). Among Israelis, perception of threat is especially marked among Arabs; while there is some differentiation in Australia among long-time Australians and those whose parents were not Australian citizens at the time of their birth, it is less marked than among Israeli Jews and Arabs.

The data reveal that compared to Israel, a substantial number of respondents in Australia perceive immigrants in a positive way in the economic and cultural arenas, again bearing in mind the narrower application of the term 'immigrant' for Jews in Israel. Thus for example, 68 per cent of Australians perceive immigrants as having a positive impact on the country's economy, compared to only 48 per cent of Israelis. Likewise, 73 per cent of Australians think that immigrants improve society by bringing in new ideas and culture, compared to only 46 per cent of Israelis. As expected, positive views concerning the impact of immigrants on the receiving society are more widely held among respondents born to noncitizen parents in Australia and among Jews in Israel.

Table 5.5 indicates attitudes to the level of immigration, access to citizenship rights and illegal immigrants. One indicator of tolerance for the incorporation of immigrants is the disposition to grant citizenship to children of immigrant parents (that is, second- or third-generation immigrants) by the *jus solis* principle. This is considered the most crucial test of a liberal attitude to foreigners' incorporation into the host society. The data show that in both countries support for grant of citizenship to

Table 5.4 *Perception of threat (per cent agree/strongly agree)*

Immigrants . . .	Australia			Israel		
	Born to Australian citizen parents	Born to non-citizen citizen parents	Total	Arab	Jew	Total
increase crime rates	37.8	24.6	33.5	85.5	44.2	49.4
generally good for country's economy	64.1	77	67.6	28.3	50.5	47.7
take jobs away from people who were born in the country	29.6	13.1	24.3	85.6	46.3	51.5
Improve society by bringing in new ideas and cultures	68.6	83.3	72.9	25.6	48.7	45.8
government spends too much money assisting immigrants	45.3	33.8	41.8	83.5	31.2	37.8
N	1481	569	2183	152	1066	1218

Table 5.5 Attitudes towards granting rights and citizenship and exclusion of illegal immigrants (percentages)

	Australia			Israel		
	Born to Australian citizen parents	Born to non-citizen parents	Total	Arabs	Jews	Total
Children born in [country] of parents who are not citizens should have the right to become citizens (% supporting)	87.3	89.4	89.8	79.6	79.5	79.6
Legal immigrants to [country] who are not citizens should have the same rights as citizens (% supporting)	53.8	65.1	57.5	68.3	60.6	61.3
[Country] should take stronger measures to exclude illegal immigrants (% agree)	73.0	71.6	72.6	84.2	77.5	78.4
Number of immigrants coming to the country (% reduce a lot)	21.1	11.0	17.9	46.0	25.1	27.8
N	1481	569	2183	152	1066	1218

locally-born children of immigrant parents is high (90 per cent and 80 per cent for Australia and Israel, respectively).

The level of support for the grant of citizen rights to the second-generation of immigrants was higher than for the first generation, although granting of rights to the first generation was endorsed by a clear majority in both countries. Support for the *jus domicile* principle, that is, rights based on residency, was at a similar level in Australia (58 per cent) and Israel (61 per cent). In both countries close to three out of four respondents support taking 'stronger measures' to exclude illegal immigrants (73 per cent and 78 per cent for Australia and Israel, respectively). When asked for views on reduction of immigration, there is only a marginal difference between long-time Australians and Jewish Israelis and, as expected, lower level of opposition by those whose parents were not Australian citizens and the highest level among Israeli Arabs.

Explaining Threat and Attitudes Towards Granting Rights to Foreigners

First, in keeping with the earlier discussion, perception of threat and exclusionary attitudes towards immigrants in both countries tends to decrease with age and education. Threat is also less pronounced among left-oriented respondents and among white collar workers. Other things being equal, we find that perception of threat is less pronounced in Australia than in Israel.

Second, the effect of ethnic origin on perception of threat is in the expected direction in both countries. Specifically, in Israel perceived threat is more evident among subordinate populations, notably Arab Israelis. In Australia, threat is more evident among long-time Australians.

Third, again as expected, the individuals who are members of socio-economic groups most likely to suffer the detrimental consequences of competition perceive immigrants as more damaging to their socio-economic well-being. There is indication that labour force status exerts differential effects on perception of threat in the two countries. Compared to blue collar workers, level of threat is more pronounced among white collar workers in Israel and those out of the labour force. By contrast, level of threat is less pronounced in Australia among white collar workers and those out of the labour force.

CONCLUSION

The evidence presented in this chapter indicates that dominant groups in both Australia and Israel accept that their homelands are countries of immigration – that immigration confers major benefits. In this regard they are in contrast with most advanced western economies, where a majority of the population does not share this perspective.

Public opinion in Australia and Israel is, however, variable – in the context of economic downturn and rising unemployment the positive attitude in both countries shifts. This was evident in surveys conducted in the early 1990s, with opposition to the immigration intake peaking at over 70 per cent in Australia and with heightened opposition in Israel at the time of the massive immigration from the FSU.

Ethnic divisions in both countries add a layer of complexity to generalization. In Australia there is a difference in the attitudes of long-time Australians and immigrants, particularly those of non-English speaking background in their early years of settlement. The views of Aboriginal Australians have not been polled.

In Israel the known difference is more sharply delineated, with a marked difference in the attitudes of Jewish and Arab populations. Arab Israelis indicated negative views to all immigration streams. Jewish Israelis' attitudes differ with regard to Jews making *aliyah*, non-Jewish *olim,* labour immigrants who gain entry legally for limited terms of residence and those who enter without documentation. The positive attitude is particularly in evidence with regard to Jewish *olim.*

NOTES

1. We acknowledge that it is difficult to argue about the causal sequence of perception of threats and discriminatory attitudes. For the causal relationship of threat and prejudice we follow Schlueter et al. (2008) who in their longitudinal study based on attitudes to minorities in Germany and Russia, clearly show that perception of threat is causally antecedent to out-group derogation.

2. Most of the data in which the present analysis is based rests on Leshem (1998), who compiled data from these independent surveys extracting questions that were nearly identical, thus making it possible to follow public views over time (see Leshem 1998: Tables 1 to 7). See also Astman and Rozenbaum (1980); Damian and Rozenabum-Tamari (1992); and Al-Haj (1998).

3. The analysis reported here rests on a survey of the adult Israeli population based on a stratified sample of 1025 respondents (667 Jewish, 358 Arabs) conducted in Israel in 2007 by the B.I. and Lucille Cohen Institute for Public Opinion Research at Tel Aviv University. Interviews were face-to-face and lasted about 50 minutes. Response rate was 62 per cent, which is high by any standard in Israeli society. Respondents were asked about attitudes to three types of migrants: labour migrants, Jewish migrants arriving under the Law of Return and non-Jewish migrants arriving under the Law of Return. For further information regarding the 1999 data, please contact the author of this chapter.

4. As Table 5.3 shows, the only possible direct comparison between the two surveys is for attitudes to labour migrants. Immigrants arriving under the Law of Return were considered as a group in the 1999 survey, but were divided in two groups in the 2007 survey

to differentiate Jewish from non-Jewish *olim*. For this reason, our analysis focuses on attitudes to immigrants in 2007 and relates to changes over time when possible.

5. Immigrant workers are not entitled to any welfare services granted by the state to its citizens. Nevertheless, 26 per cent of Jewish respondents and 74 per cent of Arabs perceive that the presence of labour migrants in society negatively affects their welfare rights.

6. Social distance from migrants was measured on a 1–7 scale based on response to the following four questions: 'Would it be unpleasant if . . . (1) your neighbour is [group]; (2) a relative marries a [group]; (3) your child studies with [child of group]; (4) your boss is [group]?'

7. Respondents were asked whether Jewish migrants arriving under the Law of Return/ non-Jewish migrants arriving under the Law of Return/labour migrants deserve the same rights as established citizens.

8. We are cautious in interpreting changes over time when analysing this specific variable because the categories of response were changed. In 1999 respondents had three categories of choice: (1) unlimited entrance; (2) restricted entrance; (3) forbid entrance. In 2007 there were five categories: (1) unlimited entrance; (2) limited entrance, but less limited than at present; (3) limited the same as at present; (4) limited more than at present; (5) forbid entrance.

9. Numerous studies have documented a hierarchy of social distance preferences in the USA and in Europe (see for example Dovidio et al. 1996). These studies reveal that social distance hierarchies tend to be consensual within social groups when at the top of this hierarchy are Europeans, then Asians, and finally African-Americans.

10. We conducted six focus groups in Israel: three with Jewish respondents and three with Arab respondents. The sessions were recorded and transcribed.

11. Perception of threat is a variable measuring perceptions of the consequences of the presence of immigrant minorities. It was measured on a 1–5 scale (from 1 = strongly disagree to 5 = strongly agree) based on response to the questions: 'How much do you agree or disagree with each of the following statements? (a) Immigrants improve [country's] society by bringing in new ideas and culture; (b) Immigrants are generally good for [country's] economy; (c) Immigrants take jobs away from people who were born in [country]; (d) Immigrants increase crime rates; (e) Government spends too much on assisting immigrants'. Factor analysis showed that all measured items measured only one latent variable, which we labelled 'threat of socio-economic threat'.

12. Exclusion was measured as a latent variable composed by the following questions (measured on a 1–5 scale from 1 = strongly disagree to 5 = strongly agree): (1) Children born in [country] to parents who are not citizens should become citizens of [country] at birth; (2) Legal immigrants should have the same rights as citizens; (3) Country should take stronger measures to exclude illegal immigrants. Factor analysis lent support to the argument that these items measured the latent variable 'exclusion'.

APPENDIX: DATA AND METHODS

The political and social significance of immigration within host societies has attracted substantial academic research within a range of disciplinary specializations. The extent of research into public opinion varies from country to country, with some governments providing substantial government funding for opinion polling. Within the European Union (EU) and its predecessors regular surveys have been undertaken since 1973. Special attention has been devoted to racism and xenophobia, with reports published every three to five years since 1988. Individual EU states also undertake their own public opinion research. In the UK comprehensive citizenship surveys have been conducted since 2001. In Canada, the Department of Citizenship and Immigration conducts an ongoing research program to develop a better and ongoing understanding of Canadian attitudes. A survey to track attitudes to immigration was conducted several times each year for more than 20 years. The Ethnic Diversity Survey of 2002, developed by Statistics Canada, is the largest survey of its type and achieved a sample of 42 500 people (Statistics Canada 2003).

In Australia, relatively minor and infrequent surveys are undertaken by the standards of Europe and Canada. Some research is conducted within the universities, notably the Australian National University. Small-scale, narrowly focused surveys are commissioned on a regular basis for major newspaper groups. A private philanthropic trust, the Scanlon Foundation, in 2007 and 2009 funded surveys related to immigration and social cohesion issues (Markus and Dharmalingham 2008; Markus 2009).

In Israel, unlike other major countries of immigration, there is no systematic public surveying of opinion concerning immigration. Since early 1970s the Ministry of Absorption and other independent organizations have conducted surveys on attitudes of Jewish Israelis to *olim* but these data files are not available for public use. The discussion of Israel focuses on four relatively small surveys conducted in the period 1974–92, and more detailed analysis of surveys in 1999 and 2007. While these six surveys are available for analysis, there is no set of common questions allowing precise plotting of change over time.

The Australian surveying record is in the mid- to low-range when compared with other developed nations. Australia has a relatively rich record of polling on a staple of key questions and has participated in some international survey projects, including the World Values Survey, but is lacking detailed studies. Israel, on the other hand, lacks even a continuous record of public polling, so the findings reported in this study rest on a handful of surveys.

For the final comparison of Ausralian and Israeli attitudes based on the ISSP data, in order to examine the extent to which attitudes towards immigrants differ, we pooled the data sets from the two countries into one file and estimated three regression models. In Model 1 we predict 'threat' as a function of a respondent's characteristics. In Model 2 we estimate 'exclusion' as a function of a respondent's characteristics plus threat and country. In Model 3 we use a logistic regression model to estimate the effect of a respondent's characteristics, country effects and threat on the variable 'Reduce number of Immigrants'.

6. The second generation

Haya Stier and Siew-Ean Khoo

The children of migrants are a particularly intriguing group. Whether one or both parents were born overseas, the children are intimately exposed to an immigrant inheritance, in culture, in ethnicity and in language. At the same time, these children grow up, are educated and work in the country of their birth, not that of their parent or parents. How does this exposure to two cultures affect their lives? What difference does it make to their education, their jobs, their income, whom they marry and their own children? To what extent do they adopt the habits of the new country?

THE SECOND GENERATION IN OTHER COUNTRIES

There has been much research interest in the US, as a nation of immigrants, in the second generation and their incorporation into American society. Sociologists are particularly interested in the economic and social adaptation of the 'new' second generation, the children of immigrants who arrived after the change in migration policy in 1965 which led to an increase in the migration of non-Europeans, notably Latin Americans and Asians, to the US. Since these children are of non-European and non-English-speaking background, there is particular interest in their educational and labour market outcomes and how they compare with their third or more generation American peers on these characteristics.

Research by Portes and Zhou (1993) on the children of immigrants in the US has led them to introduce the concept of 'segmented assimilation' to describe the diverse outcomes they observed among the second generation of post-1965 immigrants. Some are integrating into the white middle class while others are assimilating into the underclass. A third pattern of adaptation is that of rapid economic advancement with deliberate preservation of ethnic values and community cohesion. Portes and Zhou (1993) suggested that differences in second generation outcomes could be explained by the social contexts faced by immigrant youth, in particular the factors of race, location of residence and types of resources made available through government programs (schools) and networks within their own ethnic community (social capital). The immigrant parents' legal status has also been shown to be important (Portes and Rumbaut 2001, 2006). More recent studies by Portes and Fernandez-Kelly (2008) and others (see chapters in Fernandez-Kelly and Portes 2008) have also suggested the importance of other factors such as middle class cultural capital brought from the country of origin, access to public colleges and universities and a mentor or significant other who takes an interest in the young person.

A study of second-generation children based on the US 1990 Census data also showed a mixed picture of disadvantage and advantage in their household situation (Jensen and Chitose 1994). The second-generation children were more likely than other American children to live in poor households, where the household heads were in the lowest education categories, but also more likely to live in households where the heads were highly educated, married and not receiving welfare support from government. In reviewing the US studies, Waldinger and Perlman (1998) concluded that while there was concern that some second-generation youth might be assimilating into the urban underclass, there were also indications that others were adapting well in relation to educational outcomes and this was important for their integration into American society.

Recent findings from Europe also suggest a diverse experience of the second generation, with some outperforming the majority population in education while others have lower attainment (Crul and Vermuelen 2003; Heath et al. 2008). In particular, Heath et al. found that second-generation minorities from non-European less-developed countries attained lower levels of education and had higher risks of unemployment, while those who originated from European countries were more successful, both in their educational attainment and labour market achievements. They attribute this diversity to differences in socio-economic background but also to ethnic segregation and discrimination.

The second generation of adult age in Canada is one of successful adaptation in terms of social mobility (Boyd and Grieco 1998). While the study is of Canadian-born children of immigrant cohorts before 1970, and therefore is not concerned with the children of more recent immigrant cohorts, it shows that the second generation had high levels of education and labour market achievements. This finding is similar to those of studies of the second generation in Australia whose parents immigrated before 1970, as discussed in the next section.

PREVIOUS STUDIES OF THE SECOND GENERATION IN AUSTRALIA AND ISRAEL

There have been a number of studies in Australia of the second-generation's educational outcomes dating back to the 1970s when there were concerns about how the children of Southern European migrants would fare in Australian schools. However, a study of secondary school students in Sydney in the mid-1970s found that a higher percentage of second-generation children whose parents had migrated from Southern European countries had completed high school than did the children of Australian-born parents (Martin and Meade 1979; Meade 1983). Other studies in the 1980s and 1990s also showed that the second generation of Southern and Eastern European background had better educational and occupational outcomes than third or more generation Australians of the same age (Hugo 1986; Birrell and Khoo 1995; Giorgas 1999). The second generation of Southern and Eastern European background were more likely to have tertiary education qualifications and to be in professional occupations than their counterparts of Western European origins who were more likely to have vocational or trade qualifications. In discussing these findings, Birrell and Khoo (1995: 16) suggested that the better educational outcomes of the second generation of Southern and Eastern European background might be related to the importance on educational attainment placed by their immigrant parents, although the second generation themselves must be given credit for their motivation to invest in their own education.

In 2001, the Australian Government's Department of Immigration and Multicultural Affairs commissioned a study of the second generation based on data from the Australian 1996 Census (Khoo et al. 2002). The study examined three different age cohorts of the second generation – those aged 0–14 years, 15–24 years and 25–44 years – by their parents' country of origin (Khoo et al. 2002). These age cohorts are associated with different waves of immigration to Australia, with the younger cohorts including the children of non-European immigrants arriving after 1975, while the older cohorts are predominantly the children of immigrants who are part of the post-1945 migration from Europe. The study shows that the second generation as a group is doing better than their third-generation peers in terms of educational attainment and occupational status; however, there is considerable diversity in outcomes by origin. The second generation of some Southern European and Asian origins are more likely to achieve better educational and occupational outcomes than those of other origins. The second generation of English-speaking or Western European origins is more similar to third-generation

Australians in their socio-economic characteristics. There are also differences in language and cultural maintenance among the second generation by origin, indicated by differences in the shift to speaking English only at home and in demographic behaviours such as having children without being married, living with a partner without being married and independent living. The second generation of Mediterranean or Asian origins is more likely to differ from the third or more generations in these demographic behaviours (Khoo et al. 2002). The authors of the study concluded that the differences in educational and demographic outcomes among the second generation by ethnic origin would appear to support the segmented assimilation theory of Portes and Zhou (1993) although it was not clear that the factors contributing to the diversity in outcomes of the second generation in Australia were necessarily the same as those affecting the second generation in the USA.

Previous studies in Israel have focused on the socio-economic achievements of second-generation Israelis, highlighted mainly by ethnic cleavages within groups (for example Cohen and Haberfeld 1998; Friedlander et al. 2002; Cohen et al. 2007). Most of these studies reported a narrowing gap between the ethnic groups in educational attainment and family formation (Friedlander et al. 2002; Gshur and Okun 2003; Okun and Khait-Marelly 2008). Friedlander et al. (2002) compared a selection of cohorts alongside the three generations of Israelis. Findings pointed to lower educational achievement in first-generation North African and Middle Eastern immigrants from early birth cohorts (1925–29), compared to their third-generation counterparts, and a first-to-third generation gap not nearly as pronounced in American-European descendants. However, the first-to-third generation gap in later birth cohorts (1950–54) showed evidence that the educational gap had significantly narrowed – and in some cases, closed – for Asian-African immigrants at the primary and secondary school level. Findings also pointed to ethnic gaps in the second generation disappearing or becoming significantly smaller by the third generation in the higher levels of education (that is secondary, matriculation degree, post-secondary, academic). These results, then, showed trends towards the ethnic gap in educational achievement decreasing between generations and cohorts, a sign of ethnic assimilation.

Yet, when higher education is considered, there is evidence that there are still persisting ethnic differences among the Israeli-born Jews, with those from European-American descent still having higher rates of university graduation than those of Asian-African origin (for example Cohen and Haberfeld 1998; Cohen et al. 2007). A study by Cohen et al. (2007) examined whether Israelis from Asian-African or mixed ethnic origins were as likely to graduate from university as those of European-American origin from similar parental backgrounds. Findings showed no difference in graduation rates between second-and third-generation Asian-African men, although the generation-ethnic gap was less pronounced in women. According to Cohen et al. (2007), these findings suggest that the ethnic hierarchy in Israel has not changed much from generation to generation. Cohen and Haberfeld (1998) report that despite a narrowed educational gap between second-generation Israelis from Eastern and Western origins, there is still an increase in the earnings gap between the groups. The main explanation for the widening earnings gap relates to the increased earnings inequality mainly due to increasing returns on higher education. Since more of the European-American than Asian-African origin acquire a tertiary qualification, the earnings gap between the two groups has been increasing (Haberfeld and Cohen 2007).

In terms of generational differences, studies show that in general, the second generation from European-American origin converged with the third generation in terms of socio-economic characteristics and family formation, while generational gaps still exist among the Asian-African origin (Friedlander et al. 2002; Cohen et al. 2007; Okun and Khait-Marelly 2008). Studies on Israeli marriage patterns also reveal generational endogamy – a tendency to marry within the same generation. Further, first-generation immigrants tend to marry those of the same ethnicity (ethnic endogamy) more so than in the second and third generations, and ethnic endogamy in the second and third generations has decreased over time (Gshur and Okun 2003). Overall, these studies show that ethnic cleavages still persist, even among the third generation, while generational gaps are narrowed within each ethnic group.

The studies cited above used data obtained from Israeli censuses, with the latest data from the Israeli 1995 Census. This is because the ethnic identity of the third generation can only be determined from the Israeli 1995 Census (see Friedlander et al. 2002; Cohen et al. 2007). In this chapter, socio-economic and family formation patterns of the second generation in Israel are compared to earlier and later generations using more recent data (2005–07). The main focus is on educational attainment, labour market status and family characteristics of the cohort group aged 15 to 44. Comparisons are made with the same age cohort in Australia using data from the 2006 Census. The second generation in both countries is also examined by their region of ethnic origin to see whether patterns of integration are similar in the two countries, or whether differences are observed that may be related to different policies regarding the selection, settlement and integration of immigrants in the two countries.

THE SECOND GENERATION IN AUSTRALIA AND ISRAEL: WHO ARE THEY?

In 2006, there were 3.6 million second-generation Australians – about 18 per cent of the total population. In terms of their age distribution, 28 per cent of second-generation Australians are children aged 0–14 years, 49 per cent are aged 15–44 years and 23 per cent are aged 45 and over. Two-thirds (68 per cent) of the second generation in Australia in 2006 stated a European ancestry, 8 per cent stated an Asian ancestry and 4 per cent reported a Middle Eastern ancestry. One-third (33 per cent) identified their ancestry in the Australian 2006 Census as 'Australian' either as a single response or in combination with another ancestry.

The age distribution of second-generation Australians of European and Asian origins is quite different and reflects the different period of migration of their parents' generation. Most of the second generation of Asian background are still very young because their parents migrated after 1975, while the second generation of European origins comprises mostly the children of European migrants who arrived in Australia during the 1950s and 1960s. Of the second generation of Asian origins 63 per cent were aged 0–14 years in 2006 compared with 19 per cent of the second generation of European ancestry. Less than 3 per cent of the second generation of Asian ancestry were aged 45 years and over compared with 28 per cent of the second generation of European ancestry. In this chapter we focus on the second generation aged 15–44 years which accounted for one-third (34 per cent) of the second generation of Asian ancestry and just over one-half (53 per cent) of the second generation of European ancestry in Australia. Of the second generation aged 15–44, 73 per cent stated a European ancestry, 14 per cent reported Australian ancestry, 5 per cent were of Asian ancestry and less than 4 per cent claimed Middle Eastern ancestry.

In Israel, the second generation numbers around 3.8 million, which is about a third of the total Jewish population, a much higher proportion than in Australia. Of these, 17 per cent are children aged 0–14 and another 53 per cent are between the ages 15 and 44. The first generation immigrants also comprise a third of the Jewish population, but they are significantly older – only 3 per cent are young children and 28 per cent are in the age range 15 to 44. The third generation is much younger, with 36 per cent of children and 48 per cent between the ages 15 and 44.

In Israel 44 per cent of the second generation is of European origin, 30 per cent originate from North African countries and the remaining 26 per cent are of Asian (mainly Middle Eastern) origin. The three regional groups differ in their age distribution, with a higher percentage of children among those of European origin (about 19 per cent compared to 14 per cent among North Africans and only 6 per cent among those of Asian origin). In the age range 15 to 44, our main focus in this study, the minority originated from Europe (40 per cent) compared to 68 per cent and 58 per cent among Africans and Asians, respectively. This reflects in part the different waves of immigration to Israel, which are highly related to ethnicity, with Europeans constituting both the more veteran groups and the recent comers. Ethnic differences in age are more pronounced among immigrants. The Asian group is much older than the two others, with about 90 per cent aged 45 years or older and only 8 per cent aged 15–44. Nineteen per cent of North Africans and a third of all immigrants are in the 15–44 age group, reflecting the more recent (since 1989) mass migration from the former Soviet Union (FSU) to Israel.

THE SECOND GENERATION AT SCHOOL AND UNIVERSITY: HOW WELL DO THEY DO?

Studies of the second generation have usually focused on their educational participation and outcomes as these measures are considered to be important indicators of their social and structural integration. Table 6.1 compares the educational participation of young people aged 15–24 years of the first, second and third generations in Australia in 2006 and Israel in 2005–07. The second generation in both age groups 15–18 and 19–24 in Australia are more likely than their Israeli counterparts to be still studying. Australian youth in general are also more likely to combine studying with paid work than Israeli youth. The percentage of Australians aged 15–18 years who are working only is also higher than the percentage of Israeli youth in the same age group, while the percentage that is neither studying nor working is lower in Australia than in Israel. It should be pointed out that the overseas-born first generation in Australia includes international students studying at Australian educational institutions. Therefore, the higher percentage studying among the first generation in Australia is partly due to this factor. In Israel, a relatively low level of school enrollment or work at ages 19–24 results mainly from the three-year (two years for women) mandatory army service. Consequently, young men and women attend higher education at older ages than their counterparts in most of the industrialized world.

Table 6.2 compares the educational participation of first and second generation youth in Australia and Israel by their geographic region of origin. The first and second generations aged 15–18 of Asian or African origin in Australia are more likely to be in education compared with their counterparts in Israel. However, the percentage still studying among the

Table 6.1   *Participation in education and work at ages 15–18 and 19–24*
                by generation, Israel and Australia

	Country	First generation	Second generation	Third generation
Age 15–18				
% studying	Israel	80.5	78.8	76.6
	Australia	88.6	84.4	79.3
% studying only	Israel	70.9	70.6	69.5
	Australia	69.9	56.4	48.4
% studying and	Israel	9.6	8.2	7.2
working	Australia	18.7	27.9	30.9
% working only	Israel	5.4	5.8	7.2
	Australia	6.7	10.8	13.7
% not studying,	Israel	13.8	14.6	18.2
not working	Australia	4.7	5.4	7.0
N	Israel	3 383	5 924	9 812
	Australia	118 455	280 083	614 395
Age 19–24				
% studying	Israel	32.2	34.7	27.6
	Australia	58.2	37.7	32.3
N	Israel	5 975	10 282	13 845
	Australia	290 038	375 234	806 155

Sources: Israel Central Bureau of Statistics (2005–07); Australian 2006 Census.

first and second generations of European-American origin is about the same in the two countries. While a higher proportion of second-generation youth of Asian or African origin in Australia is studying compared with those of European origin, the reverse pattern is seen in Israel. In Australia, youth of Asian or African origin are also more likely to be studying only while those of European origin are more likely to combine study with paid work. Second-generation youth of European background in Australia are more likely than their counterparts of non-European background to be working.

Differences in school enrollment between ethnic groups are similar in Israel, although some interesting patterns emerge. Immigrants of Asian origin have relatively low rates of school attendance (74 per cent) while immigrants from Africa have the highest rates (86 per cent). Immigrants from European countries are in between with 80 per cent of youth still in school. The figures are different for the second generation – those of African origin have the lowest rate of school attendance (76 per cent

Table 6.2 Participation in education and work by region of origin and generation, Israel and Australia

		First generation			Second generation		
		Asia	Africa	EU/AM	Asia	Africa	EU/AM
Age 15–18							
% studying	Israel	73.6	86.0	80.0	78.9	75.9	81.4
	Australia	93.7	92.1	83.1	92.9	90.7	82.4
% studying	Israel	64.2	75.7	70.6	74.2	67.5	71.5
only	Australia	81.4	81.5	56.2	75.5	71.5	51.3
% studying	Israel						
and	Australia	9.4	10.3	9.4	4.7	8.4	9.9
working		12.3	10.7	26.9	17.4	19.2	31.1
% working	Israel	10.7	1.0	5.8	4.4	7.1	5.4
only	Australia	2.2	2.7	11.1	3.3	4.9	12.0
% not	Israel						
studying,	Australia						
not		15.7	13.0	14.2	16.7	17.0	13.2
working		2.4	5.2	5.8	3.7	4.4	5.6
N	Israel	318	585	2480	1284	2236	2404
	Australia	51737	8582	42019	45192	4367	160752
Age 19–24							
% studying	Israel	26.5	26.4	33.9	36.9	31.5	36.5
	Australia	70.1	63.5	41.6	51.7	35.5	35.0
N	Israel	692	651	4632	2772	3734	377
	Australia	160760	15793	85216	47494	4840	245845

Sources: Israel Central Bureau of Statistics (2005–07); Australian 2006 Census.

compared to 79 per cent among those of Asian origin and more than 81 per cent among those of European origin). Almost 16 per cent of immigrant children of Asian origin compared to 13 per cent of those arriving from Africa and 14 per cent of the Europeans are neither working nor studying, but differences between Asian and African origins in the second generation disappear and both groups are more likely than their European counterparts to be dislocated. The differences among all groups, however, are rather small. In Australia, the percentage neither studying nor working in the age group 15–18 is quite small (6 per cent or less) in both the first and second generations.

The educational advantage of immigrants disappears in the older age groups. Among the age groups 25 to 44, the third generation has the highest educational achievement, with more than 42 per cent having a tertiary education, compared to 30 per cent and 34 per cent for second generation and immigrants, respectively. It appears that the lowest educational achievements are at the second generation, with only 49 per cent with post high-school education, compared to more than 57 per cent of the immigrants and 63 per cent of the more veteran group.

Among those 19 to 24 years of age, some differences in educational attainment appear between ethnic groups. Educational attainment is lower for immigrants and Israeli-born of North African origin. Only 10 per cent of the immigrants and 24 per cent of the Israeli-born North African have post-high school or academic education, compared to more than 30 per cent of Israeli-born of the two other groups. Interestingly, however, the difference in education between immigrants and second-generation Israelis of North African origin are higher than in the other two groups. More pronounced differences between the ethnic groups emerge among the older groups, mainly in higher education (Table 6.3). More than 65 per cent of the second generation from European-American origins have post-high school education compared to 44 per cent of their Asian and only 37 per cent of their African origin counterparts. Compared to immigrants of the same ethnic origin, all second-generation ethnic groups have a better position – for example, a quarter of the second-generation Asian sample has a college education compared to 21 per cent of the immigrants from the same origin; the comparable figures for Africans are 21 per cent and 11 per cent respectively and for Europeans are 46 per cent and 40 per cent. More of the European groups are still in school at these age groups, further improving their level of education. Overall, Table 6.3 shows that much of the gaps in education can be attributed to ethnicity, but for some ethnic groups (mostly of North African origin) there are more substantial differences between the second generation and immigrants. More importantly, the second-generation disadvantages compared to the first generation can be fully accounted for by the ethnic composition of the two groups.

We next compare the educational attainment of the second generation in Australia and Israel by examining the proportion with post-school qualifications in the age group 25–44. It appears that the lowest educational achievements are at the second generation in Israel, with only 49 per cent having some post-high school education, compared to 57 per cent of the immigrants and 63 per cent of the third generation (Table 6.3). This is in contrast to the pattern in Australia where the proportion with post-school qualifications is higher in the second generation than in the third (or more) generations. The percentage with post-school qualifications was also higher in the first generation than the second generation in Australia because of the emphasis on skilled migration in Australia's permanent

Table 6.3   Educational attainment of persons aged 25–44 by generation and region of ethnic origin, Israel and Australia

	% degree	% other qualifications	Total % with a qualifications[a]	N
Australia				
First generation	33.8	28.3	64.2	1 358 534
Second generation	20.9	38.5	60.7	1 145 694
Third+ generation	17.4	38.8	57.4	2 650 758
Second generation				
NW Europe	23.1	33.8	58.3	570 342
SE Europe	24.0	34.3	59.7	346 612
Middle East/	23.9	31.4	56.9	32 386
North Africa				
Other Africa	29.4	30.3	61.0	3 058
SE Asia	35.7	23.1	59.9	4 764
NE Asia	61.5	16.4	79.0	15 207
S Asia	43.2	25.4	70.0	8 252
Israel[b]				
First generation	33.5	23.6	57.1	19 643
Second generation	30.2	18.4	48.6	36 514
Third+ generation	42.5	20.7	63.2	17 776
Second generation				
Europe/America	45.5	20.2	65.7	11 108
Asia	25.8	17.9	43.7	12 986
Africa	21.0	17.2	37.2	12 420

Notes:

[a]   Includes those whose qualifications were inadequately described.

[b]   For Israel, degree refers to academic degree, other qualifications – for post-high-school non-academic degree.

Sources: Australian 2006 Census; Israel Central Bureau of Statistics (2005–07).

migration program since 1996, with skilled migrants most likely to be in the 25–44 age group.[1]

Among the second generation, educational differences are more pronounced by region of ethnic origin. As Table 6.3 shows, in Israel, the level of education is substantially higher among those of European origin where 66 per cent had some post-high school education and 45.5 per cent had an academic degree. Among Asians only a quarter had academic degrees and

44 per cent had some higher education while the numbers are lower (21 per cent and 37 per cent, respectively) among those originated in North Africa. In Australia, the European and Asian groups have been further disaggregated into sub-region-of-origin groups for a more detailed examination of ethnic diversity in the second generation's educational outcomes. The second generation of Asian origin in this age group is relatively small compared to the second generation of European origin because of the more recent migration of Asians to Australia; however they have overtaken the second generation of European origin in educational attainment, with higher proportions having post-school qualifications, particularly university degree qualifications. The Middle Eastern and African second generation is more similar to the second generation of European origin in their educational qualifications. The second generation of North-east Asian background, which is dominated by people of Chinese ethnicity, has the highest proportion with post-school qualifications and the highest proportion with university degrees, followed by the second generation of South and Central Asian background, which is dominated by people of Indian ethnicity.

WHAT WORK DOES THE SECOND GENERATION DO?

Employment outcomes are important indicators of the second generation's economic integration. Table 6.4 presents labour force characteristics of men and women (25–44 years old) within the three generational groups in Israel and Australia. Immigrant men in Israel have higher rates of labour force participation than the two Israeli-born groups.

Among the employed population, however, the level of attainment of Israeli-born is higher than that of immigrants. A higher percentage of third-generation men are employed in professional or managerial jobs (49 per cent) compared to 38 per cent of the second generation and only 35 per cent of immigrants. A somewhat higher percentage of second and third generation men work in trades (about 15 per cent) than the immigrants but the differences are rather small. Among women, participation rate is somewhat lower among the second generation compared to the two other groups but the differences are small. The same patterns of differences in attainment is evident for women – almost half of the third-generation women have professional occupations compared to 41 per cent of the second generation and only 34 per cent of immigrants. Second- and third-generation women in Israel are less likely to work in trades, where almost a quarter of immigrants to Israel are occupied. In Australia, a higher proportion of the second generation aged 25–34 is employed compared to

Table 6.4   Labour force characteristics by generation and gender, Israelis and Australians age group 25–44

		First generation	Second generation	Third generation
Men				
% employed	Israel	73.5	69.2	68.9
	Australia	84.6	88.1	87.4
Employed only				
% managers/	Israel	35.1	38.2	49.0
professionals	Australia	38.9	35.7	33.8
% trades	Israel	12.7	15.0	14.3
	Australia	21.0	24.8	24.2
Women				
% employed	Israel	69.9	66.1	69.7
	Australia	64.1	73.0	71.8
Employed only				
% managers/	Israel	34.0	40.5	48.9
professionals	Australia	38.7	38.6	37.1
% trades	Israel	22.0	14.9	13.2
	Australia	5.0	4.8	4.7

the first and third generations, among both men and women. The proportion working in skilled occupations is also higher in the second generation than in the third generation, which is the reverse of the pattern observed in Israel. The higher proportion of the first generation in skilled occupations is a reflection of the recent emphasis on skilled migration in Australia's immigration policy.

Table 6.5 repeats the analysis for the second generation immigrants in the different ethnic groups. The table shows that among Israeli men and women alike, the employment rate is lower among those of North African origin (data not shown here indicate that this group has the highest rate of unemployment). The comparison within ethnic groups reveals again higher achievements in terms of occupation among groups of European origin – about 55 per cent of men and women in this group hold professional occupations, compared to only a third of the two other groups. The rate is especially lower among North African men (29 per cent). The differences in trade occupations are much lower, with fewer Europeans holding such occupations. While Asian women and African men and women of the second generation considerably improved their occupational standing compared to immigrants (and especially immigrants of similar origin, data not shown here) they still lag behind those originated

Table 6.5   *Labour force characteristics of men and women of the second*
             generation aged 25–44, by region of ethnic origin, Israel and
             Australia

	% Employed		% Professional/ managerial		% Trade	
	Men	Women	Men	Women	Men	Women
Israel						
Europe/America	73.5	69.6	54.0	54.7	12.6	12.8
Asia	71.9	66.8	33.9	35.1	15.9	15.0
North Africa	52.9	61.2	28.9	34.4	16.2	16.6
Australia						
NW Europe	88.4	72.9	34.4	38.3	25.5	4.9
SE Europe	89.5	74.9	36.8	37.5	25.0	4.4
Middle East/						
North Africa	82.8	60.4	38.3	41.4	21.7	4.0
Other Africa	91.3	76.0	40.5	43.3	20.7	4.0
SE Asia	86.4	77.5	38.9	43.5	18.5	4.4
NE Asia	89.3	83.7	60.4	60.0	11.7	3.8
S Asia	90.4	79.6	51.8	51.2	14.7	3.1

in Europe. To summarize, the labour force experience of immigrants and later generations is similar in terms of participation rates, but the second generation is in a better position in terms of occupational attainment. Also, ethnic gaps in occupational standing and earnings persist in the second generation.

Turning to the Australian figures, it can be seen that while the second generation as a group compares well with the third or more generations in their employment outcomes, differences are seen by ethnic origin. Lower proportions of men and women of the second generation of Middle Eastern/North African origins are employed compared to their counterparts of other ethnic backgrounds and the third generation. The proportion with post-school qualifications is also lowest in this group compared to the others (Table 6.3) and it is less than that in the third generation. Men of South-east Asian origin, the majority of whom are of Vietnamese ethnicity, also have a lower employment rate than the average for second generation men.

Among the employed second generation, the proportions working in managerial or professional occupations are higher in the groups of Asian and African origins than in the groups of European origins, for both men and women. The second generation of European origin are more likely to be working in trade occupations compared to the second generation of non-European origin. Trade occupations are not so favoured among the Asian second generation where there appears to be more emphasis on professional employment, particularly among the second generation of North-east and South Asian backgrounds.

MARRIAGE AND FAMILY

Our second major focus is on patterns of family formation. The partnering and childbearing patterns of the second generation show the extent of the maintenance of the social and cultural traditions of their ethnic background in relation to their demographic behaviour. Does the second generation resemble their parents' generation in relation to their partnering and childbearing patterns or is there evidence of social integration and convergence with the broader community as represented by the third generation? In this section we examine some indicators of family formation of the second generation by ethnic background and in comparison with the first and third generations.

As Table 6.6 shows, there are some similarities, but also interesting differences between the second generation in Israel and the other two groups (immigrants and the more veteran population). The rate of marriage among second-generation Israeli men (65.7 per cent) is similar to that of immigrants and somewhat higher than that of third-generation men, probably because on average, the latter group is younger. Similar patterns are seen among women – second-generation women are more likely to be married compared to immigrants. The rate of marriage is lower among third-generation women, again, probably due to the age composition of the groups. Women of the second generation are similar to the more veteran group in the number of children younger than 17 still living with their mother. This number is higher than that of immigrants, as data for Israel have indicted for adult groups (Goldscheider 1996). The difference is especially pronounced in the rate of large families – 26 per cent of second generation women have three children, and 14 per cent have four or more. (Of course, men have the children too, but demographic statistics ignore that fact!) This is in comparison to immigrants, among whom only 17 per cent of women have three children and less than 14 per cent have four or more. The number of children of the third generation is also similar to that of the second generation.

Data on partnering patterns for Australians refer only to current marital status of men and women in each generation. They do differentiate between legal marriage and de facto relationships, providing some insight

Table 6.6   Familial characteristics by generation and gender, Israelis and Australians aged 25–44.

		First generation	Second generation	Third generation
Men				
% married	Israel	67.7	65.7	59.7
	Australia	57.9	48.2	48.9
% in de facto relationships	Australia	11.7	14.5	17.6
Total % partnered	Australia	69.5	62.7	66.5
Women				
% married	Israel	65.9	71.6	66.9
	Australia	62.7	53.9	53.3
% in de facto relationships	Australia	10.5	13.7	15.7
Total % partnered	Australia	73.2	67.6	69.0
Mean number of children	Israel	2.2	2.6	2.6
	Australia	1.4	1.3	1.6
1–2 children	Israel	69.6	56.4	59.4
	Australia	72.4	71.6	65.7
3 children	Israel	16.8	26.2	22.0
	Australia	18.4	20.4	23.1
4+children	Israel	13.6	17.4	18.6
	Australia	9.3	8.1	11.3

Note: Percentages with children based on only women with one or more children.

into patterns of cohabitation by generation and ethnicity. As Table 6.6 shows the percentage married for men and women aged 25–44 is lowest for the second generation compared to the first and third generations. This is different from the Israeli pattern. The proportion in de facto relationships in the second generation is intermediate between that of the first and third generations, suggesting that the second generation is moving towards the third generation pattern in terms of this form of partnering.

The measures of family size for Australia differ from those for Israel. The mean number of children is based on the Census question asking each woman how many babies she has ever given birth to. Women aged 25–44 have an average of 1.5 children and women in the second generation have fewer babies than those in the first and third generations. This may be related to their lower proportion married or partnered. Among women

Table 6.7   *Familial characteristics by generation, gender and ethnicity,*
Israeli Jews aged 25–44.

	First generation			Second generation		
	Asia	Africa	EU-AM	Asia	Africa	EU-AM
Men						
% married	67.9	64.5	68.2	65.8	64.7	66.7
No. of children 0–17						
Mean (SD)	2.3	2.8	2.2	2.6	2.5	2.6
	(1.3)	(1.4)	(1.4)	(1.4)	(1.3)	(1.6)
Women						
% married	55.6	63.7	68.6	71.2	73.1	70.5
No. of children 0–17						
Mean (SD)	2.3	3.0	2.1	2.6	2.6	2.6
	(1.2)	(1.5)	(1.3)	(1.4)	(1.4)	(1.5)
% 1–2 children	67.6	42.4	739	55.9	54.9	58.8
% 3 children	18.5	25.8	15.1	26.8	26.2	25.5
% 4+children	13.9	31.8	11.0	17.3	19.0	15.7

with children, the second generation also has the lowest proportion with four or more children compared to the first and third generations.

Comparing the second generation of the two countries, a lower proportion of the Australian men and women are married/living with a partner compared to their Israeli counterparts. The second generation in this age group in Australia also has smaller families than their Israeli counterparts, with a higher proportion having only 1–2 children and lower proportions having three, four or more children. Israel is indeed unique among industrialized countries in the number of children each woman has, or its fertility rate (which amounts to 2.8 among Jews) and in being more 'family centred' as the data indeed demonstrate (for reference see Israel, Central Bureau of Statistics 2008a; Toren 2003).

Table 6.7 presents ethnic differences in family patterns within each generation in Israel. The table indicates that differences are relatively small, with the exception of African immigrants having more children than immigrants from European countries (32 per cent of immigrant women had more than three children compared to about 14 per cent of Asians and 11 per cent of Europan immigrants). Patterns in the number of children a person has are similar among Israeli-born women of the three ethnic groups. These differences point to the integration between ethnic (and

*Table 6.8   Partnering and number of children by gender and region of
            ethnic origin, second-generation Australians aged 25–44.*

	NW Europe	SE Europe	Middle East North Africa	Other Africa	SE Asia	NE Asia	S Asia
Men							
% married	46.2	55.0	51.1	46.2	26.8	34.2	41.5
% in de facto relationships	18.3	9.0	4.7	15.5	13.3	9.6	12.4
Total % partnered	64.6	64.0	55.8	61.7	40.1	43.8	53.9
Women							
% married	50.9	61.4	60.6	52.2	35.1	38.4	51.7
% in de facto relationships	17.3	7.8	3.3	15.7	15.6	14.4	10.7
Total % partnered	68.2	69.2	63.9	67.9	50.7	52.8	62.4
Mean number of children	1.4	1.3	1.3	1.0	0.8	0.6	0.9
% 1–2 children	69.8	75.2	64.8	80.5	76.9	81.7	80.7
% 3 children	20.9	19.4	23.0	14.8	14.7	14.1	14.2
% 4+ children	9.3	5.1	12.2	4.8	8.4	4.2	5.1

Note: Percentages with children based on only women with one or more children.

Source: Australian 2006 Census.

Israeli-born of different generations) groups in family patterns reported
by Goldscheider (1996).

Ethnic differences in family formation patterns are more significant for
the second generation in Australia than their counterparts in Israel (Table
6.8). The second generation of European origins has higher proportions
partnered while those of Asian origins have much lower proportions.
Part of this difference is due to the younger age distribution of the Asian
second generation within this age group, most of whom are clustered in
the age range 25–34. Of more interest in terms of the influence of cultural
and social norms are the large differences in the proportion living in
de facto relationships seen in the second generation by region of ethnic
origin and even between the European sub-regional groups. The proportion of men and women of Northern and Western European origins in
de facto relationships is twice as high as the proportion among men and

women of Southern and Eastern European origins. Cohabitation is the least common among men and women of Middle Eastern/North African origins; less than 5 per cent of those aged 25–44 are in de facto relationships. Second-generation men of Asian origin and second-generation women of South Asian origin also have lower than average proportions in de facto relationships.

Cohabitation before marriage is now common among Australians and three out of four marriages in recent years have been preceded by the couple living together (Australian Bureau of Statistics 2009b). It has been suggested that the incidence of cohabitation is likely to be a good indicator of the extent to which the second generation of various ethnic origins has taken on the values of the host culture (Khoo et al. 2002). It would seem therefore that the second generation of Southern/Eastern European and Middle Eastern/North African origins has not integrated into the Australian culture in relation to this partnering pattern. An earlier study based on data from the Australian 1996 Census had also shown that the second generation of parents born in Italy, Greece, Lebanon and the Former Yugoslav Republic of Macedonia had almost no cohabitation for women and low levels for men (Khoo et al. 2002), prompting the authors to suggest that 'the original culture has been strong enough to resist the pattern of the host culture even for those who are born in Australia . . .This probably reflects a continuing level of control of the parental generation over the formation of relationships by their children' (Khoo et al. 2002, p. 131).

Differences in family size by ethnic origin in the second generation are also more pronounced in Australia than in Israel. The three Asian origin groups shown in Table 6.8 have fewer children (lower fertility in the demographic sense) than the European, Middle Eastern or African origin groups. This is likely to be related to their later marriage and partnering as shown by their lower proportion partnered compared to the women of European or Middle Eastern/African origins. Among the women who have children, family size is also smallest among North-east Asian women, who have the highest proportion with 1–2 children and the lowest proportion with four or more children. The second generation of Middle Eastern/North African origins has the highest proportion with four or more children and the lowest proportion with 1–2 children. First-generation women of Middle Eastern/North African origin in the 25–44 age group have an average of 2.3 children, with 24 per cent having four or more children, so there has been some decline in the number of children that women from this region have from the first to the second generation, suggesting some integration in family formation behaviour with the Australian pattern.

Intermarriage between people of different national origins or ethnic

Table 6.9   Patterns of intermarriage, by generation and ethnicity, Israel

	First generation	Second generation	Third generation
Total			
% married within generation	73.4	65.9	51.9
% married within ethnicity	77.9	38.6	
% married within generation and ethnicity	67.9	34.9	
Asia			
% married within generation	71.9	69.4	
% married within ethnicity	68.3	36.1	
% married within generation and ethnicity	55.0	34.9	
Africa			
% married within generation	58.7	71.1	
% married within ethnicity	69.4	41.7	
% married within generation and ethnicity	51.6	40.2	
Europe-America			
% married within generation	75.6	56.4	
% married within ethnicity	80.6	38.2	
% married within generation and ethnicity	72.2	29.3	
N	2757	5612	2547

background has been considered as a powerful indicator of integration of immigrants or ethnic groups in immigrant nations. The last part of our discussion on family patterns of the second generation examines intermarriage by generation and ethnicity. As shown in Table 6.9 and as expected, the practice of marrying someone of the same generation is highest among immigrants in Israel, followed closely by the second generation and declining substantially in the third generation. Table 6.9 further shows that the rate of ethnic intermarriage is higher for the second generation than for immigrants (39 per cent of the former compared to 78 per cent of the latter married within their broad ethnic groups). Only a third (35 per cent) of the second-generation members married within ethnicity and generation (compared to two-thirds of the immigrants).

There are some interesting ethnic differences when looking at the likelihood of crossing ethnic and generational boundaries. The likelihood of having a spouse from the same generation and ethnic background is highest among immigrants from European countries, followed closely by immigrants from Asia. Among African immigrants, ethnic intermarriage rate is as high as in the Asian groups but more of the Africans than immigrants in the two other groups married cross generation. Among the second generation the picture is entirely different. Only 56 per cent of those originated in Europe married within generation and 29 per cent within generation and ethnicity. Marriage to someone from within a similar age range is much higher among the two other groups (69 per cent of Asians and 71 per cent of Africans married within their generation) but they have similar rates of ethnic intermarriages as Europeans. Marriages within one's generation and ethnicity are more common among second-generation Africans (40 per cent) than among the other groups, indicating again that there are important differences within continent of birth across generations that cannot be fully explored in this study. However, it is possible that the data does not show the extent of marriage within an ethnic group, since many Israelis of the second generation marry members of the third generation (a third of Europeans compared to only 17 per cent and 15 per cent of Asians and Africans, respectively), for which there is no data on ethnicity. It is likely that these Israelis are of European origin, which composes the majority of the third generation in Israel (Cohen et al. 2007).

As in Israel, ethnic intermarriage increases from the first to the second generation in Australia. The increase is seen in ethnic groups from all regions (Table 6.10) and indicates the social integration of the second generation in Australia's multicultural society. However, differences seen in the first generation by ethnic origin persist in the second generation. First-generation Australians of Northern and Western European origins have higher rates of intermarriage than those of Southern and Eastern European origins. Low intermarriage rates are also seen in the first generation of non-European ethnicities. The low rates of ethnic intermarriage in the first generation are largely due to the immigrants being already married in their home country before their migration to Australia. The second generation, being born and growing up in Australia, has more opportunities to mix with Australians of other ethnicities, resulting in an increase in the proportion intermarried from the first to the second generation. In the second generation, Australians of Northern and Western European ethnicities have the highest rates of ethnic intermarriage, with over 80 per cent married to someone of different ethnic origin.

Over 70 per cent of the second generation of Eastern European origins have also intermarried, as are two-thirds of the second generation of Maltese or Serbian origin. Although the proportion intermarried in the second generation is lower for the second generation of Greek or Italian

Table 6.10   *Patterns of intermarriage, by generation and ancestry, Australia 2006*

	% of partnered men and women with spouse of a different ancestry			
	First generation		Second generation	
Ancestry	Men	Women	Men	Women
NW European				
English	41	36	49	48
Irish	62	59	86	83
Scottish	65	60	90	88
Dutch	62	55	89	88
German	59	56	91	90
SE European				
Greek	12	9	37	31
Italian	22	12	51	42
Maltese	33	28	67	64
Croatian	26	21	60	59
Macedonian	10	8	39	35
Serbian	26	17	67	62
Hungarian	47	36	89	88
Polish	34	34	84	80
Russian	28	43	74	76
Middle Eastern				
Lebanese	11	8	31	21
Turkish	11	7	25	16
Asian				
Filipino	8	52	47	76
Vietnamese	7	13	48	48
Chinese	6	13	35	48
Indian	11	11	56	58
Sinhalese	14	13	95	86

Sources: Australian 2006 Census.

origin, the increase in intermarriage rate has nonetheless been substantial. The same is observed for the second generation of Asian or Middle Eastern origins. Lowest intermarriage rates are seen among the Lebanese and Turkish second generation, suggesting less social integration among the second generation of these Middle Eastern groups within Australian society.

SUMMARY AND CONCLUSION

The findings so far suggest that generational gaps among the Israeli-born are not as extensive as the gaps between ethnic groups. There is an overall convergence between generations, especially in education and family formation, and most of the observed differences are due to the different ethnic composition among second and third generations. Clearly, while Asians and Africans of the second generation improved their standing relative to immigrants from the same origin, their disadvantage is still significant. Not only that Asian and especially Africans of the second generation are less educated and have lower achievements in the labour market than their European counterparts, they are also less likely to outmarry. This further strengthens the possibility that ethnic disparities will persist also in the third generation, as some studies already indicate (Cohen et al. 2007).

In Australia, the second generation has better educational and employment outcomes than the third or more generations. However, differences by region of ethnic origin are also observed. The second generation of North-east and South Asian origins have better educational and occupational outcomes than the second generation of other ethnic origins, with a higher proportion enrolled in tertiary education, having university qualifications and being employed in professional occupations. They are the offspring of mainly Chinese and Indian immigrants, many of whom arrived in Australia after 1970 as skilled migrants, or overseas students who became permanent residents. In contrast, the second generation of Middle Eastern and South-east Asian origins are the offspring of immigrants who arrived on family reunion or humanitarian/refugee visas. While it is not possible to show this with the census data, some of the differences in educational and employment outcomes of the second generation may be related to the context of their parents' migration and associated level of human capital resources brought by their immigrant parents. Studies of Chinese and Vietnamese school children in Australia have also found evidence that they put more effort into studying and they and their parents have higher educational and occupational aspirations – and a greater preference for university education – compared to their counterparts of Anglo-Celtic background (Dandy and Nettelbeck 2000, 2002a, 2002b).

The ethnic differences in family formation patterns of the second generation in Australia point to different degrees of social integration and maintenance of family norms and values brought from their parents' country of origin. Partnering by cohabitation is much less common in the second generation of some ethnic origins than others. Differences in family size by ethnicity are also evident. It would appear that while the second generation has integrated structurally in terms of their educational and occupational outcomes, they have not integrated to the same extent socially and culturally in terms of their family formation patterns. Studies of intermarriage patterns by generation in Australia have shown that it is only in the third generation that differences in intermarriage rates by ethnicity are reduced and a pattern of convergence emerges (Khoo 2004; Khoo et al. 2009).

The Australian and Israeli second generation's diversity in educational, occupational and family formation outcomes does not appear to fit with the segmented assimilation concept as there is no indication of a downward mobility and integration into an existing underclass. The differences in Australia appear more indicative of a pattern of 'selective acculturation' among some groups more than others. This refers to the preservation of elements of the immigrant parents' culture while achieving integration into the broader community through education and employment and has been suggested in recent studies of the second generation in the US (for example, Portes and Fernandez-Kelly 2008). In Israel, cultural assimilation seems to be stronger especially as it pertains to the adaptation of common family formation patterns, which characterize Israeli-born of all generations and distinguishes them from the immigrants. However, ethnic differences which result probably from family background and class differences between different ethnic groups carry over to second (and probably third) generations as some studies indicate (for example, Cohen et al. 2007; Okun and Khait-Marelly 2008) and affect the full integration of the different groups.

The differences in integration levels between Australia and Israel can be attributed to several factors at the societal level – the different policies regarding selection of immigrants, for example, may affect the differences in the second generation's achievements; state investment in immigrants' integration can also account for success or failure of certain groups to advance in the new country; and different patterns of residential segregation may affect their social integration and cultural disparities. Australia's immigration policy allows for three types of permanent migration – skilled, family reunion and humanitarian – while its settlement policy expects all immigrants to achieve full and active participation in Australian society while recognizing ethnic diversity. While immigrants to Australia in each of the three migration visa categories face different entry criteria and bring different levels of human capital and other resources, the second generation's educational and employment outcomes compared with those of the third generation suggest that the long-term impact of the immigration and settlement policies has been generally positive, although some ethnic disparities are observed. It is possible that these disparities may be related to the immigrant parents' socio-economic status and other characteristics associated with the context of their migration. Israel's immigration policy is non-selective in terms of educational and occupational qualification, age or family status. All Jews can enter the country and establish citizenship upon arrival, thus, systematic ethnic differences among immigrants in terms of human, economic and social capital affect the achievement level of their offspring, and shape the pattern of assimilation for the next generations. The data analyses in this chapter have been largely descriptive and have not controlled for the effects of these variables.

This chapter has also not addressed the issues of identity and belonging among the second generation. These issues can also have important implications for the second generation's integration, but would have to be the focus of future studies that include qualitative data. However, positive outcomes in education and employment among second-generation youth are generally less likely to result in feelings of social exclusion and therefore can also contribute to a greater sense of belonging. The educational, employment and demographic outcomes of the second generation in Australia and Israel examined in this chapter can be considered to be important indicators of their social and economic integration in the two countries.

NOTE

1. Potential immigrants applying for permanent skilled migration visas to Australia have to be less than 45 years of age.

APPENDIX: DATA AND APPROACH

Data used for Israel are based on pooled labour force surveys (and for income data – the pooled income surveys) conducted by the Israeli Central Bureau of Statistics (CBS) during the years of 2005 to 2007. The sample is limited to include Jews aged 15 to 44 (although most analyses were based on the 25–44 age group). Using information on birthplace of the respondent and respondent's father, the sample was further divided into three generations: the 'first generation', which includes respondents born outside of Israel; 'second generation', including respondents born in Israel to a father who was born abroad; and 'third generation', Israelis whose fathers are also Israeli-born. Within the first and second generations, we further differentiate between three major ethnic groups – Europeans/ Americans, including those who themselves or their fathers were born in Europe, America or South Africa; Asian origin including those born or originated in Asian countries (mainly the Middle East and former Asian Soviet Union republics); and African origin, including those who were born in or originated from North African countries. The data set does not provide information on the ethnic origin of those whose fathers were born in Israel; therefore no ethnic distinction can be made among the third generation. Also, because of the relatively limited sample size, it was impossible to separate 'mixed generations' (for example where the father is Israeli-born and the mother is an immigrant, or vice versa), or mixed ethnicities, for the current study.

Data for Australia are from the 2006 Population Census. The census is the only national data source that identifies the second generation and provides information on their characteristics by ethnic origin. As in the case for Israel, the first generation in Australia refers to persons born overseas. The definition of the second generation differs slightly from that used for Israel in that it is based on both parents' birthplace and not just the father's birthplace, and refers to persons born in Australia who have either one or both parents who are born overseas. The third or more generation refers to persons born in Australia whose parents are also born in Australia. It is not possible to differentiate the third generation from the fourth or more generations.

Then, three region-of-origin groups – Asian, African and European/ American – are defined for comparison with the Israeli data. However, the composition of the three groups in Australia is somewhat different from that for Israel. While the Asian group in Israel comprises mainly people from the Middle East and former Asian Soviet Union republics, the Asian group in Australia is dominated by people from East, South-east and South Asian countries, which have become major sources of immigration to Australia after 1975, with the end of the White Australia Policy in the early 1970s. The two main Middle Eastern ethnic groups included with the Asian group are Lebanese and Turks. The European group in Australia is dominated by people of Anglo-Celtic, other Western European and Southern and Eastern European backgrounds, the result of past immigration patterns. The group of African origin is relatively small since African countries, aside from South Africa, are not significant sources of immigration to Australia. Since the Asian and European groups are quite large in Australia, they are further differentiated into sub-regional groups for some of the discussion to observe within-region diversity in integration patterns. The sub-regional ancestry groups are Northern and Western European; Southern and Eastern European; Middle Eastern and North African; Other (Sub-Saharan) African (which includes South African ancestry); South-east Asian, North-east Asian and South Asian.

Unlike in the Israeli data, the ethnic/region of origin identification for Australia is based on a person's ancestry or ethnic origin rather than birthplace of the father. In the Australian 2006 Census, each person was asked to identify up to two ancestries based on the person's parents' or grandparents' ethnic background. In this chapter, ethnic or region of origin is based on a person's first or sole ancestry response. Ancestry is a more subjective identifier of the second generation's ethnic origin than birthplace of parents; however, country of birth of parents is not asked in the Australian 2006 Census and therefore it is not possible to identify the second generation's ethnic origin by their father's country or region of birth, as in the data for Israel.

References

Al-Haj, M. (1998), 'Soviet immigration as viewed by Jews and Arabs: divided attitudes in a divided country', in E. Leshem and J.T. Shuval (eds), *Immigration to Israel: Sociological Perspectives,* New Brunswick and London: Transaction Publishers, pp. 211–27.

Amir, Shmuel (1987), 'Trends in earnings gaps among Jewish men during the 1970s by country of origin', Survey no. 63, Jerusalem: Bank of Israel, pp. 43–64 (Hebrew).

Amit, Karin (2005), 'The Binary Ethnic Classification and the economic assimilation of first and second generation immigrants in the Israeli labor market', *Megamot,* **44** (1), 3–28 (Hebrew).

Amit, Karin and I. Riss (2007), 'The role of social networks in the immigration decision-making process: the case of North American immigration to Israel', *Immigrants and Minorities*, **25** (3), 290–313.

Ang, Ien, Jeffrey E. Brand, Greg Noble and Derek Wilding (2002), *Living Diversity: Australia's Multicultural Future*, Sydney: SBS, available at: www20.sbs.com.au/sbscorporate/index.php?id=547 (accessed 8 April 2009).

Antecol, Heather, D. Cobb-Clark and S. Trejo (2003), 'Immigration policy and the skills of immigrants to Australia, Canada and the United States', *Journal of Human Resource*, **38** (1), 192–218.

ANU Poll (various), 'A quarterly survey of public opinion', available at: www.anu.edu.au/anupoll/ (accessed 18 December 2009).

Arian, Asher et al. (2009), *The 2009 Israel Democracy Index,* Jerusalem: The Israel Democracy Institute, available at: http://www.idi.org.il/ sites / english / events / ThePresidentsConference / Pages / 2009Presidents Conference.aspx (accessed 15 February 2010).

Artsieli, Yoav (2004), *The Gavison-Medan Covenant – Main Points and Principles*, Jerusalem: Israel Democracy Institute, pp. 22–41, available at: http://www.gavison-medan.org.il/FileServer/792c573c471c12fd8eac 98ae9e21cc89.pdf (accessed 17 June 2010).

Astman, R. and Y. Rosenbaum (1980), *Attitudes and Behavior of the Israeli Public on Immigration and Absorption,* Jerusalem: Ministry of Absorption, Planning and Research Department (Hebrew).

Australia Department of Immigration and Multicultural Affairs (2006), *Sudanese Community Profile,* Canberra: Commonwealth of Australia.

Australia Joint Standing Committee on Migration (1994), *Australian All: Enhancing Australian Citizenship*, Canberra: Australian Government Publishing Service.

Australia: Review of Post-Arrival Programs and Services to Migrants (1978), *Migrant Services and Programs: [Report of the Review of Post-arrival Programs and Services for Migrants]* (Galbally Report), Canberra: AGPS.

Australian Bureau of Statistics (2008a), *Australian Historical Population Statistics,* (Catalogue No. 3105.0.65.001), ABS, Canberra.

Australian Bureau of Statistics (2008b), *Australian Demographic Statistics, June Quarter,* (Catalogue No. 3101.0), Canberra: Australian Bureau of Statistics.

Australian Bureau of Statistics (2008c), *Births Australia, 2007,* (Catalogue No. 3301.0), Canberra: Australian Bureau of Statistics.

Australian Bureau of Statistics (2008d), *Australian Social Trends 2008,* (Catalogue No. 4102.0), Canberra: Australian Bureau of Statistics.

Australian Bureau of Statistics (2008e), *Year Book Australia 2008,* (Catalogue No. 1301.0), Canberra: Australian Bureau of Statistics.

Australian Bureau of Statistics (2009a), *Australian Demographic Statistics, March Quarter,* (Catalogue No. 3101.0), Canberra: Australian Bureau of Statistics.

Australian Bureau of Statistics (2009b), *Australian Social Trends 2009,* (Catalogue No. 4102.0), Canberra: Australian Bureau of Statistics.

Australian Bureau of Statistics (ABS) (2009c), *A Picture of a Nation: The Statisticians Report on the 2006 Census*, (Catalogue No. 2070.0), Canberra: Australian Bureau of Statistics.

Australian Bureau of Statistics (2010), *Australian Demographic Statistics, September Quarter*, (Catalogue No. 3101.0), Canberra: Australian Bureau of Statistics.

Australian Citizenship Council (2000), *Australian Citizenship for a New Century*, Canberra: Australian Citizenship Council.

Australian Council of Social Service (ACOSS) (2007), 'Civil society organisations call for legislation to be delayed', ACOSS News, 7 August, available at: www.acoss.org.au/News.aspx?displayID=99&articleID=2999 (accessed 26 December 2009).

Australian Education International (2008), *Monthly Summary of International Student Enrolment Data – Australia – September 2008,* Canberra: Australian Government.

Australian Government (n.d.), 'Social inclusion' available at: http://www.socialinclusion.gov.au (accessed 17 June 2010).

Australian Human Rights Commission (2008), *2008 Face the Facts,* Sydney: The Commission.

Bachi, R. (1977), *The Population of Israel*, CICRED series in conjunction with ICJ and the Demographic Center, Prime Minister's Office, Jerusalem, Institute of Contemporary Jewry, The Hebrew University, Jerusalem.

Barak-Erez, Daphne (2008), 'Israel: citizenship and immigration law in the vise of security, nationality, and human rights', *International Journal of Constitutional Law*, **6** (1), 184–92.

Baumgartl, B. and A. Favell (1995), *New Xenophobia in Europe*, London: Kluwer Law International.

Beggs, John and Bruce Chapman (1988), 'The international transferability of human capital: immigrant labour outcomes in Australia', in Paul Miller and Meredith Baker (eds), *The Economics of Immigration: Proceedings of a Conference*, Canberra: Australian Government Publishing Service, pp. 43–71.

Ben-Bassat, Avi (ed.) (2002), *The Israeli Economy, 1985–1998: From Government Intervention to Market Economics,* Cambridge, MA: MIT Press.

Ben-Porath, Yoram (1986), *The Israeli Economy: Maturing Through Crises*, Cambridge, MA: Harvard University Press.

Ben-Rafael, E. (1982), *The Emergence of Ethnicity: Cultural Groups and Social Conflict in Israel*, Westport, CT: Greenwood Press.

Berkovic, Nicola (2009), 'Migrant jobs to attract local wages', *The Australian,* Thursday 2 April, p. 5.

Betts, Katharine (2001), 'Boat people and public opinion in Australia', *People and Place*, **9** (4), 34–48.

Betts, Katharine (2008), 'The 2007 Australian election: blue-collar voters, migrants and the environment', *People and Place,* **16** (2), 71–85.

Birrell, Bob and Siew-Ean Khoo (1995), *The Second Generation in Australia: Educational and Occupational Characteristics,* Statistical Report No. 14, Canberra: Bureau of Immigration, Multicultural and Population Research.

Birrell, Bob and Earnest Healy (2008), 'How are skilled migrants doing?', *People and Place*, **16** (1), 1–19.

Birrell, Bob, Ernest Healy and Bob Kinnaird (2009), *Immigration and the Nation Building and Jobs Plan,* CPUR bulletin, Clayton, VIC: Centre for Population and Urban Research, Monash University.

Bogardus, E.S. (1928), *Immigration and Race Attitudes*, Boston, MA: Heath.

Borjas, George (1990), *Friends or Strangers: The Impact of Immigrants on the American Economy*, New York: Basic Books.

Borowski, Allan (2000), 'Creating a virtuous society: immigration and Australia's policies of multiculturalism', *Journal of Social Policy,* **29** (3), 459–75.

Borowski, Allan and Peter McDonald (2007), 'The dimensions and impli-cations of Australian population ageing', in Allan Borowski, Sol Encel and Elizabeth Ozanne (eds), *Longevity and Social Change in Australia*, Sydney: University of New South Wales Press, pp. 15–39.

Borowski, Allan and Jing Shu (1992), *Australia's Population Trends and Prospects*, Canberra: Australian Bureau of Immigration Research.

Borowski, Allan and Uri Yanay (1997), 'Temporary and illegal labour migration: the Israeli experience', *International Migration,* **3** (4), 495–511.

Boyd, Monica and Elizabeth Grieco (1998), 'Triumphant transitions: socioeconomic achievements of the second generation in Canada', *International Migration Review*, **32** (4), 853–76.

Boyd, Monica, David Featherman and Judah Matras (1980), 'Status attainment of immigrants and immigrant categories in the US, Canada, and Israel', *Comparative Social Research*, **3**, 199–228.

Bratton, M. (1989), 'The politics of NGO government relations in Africa', *World Development* **17** (4), 569–87.

Brown, J. and J. Miller et al. (2006), 'Interrupted schooling and the acquisition of literacy: experiences of Sudanese refugees in Victorian secondary schools', *Australian Journal of Language and Literacy,* **29** (2), 150–62.

Canetti-Nissim, D., G. Ariely and E. Halperin (2008), 'Life, pocketbook, or culture: the role of perceived security threats in promoting exclusion-ist political attitudes toward minorities in Israel', *Political Research Quarterly*, **61** (1), 90–103.

Carliner, Geoffrey (1980), 'Wages, earnings and hours of first, second, and third generation American males', *Economic Inquiry*, **18** (1), 87–102.

Carmi, Na'ama (2003), *Immigration and the Law of Return; Immigration Rights and Their Limits* (Hebrew).

Carmi, Na'ama (2006), '"Shall be Deemed to be a Person Who Has Come to this Country as an *Oleh* under this Law": the Stamka Dilemma, the purpose of the Law of Return and the connection between return and citizenship', *Mishpat Umimshal*, **10** (1), 151–83 (Hebrew).

Cassity, E. and G. Gow (2005), 'Making up for lost time: the experiences of Southern Sudanese young refugees in high schools', *Youth Studies Australia*, **24** (3), 51–5.

Castles, S. and A. Davidson (2000), *Citizenship and Migration. Globalization and the Politics of Belonging,* New York: Routledge.

Centre for Civil Society, London School of Economics (n.d.), 'Definition of civil society', available at: http://www.lse.ac.uk/collections/CCS/introduction/default.htm (accessed 17 June 2010).

Chapman, Bruce and Paul Miller (1985), 'An appraisal of immigrants' labour market performance in Australia', in M.E. Poole, P.R. de Lacey and B.S. Randhawa (eds), *Australia in Transition: Culture and Life Possibilities*, Sydney: Harcourt Brace Jovanovich, pp. 3–310.

Chazan, N. (1992), 'Africa's democratic challenge', *World Policy Journal*, **9** (2), 279–307.

Chiswick, Barry (1978), 'The effects of Americanization on the earnings of foreign-born men', *Journal of Political Economy*, **86** (5), 897–921.

Chiswick, Barry and Paul Miller (1985), 'Immigrant generation and income in Australia', *Economic Record*, **61** (2), 540–53.

Chiswick, Barry and Paul Miller (2008), 'Occupational attainment and immigrant economic progress in Australia', *The Economic Record*, **84** (S1), S45–S56.

Cobb-Clark, Deborah (2000), 'Do selection criteria make a difference? Visa category and the labour market status of immigrants to Australia', *The Economic Record*, **76** (232), 15–31.

Coenders, Marcel, Mérove Gijsberts and Peer Scheepers (2004), 'Resistance to the presence of immigrants and refugees in 22 countries', in M. Gijsberts, L. Hagendoorn and P. Scheepers (eds), *Nationalism and Exclusion of Migrants. Cross-National Comparisons*, Aldershot: Ashgate, pp. 97–120

Cohen, Yinon (1998), 'Socioeconomic gaps among Jews, 1975–1995', *Israeli Sociology* **1** (1), 134 (Hebrew).

Cohen, Yinon (2002), 'From haven to heaven: changing patterns of immigration to Israel', in D. Levy and Y. Weiss (eds) *Challenging Ethnic Citizenship: German and Israeli Perspectives on Immigration*, New York and Oxford: Berghahn Books, pp. 33–56.

Cohen, Yinon (2002), 'Immigration and the changing composition of Israel's population, 1948–1999', in D. Levy and Y. Weiss (eds), *Challenging Ethnic Citizenship: German and Israeli Perspectives on Immigration*, New York: Berghahn Books, pp. 36–56.

Cohen, Yinon (2007), 'The demographic success of Zionism', *Israeli Sociology*, **8** (2), 151–8 (Hebrew).

Cohen, Yinon and Yitchak Haberfeld (1998), 'Second generation Jewish immigrants in Israel: have the ethnic gaps in schooling and earnings declined?', *Ethnic and Racial Studies*, **21** (3), 507–28.

Cohen, Yinon and Yitchak Haberfeld (2003), 'Economic assimilation among children of Israeli immigrants in the US', *International Migration*, **41** (4), 141–60.

Cohen, Yinon and Yitchak Haberfeld (2007), 'Self selection and earnings assimilation: immigrants from the former Soviet Union in Israel and the United States', *Demography*, **44** (3), 649–68.

Cohen, Yinon and Irena Kogan (2007), 'Next year in Jerusalem . . . or in Cologne? Labor market integration of Jewish immigrants from the former Soviet Union in Israel and Germany in the 1990s', *European Sociological Review*, **23** (2), 155–68.

Cohen, Yinon, Yitchak Haberfeld and Tali Kristal (2007), 'Ethnicity and mixed ethnicity: educational gaps among Israeli-born Jews', *Ethnic and Racial Studies*, **30** (5), 896–917.

Cohen, Yinon, Yitchak Haberfeld and Irena Kogan (2008), 'Jewish immigration from the Former Soviet Union: a natural experiment in immigrants' destination choices', *KZfSS – Kölner Zeitschrift für Soziologie und Sozialpsychologie*, **48**, 185–201 (German).

Community Relations Commission for a Multicultural NSW (2005), *Community Relations Report 2004*, available at: http://www.crc.nsw. gov.au/about_crc/annual_report/2004-2005 (accessed 18 June 2010).

Cope, B. and S. Castles et al. (1991), *Immigration, Ethnic Conflicts and Social Cohesion,* Melbourne: Bureau of Immigration Research.

Crul, M. and H. Vermuelen (2003), 'The second generation in Europe: introduction', *International Migration Review*, **37** (4), 965–86.

Curthoys, Ann and Andrew Markus (1978), *Who Are Our Enemies: Racism and the Australian Working Class,* Sydney: Hale and Iremonger.

Damian, N. and Y. Rozenbaum-Tamari (1992), *Trends in the Public's Attitudes on Immigration and the Absorption of New Immigrants,* Jerusalem: Ministry of Absorption, Planning and Research Department (Hebrew).

Dandy, J. and T. Nettelbeck (2000), 'The model student? An investigation of Chinese Australian students' academic achievement, studying, and causal attributions for academic success and failure', *Australian Psychologist*, **35** (3), 208–15.

Dandy, J. and T. Nettelbeck (2002a), 'The relationship between IQ, homework, aspirations and academic achievement for Chinese, Vietnamese and Anglo-Celtic Australian school children', *Educational Psychology*, **22** (3), 267–75.

Dandy, J. and T. Nettelbeck (2002b), 'A cross-cultural study of parents' academic standards and educational aspirations for their children', *Educational Psychology,* **22** (5): 621–7.

Davidson, A. (1997), *From Subject to Citizen: Australian Citizenship in the Twentieth Century*, Melbourne: Melbourne University Press.

DellaPergola, Sergio (1998), 'The global context of migration to Israel', in E. Leshemm and J. Shuval (eds), *Immigration to Israel: Sociological Perspectives*, New Brunswick: Transaction Publishers, pp. 51–92.

DellaPergola, Sergio (2003), 'Demographic trends in Israel and Palestine: prospects and policy implications', *American Jewish Year Book*, **103**, 3–68, The American Jewish Committee, New York.

DellaPergola, Sergio (2007), 'Sephardi and oriental migrations to Israel: migration, social change and identification', in P. Medding (ed.), *Studies in Contemporary Jewry*, **22**, 3–43, Oxford University Press, New York.

DellaPergola, Sergio (2008), 'World Jewish Population 2008', *American Jewish Year Book*, **108**, 569–620.

DellaPergola, Sergio (2009a). 'International migration of Jews', in E. Ben-Rafael and Y. Sternberg (eds) *Transnationalism: Diasporas and the Advent of a New (dis)order*, Leyden and Boston: Brill, pp. 213–36.

DellaPergola, Sergio (2009b), 'Fertility prospects in Israel: ever below replacement level?', *United Nations Expert Group Meeting on Recent and Future Trends in Fertility*, New York: Population Division, United Nations Department of Social and Economic Affairs, available at: http://www.un.org./esa/population/meetings/EGM-fertility2009/Della Pergola.pdf (accessed 17 June 2010).

DellaPergola, Sergio, U. Rebhun and M. Tolts (2005), 'Contemporary Jewish Diaspora in global context: human development correlates of population trends', *Israel Studies*, **11** (1), 61–95.

Department of Immigration and Citizenship (2008a), *Emigration from Australia*, (Fact Sheet 5), Canberra: Department of Immigration and Citizenship.

Department of Immigration and Citizenship (2008b), *Emigration 2007–2008,* Canberra: Department of Immigration and Citizenship.

Department of Immigration and Citizenship (2008c), *Immigration Update 2007–08,* Canberra: Department of Immigration and Citizenship.

Department of Immigration and Citizenship (2008d), *Migration Program Statistics*, Canberra: Department of Immigration and Citizenship, available at: http://www.immi.gov.au/media/statistics/statistical-info/visa-grants/migrants.htm (accessed 12 February 2009).

Department of Immigration and Citizenship (2008e), *Fact Sheet 2 – Key Facts in Immigration*, Canberra: Department of Immigration and Citizenship.

Dgani, A. and R. Dgani (2004), *Argentinian Olim: Attitudes and Beliefs Towards the Absorption Process in Israel,* Jerusalem: The Israeli Ministry of Absorption and the Jewish Agency.

Donovan, T., D. Denemark and S. Bowler (2007), 'Trust, citizenship and participation: Australia in comparative perspective', in D. Denemark, G. Meagher, S. Wilson, M. Western and T. Phillips (eds), *Australian Social Attitudes 2: Citizenship, Work and Aspirations,* Sydney: UNSW Press, pp. 81–106.

Doulman, J. and D. Lee (2008), *Every Assistance and Protection: A History of the Australian Passport,* Adelaide: Federation Press.

Dovidio, J., J. Brigham, B. Johnson and S. Gaertner (1996), 'Stereotyping, prejudice and discrimination', in N. Macrae, C. Stangor and M. Hewstone (eds), *Foundations of Stereotypes and Stereotyping*, New York: Guilford, pp. 276–319.

Dryzek, J. (1996), 'Political inclusion and the dynamics of democratization', *American Political Science Review,* **90** (3), 475–87.

Eckstein, Zvi and Yoram Weiss (2002), 'The integration of immigrants from the former Soviet Union in the Israeli labor market', in Avi Ben-Bassat (ed.), *The Israeli Economy, 1985–1998: From Government Intervention to Market Economics,* Cambridge, MA: MIT Press, pp. 349–77.

Ellman, Michael and Laacher Smain (2003), 'Migrant workers in Israel – a contemporary form of slavery', Euro-Mediterranean Human Rights Network and International Federation for Human Rights, available at: http://www.reliefweb.int/library/documents/2003/fidh-opt-25aug.pdf (accessed 17 June 2010).

Espenshade, T. and K. Hempstead (1996), 'Contemporary American attitudes toward US immigration', *International Migration Review,* **30** (2), 535–70.

Esses, V.M., J.F. Dovidio, L.M. Jackson and T.L. Armstrong (2001), 'The immigrants' dilemma: the role of perceived group competition, ethnic prejudice, and nationality identity', *Journal of Social Issues,* **53** (3), 389–412.

EU Agency for Fundamental Rights (2007), *Report on Racism and Xenophobia in the Member States of the EU,* available at: http://fra.europa.eu/fraWebsite/products/publications_reports/ar2007_part2_en.htm (accessed 8 April 2009).

Farrar, A. and J. Inglis (eds) (1996), *Keeping it Together: State and Civil Society in Australia,* Leichhardt: Pluto Press with Australian Council of Social Service, Inc.

Fernandez-Kelly, P. and A. Portes (eds) (2008), 'Exceptional outcomes: achievement in education and employment among children of immigrants', *The Annals of the American Academy of Political and Social Science,* **620**, November 2008.

Fetzer, J.S. (2000), *Public Attitudes toward Immigration in the United States, France, and Germany,* New York: Cambridge University Press.

Fisher, W.F. (1997), 'Doing good? The politics and antipolitics of NGO practices', *Annual Review of Anthropology,* **26**, 439–64.

Fitzgerald, Stephen (1988), *Committee to Advise on Australia's Immigration Policies. Immigration, a commitment to Australia,* Canberra: Australian Government Publishing Service.

Foster, L. and D. Stockley (1988), *Australian Multiculturalism:*

A Documentary History and Critique, Clevedon and Philadelphia: Multilingual Matters.

Fowler, A. (1991), 'The role of NGOs in changing state-society relations: perspectives from Eastern and Southern Africa', *Developmental Policy Review,* **9** (1), 53–84.

Fox, R. (2006), 'Promoting freedom and community: civil society organisations in Australia', *IPA Backgrounder Institute of Public Affairs,* **18** (2).

Frantz, T.R. (1987), 'The role of NGOs in the strengthening of civil society', *World Development,* **15** (Supplement), 121–27.

Friedberg, Rachel (2000), 'You can't take it with you? Immigrant assimilation and the portability of human capital', *Journal of Labor Economics,* **18** (2), 221–51.

Friedlander, D. and C. Godscheider (1979), *The Population of Israel*, New York: Columbia University Press.

Friedlander, D., B. Okun, Z. Eisenbach and L. Lion Elmakias (2002), 'Immigration, social change and assimilation: educational attainment among birth cohorts of Jewish ethnic groups in Israel, 1925–29 to 1965–69', *Population Studies,* **56** (2), 135–50.

Giorgas, D. (1999), *Social Distance, Social Capital and Segmented Assimilation: The Labour and Marriage Market Experiences of Second Generation Australians,* PhD Thesis submitted to the Australian National University.

Goldscheider, Calvin (1996), *Israel's Changing Society: Population, Ethnicity, and Development*, Boulder, CO: Westview Press.

Goot, Murray (1999), 'Migrant numbers, Asian immigration and multiculturalism: trends in the polls, 1943–1998', National Multicultural Advisory Council, *Australian Multiculturalism for a New Century*, Statistical Appendix Part 2, available at: www.immi.gov.au/media/publications/multicultural/nmac/statistics.pdf (accessed 8 April 2009).

Goot, Murray and Ian Watson (2005), 'Immigration, multiculturalism and national identity', in Shaun Wilson, Gabrielle Meagher, Rachel Gibson, David Denemark and Mark Western (eds), *Australian Social Attitudes: The First Report*, Sydney: UNSW Press, pp. 182–267.

Gorodzeisky, Anastasia and Moshe Semyonov (2008), 'Two dimensions to immigrants' economic incorporation: Soviet immigrants in the Israeli labor market', paper presented at the Canada-Israel Forum on Immigration, Toronto, September 2008.

Grattan, Michelle and Lindsay Murdoch (2009), 'Murky waters', *The Age*, Saturday 24 October, Insight, p. 5.

Gshur, B. and B.S. Okun (2003), 'Generational effects on marriage patterns: Jewish immigrants and their descendants in Israel', *Journal of Marriage and the Family*, **65** (2), 287–301.

Guild, E. and J. van Selm (eds) (2005), *International Migration and Security: Opportunities and Challenges*, London: Routledge.

Haaretz (2009), articles dealing with foreign workers, 2 July 2009, available at: https://haaretz.co.il/hasen/spages/1097062.html; and 12 July 2009, available at: https://haaretz.co.il/hasen/spages/1098035.html (accessed 17 June 2010).

Haberfeld, Yitchak (1993), 'Immigration and ethnic origin: the effect of demographic attributes on earnings of Israeli men and women', *International Migration Review*, **27** (2), 286–305.

Haberfeld, Yitchak (2009), 'Group-based differences in intra-generational earnings mobility in Israel', *Research in Social Stratification and Mobility*, **27** (2), 79–91.

Haberfeld, Yitchak (2010), 'Estimating self-selection of immigrants: comparing earnings differentials between natives and immigrants in the US and Israel', *International Migration*, online early view.

Haberfeld, Yitchak and Yinon Cohen (1998), 'Earnings gaps between Israel's native-born men and women, 1982–1993', *Sex Roles,* **39** (11–12), 855–72.

Haberfeld, Yitchak and Yinon Cohen (2007), 'Gender, ethnic, and national earnings gaps in Israel: the role of rising inequality', *Social Science Research,* **36** (2), 654–72.

Haberfeld, Yitchak, Moshe Semyonov and Yinon Cohen (2000), 'Ethnicity and labor market performance among recent immigrants from the former Soviet Union to Israel', *European Sociological Review,* **16** (3), 287–99.

Hacohen, D. (2003), *Immigrants in Turmoil*, translated from the Hebrew by Gila Brand, Syracuse University Press.

Halevi, Nadav and Ruth Klinov-Malul (1968), *The Economic Development of Israel*, New York: Praeger.

Hart, Cath (2007), 'Andrews enters visa row', *The Australian,* 26 January, p. 2.

Hasan, S. and J. Onyx (eds) (2008), *Comparative Third Sector Governance in Asia: Structure, Process, and Political Economy*, New York: Springer.

Healy, Guy (2009), 'Overseas students defy downturn', *The Australian*, Thursday 7 May, p. 6.

Heath, A.F., C. Rothon and E. Kilpi (2008), 'The second generation in Western Europe: education, unemployment, and occupational attainment', *Annual Review of Sociology,* **34**: 211–35.

Hicks, George (1997), *Japan's Hidden Apartheid: The Korean Minority and the Japanese*, Brookfield: Ashgate.

High Court of Australia (2003), *Plaintiff S441/2003 and Minister for Immigration and Multicultural and Indigenous Affairs*, Transcript, 4 August.

Horowitz, Tamar (2005), 'The Integration of immigrants from the Former Soviet Union', in Cohen-Almagor R. (ed.), *Israeli Democracy at the Crossroads*, London: Routledge, pp. 117–36.

Howard, J. (1999), 'A new agenda for a multicultural Australia: message from the Prime Minister', available at: www.immi.gov.au/media/publications/multicultural/agenda/pmforeword.htm (accessed 17 June 2010).

Hugo, G. (1986), *Australia's Changing Population: Trends and Implication*, Melbourne: Oxford University Press.

Ipsos MORI Social Research Institute (2008), *Blair's Britain: The Social and Cultural Legacy*, available at: www.ipsos-mori.com/content/research-archive/blairs-britain-the-socialand-cultural-legacy.ashx (accessed 8 April 2009).

Israel, Central Bureau of Statistics (2005–07), *Labour Force Surveys*, available at: http://www.cbs.gov.il/ts/databank/databank_main_func_e.html?i=21&ti=11&r=0&f=3&o=0 (accessed 17 June 2010).

Israel, Central Bureau of Statistics (2008a), *Statistical Abstracts of Israel No. 59*, Jerusalem.

Israel, Central Bureau of Statistics (2008b), *Labour Force Survey*, available at: http://www.cbs.gov.il/reader/?MIval=cw_usr_view_SHTML&ID=417 (accessed 17 June 2010).

Israel, Central Bureau of Statistics (2009), *Statistical Abstracts of Israel No. 60*, Jerusalem.

Israel Democracy Institute 2008, *The 2008 Democracy Index*, available at: http://www.idi.org.il/sites/english/ResearchAndPrograms/The%20Israeli%20Democracy%20Index/Pages/2008PressRelease.aspx (accessed 17 June 2010).

ISSP Research Group, International Social Survey Program (2003), 'National Identity II' (SPSS data file), Distributor: GESIS Cologne Germany ZA3910, available at: http://www.issp.org/page.php?pageId=4 (accessed 1 April 2009).

Jakubowicz, A. (2009), 'The risk of diversity: the meanings of integration in Australian political culture', *Around the Globe*, 6.

Jakubowicz, A., M. Morrissey and J. Palser (1984), 'Ethnicity class and social welfare in Australia', *SWRC Reports and Proceedings,* no. 46, Sydney: Social Welfare Research Centre, University of New South Wales.

Jamrozik, A., C. Boland and R. Urquhart (1995), *Social Change and Cultural Transformation in Australia*, Melbourne: Cambridge University Press.

Jensen, L. and Y. Chitose (1994), 'Today's second generation: evidence from the 1990 U.S. census', *International Migration Review,* **28** (4), 714–35.

Jordens, A.M. (1995), *Redefining Australians: Immigration, Citizenship, and National Identity*, Sydney: Hale and Iremonger.

Jupp, James (2002a), 'Ethnicity and Immigration', *The Centenary Election*, in J. Warhurst and M. Simms (eds), St Lucia, Brisbane: University of Queensland Press.

Jupp, James (2002b), *From White Australia to Woomera: The Story of Australian Immigration*, Melbourne: Cambridge University Press.

Jupp, James (2003), 'Trends in Australian religious demography', *Australian Mosaic,* issue 2 (Autumn), 29–31.

Jupp, James (2007), *From White Australia to Woomera: the Story of Australian Immigration*, 2nd edn, Port Melbourne: Cambridge University Press.

Jupp, James (2008), 'Citizenship in Australia', *Canadian Diversity*, **6** (4), 21–3.

Kenny, S. (2007), 'Non-government organisations and the dialectics of state and civil society', *Futures*, **39** (2–3), 185–99.

Khoo, Siew-Ean (2004), 'Intermarriage in Australia: patterns by ancestry, gender and generation', *People and Place*, **12** (2), 35–44.

Khoo, Siew-Ean and Bob Birrell (2002), 'The progress of young people of migrant origin in Australia', *People and Place*, **10** (2), 30–44.

Khoo, Siew-Ean, B. Birrell and G. Heard (2009), 'Intermarriage by birthplace and ancestry in Australia', *People and Place*, **17** (1), 15–28.

Khoo, Siew-Ean, Peter McDonald, Dimi Giorgas and Bob Birrell (2002), *Second Generation Australians*, Canberra: Department of Immigration, Multiculturalism and Indigenous Affairs, available at: http://www.immi.gov.au/media/publications/multicultural/2gen/ (accessed 12 January 2010).

Klapdor, Michael et al. (2009), *Australian Citizenship: a Chronology of Major Developments in Policy and Law*, Parliament of Australia, Department of Parliamentary Services, 11 September 2009, p. 2.

Klinov, Ruth (1991), 'Immigrants from the Soviet Union to the United States and Israel: a preliminary comparison following Barry Chiswick's study', *The Economic Quarterly*, **38**, 225–31 (Hebrew).

Kneebone, Susan (2006), 'The Pacific Plan: the provision of "effective protection"?', *International Journal of Refugee Law*, **18** (3, 4), 696–721

Kraus, Vered (2002), *Secondary Breadwinners: Israeli Women in the Labor Force*, Westport, CT: Praeger.

Kretzmer, David (1990), *The Legal Status of Arabs in Israel*, 39-40, Boulder, CO: Westview Press.

Kunovich, Robert, M. (2004), 'Social structural position and prejudice: an exploration of cross-national differences in regression slopes', *Social Science Research,* **33** (1), 20–44.

Kymlicka, Will (2003), 'Introduction', *Canadian Diversity,* **2** (1), 4–6.

Lahav, G. (2004), *Immigration and Politics in the New Europe. Reinventing Borders*, Cambridge: Cambridge University Press.

Langfield, M. (1999), *More People Imperative: Immigration to Australia 1901–39*, National Archives.

Leshem, E. (1998), 'The Israeli public's attitudes toward the new immigrants of the 1990s', in E. Leshem and J.T. Shuval (eds), *Immigration to Israel. Sociological Perspectives*, New Brunswick and London: Transaction Publishers, pp. 307–30.

Lewin-Epstein, Noah and Moshe Semyonov (1986), 'Ethnic group mobility in the Israeli labor market', *American Sociological Review*, **51** (3), 342–52.

McCormick, P.D. (1878), 'Advance Australia Fair' (Australian National Anthem).

Mark, Nili (1994), 'Ethnic gaps in earnings and consumption in Israel', *Economic Quarterly*, **41** (1), 55–77 (Hebrew).

Mark, Nili (1996), 'The contribution of education to earnings differentials among ethnic groups in Israel', *Israel Social Science Research*, **11**, 47–86.

Markus, Andrew (1995), *Australian Race Relations*, Sydney: Allen and Unwin.

Markus, Andrew (2009), *Mapping Social Cohesion 2009: The Scanlon Foundation Surveys,* Institute for the Study of Global Movements, Monash University, available at: www.globalmovements.monash.edu. au/projects/scrp.php (accessed 18 December 2009).

Markus, Andrew and Arunachalam Dharmalingham (2008), *Mapping Social Cohesion*, Institute for the Study of Global Movements, Monash University, available at: www.globalmovements.monash.edu.au (accessed 8 April 2009).

Markus, Andrew, James Jupp and Peter McDonald (2009), *Australia's Immigration Revolution*, Sydney: Allen and Unwin.

Martin, J. and P. Meade (1979), *The Educational Experience of Sydney High School Students*, Canberra: Australian Government Publishing Service.

McDonald, James and Chris Worswick (1999), 'The earnings of immigrant men in Australia: assimilation, cohort effects, and macroeconomic conditions', *The Economic Record*, **75** (1), 49–62.

Meade, P. (1983), *The Educational Experience of Sydney High School Students,* Report No. 3, Canberra: Australian Government Publishing Service.

Messimeri, V. (2008), 'Social inclusion for multicultural and faith communities', Unity in Diversity Conference Townsville, Australia, 14

August 2008, available at: http://www.culturalfest.org/PresentersNotes/Messimeri.pdf (accessed 17 June 2010).

Mikhelidze, N. and N. Pirozzi (2008), *Civil Society and Conflict Transformation in Abkhazia, Israel/Palestine, Nagorno-Karabakh, Transnistria and Western Sahara,* MICROCON Policy Working Paper 3, Brighton: MICROCON.

Miller, Paul (1986), 'Immigrant unemployment in the first year of Australian labour market activity', *The Economic Record*, **62** (176), 82–7.

Miller, Paul (1999), 'Immigration policy and immigrant quality: the Australian points system', *American Economic Review*, **89** (2), 192–7.

Miller, Paul and Leanne Neo (2003), 'Labour market flexibility and immigrant adjustment', *The Economic Record*, **79**, 336–56.

Miller, Paul and Leanne Neo (n.d.), *Immigrant Unemployment: the Australian Experience,* Department of Economics, University of Western Australia, mimeo.

Nahon, Yaakov (1987), *Education Levels and Employment Opportunities: The Ethnic Dimension*, Jerusalem: Jerusalem Institute for the Study of Israel (Hebrew).

Ndegwa, S.N. (1993), 'NGOs as pluralizing agents in civil society in Kenya', Working Paper No. 491, Nairobi: Institute of Developmental Studies.

Ndegwa, S.N. (1996), *The Two Faces of Civil Society: NGOs and Politics in Africa*, West Hartford, CT: Kumarian.

Ng'ethe, N. and K. Kanyinga (1992), 'The politics of development space: the state and NGOs in the delivery of basic services in Kenya', Working Paper No. 486, Nairobi: Institute of Developmental Studies.

NSW Community Relations Commission (n.d.), available at: http://crc.nsw.gov.au/communities/NSW_Community_Organisations (accessed 17 June 2010).

Offer, Shira (2004), 'The socio-economic integration of the Ethiopian community in Israel', *International Migration*, **42** (3), 29–55.

Okun, B.S. and O. Khait-Marelly (2008), 'Demographic behaviour of adults of mixed ethnic ancestry: Jews in Israel', *Ethnic and Racial Studies*, **31** (8), 1357–80.

Pettigrew, T.F. (1998), 'Intergroup contact theory', *Annual Review of Psychology,* **49**, 65–85.

Pink, Brian (2009), *2006 Census of Population and Housing. A Picture of the Nation: The Statistician's Report on the 2006 Census,* ABS Catalogue No. 2070, Canberra: Australian Bureau of Statistics.

Portes, A. and P. Fernandez-Kelly (2008), 'No margin for error: educational and occupational achievement among disadvantaged children of immigrants', *The Annals of the American Academy of Political and Social Science*, **620** (1), 12–36.

Portes, A. and R.G. Rumbaut (2001), *Legacies: The Story of the Immigrant Second Generation*, Berkeley: University of California Press and Russell Sage Foundation.

Portes, A. and R.G. Rumbaut (2006), *Immigrant America: A Portrait,* 3rd edn, Berkeley: University of California Press.

Portes, A. and M. Zhou (1993), 'The new second generation: segmented assimilation and its variants', *The Annals of the American Academy of Political and Social Science*, **530** (1), 74–96.

Productivity Commission (2006), *Economic Impacts of Migration and Population Growth: Research Report*, Canberra: Productivity Commission, available at: http://www.pc.gov.au/_data/assets/pdf_file/0006/9438/migrationandpopulation.pdf (accessed 17 June 2010).

Quillian, L. (1995), 'Prejudice as a response to perceived group threat: population composition and anti-Immigrant and racial prejudice in Europe', *American Sociological Review*, **60** (4), 586–611.

Raijman, Rebeca (2009), 'Immigration in Israel: a map of trends and empirical studies: 1990–2007', *Israeli Sociology*, **10** (2), 339–79 (Hebrew).

Raijman, Rebeca and Adriana Kemp (2010), 'The new immigration to Israel: becoming a de-facto immigration state in the 1990s', in U. Segal, N. Mayadas and D. Elliot (eds), *Immigration Worldwide*, Oxford: Oxford University Press.

Raijman, Rebeca and Moshe Semyonov (1997),'Gender, ethnicity and immigration: double-disadvantage and triple-disadvantage among recent immigrant women in the Israeli labor market', *Gender and Society*, **11** (1): 108–25.

Raijman, Rebeca and Moshe Semyonov (1998), 'Best of times, worst of times, and occupational mobility: the case of Russian immigrants in Israel', *International Migration*, **36** (3), 291–312.

Raijman, Rebeca and Moshe Semyonov (2004), 'Perceived threat and exclusionary attitudes towards foreign workers in Israel', *Ethnic and Racial Studies,* **27** (5), 780–99.

Raijman, Rebeca, Moshe Semyonov and Peter Schmidt (2003), 'Do foreigners deserve rights? Determinants of public views towards foreigners in Germany and Israel', *European Sociological Review*, **19** (4), 379–92.

Rebhun, Uzi (2008), 'A double disadvantage? Immigration, gender, and employment status in Israel', *European Journal of Population,* **24** (1), 87–113.

Rebhun, Uzi (2010), 'Immigration, gender, and earnings in Israel', *European Journal of Population*, **26** (1), 73–97.

Richards, Eric (2008), *Destination Australia*, Sydney: UNSW Press.

Roth, Lenny (2007), *Multiculturalism,* (briefing paper no 9/07), Sydney: New South Wales Parliamentary Library Research Service.

Rubinstein, Amnon (2000),'The problem is how to become an Israeli', *Ha'aretz,* 4 January 2000.

Rubinstein, A., L. Orgad and S. Avineri (2009), 'Facing Global Migration: Outline to an Immigration Policy for Israel – Working Paper, Jerusalem: Metzilah Center for Zionist, Jewish, Liberal and Humanistic Thought (Hebrew).

Rubenstein, K. (2000) 'Citizenship and the centenary – inclusion and exclusion in 20th century Australia', *Melbourne University Law Review* **24** (3), 576–608.

Ryang, Sonia (ed.) (2000), *Koreans in Japan: Critical Voices from the Margin,* London: Routledge.

Sadowski, Ireneusz (2009), 'The contextuality of the concept of civil society – from particular meanings to the common vector of emancipation', *Polish Sociological Review,* **1** (165), 63–80.

Sanyal, B. (1994), *Cooperative Autonomy: the Dialectics of state-NGO Relationships in Developing Countries,* Research Series 100, Geneva: ILO.

Saulwick, Irving (1999), in National Multicultural Advisory Council, *Australian Multiculturalism for a New Century: Towards Inclusiveness,* Commonwealth of Australia, available at: www.immi.gov.au/media/publications/multicultural/nmac/report.pdf (accessed 8 April 2009).

Schenkolewski-Kroll, S. (2004), 'Argentinean Jews: from a supportive Zionistic movement to a supported community', *Kivunim Hadashim,* (Bialik Institute), issue 1: 190–202 (Hebrew).

Schlueter, E., P. Schmidt and U. Wagner (2008), 'Disentangling the causal relations of perceived group threat and outgroup derogation: cross-national evidence from German and Russian panel surveys', *European Sociological Review,* **24** (5), 567–81.

Schnapper, D. (1994), 'The debate on immigration and the crisis of national identity', in M. Baldwin-Edwards and M. Schain (eds), *The Politics of Immigration in Western Europe,* Essex: Frank Cass, pp. 127–39.

Semyonov, Moshe (1996), 'On the cost of being an immigrant in Israel: the effects of tenure, ethnicity and gender', *Research on Social Stratification and Mobility,* **15**, 115–31.

Semyonov, Moshe and Vered Kraus (1983), 'Gender, ethnicity, and earnings inequality: the Israeli experience', *International Journal of Comparative Sociology,* **24** (3–4), 258–72.

Semyonov, Moshe and Tamar Lerenthal (1991), 'Country of origin, gender, and the attainment of socioeconomic status: a study of stratification in the Jewish population of Israel', *Research in Social Stratification and Mobility*, **10**, 327–45.

Semyonov, Moshe and N. Lewin-Epstein (2003), 'Immigration and ethnicity in Israel: returning diaspora and nation-building', in M. Rainer and O. Rainer (eds), *Diasporas and Ethnic Migrants*, London: Frank Cass, pp. 327–37.

Semyonov, Moshe and Andrea Tyree (1981), 'Community segregation and the cost of ethnic subordination', *Social Forces*, **59** (3), 649–66.

Semyonov, Moshe, Rebeca Raijman and Anastasia Gorodzeisky (2006), 'The rise of anti-foreigner sentiment in European societies: a cross-national multi-level analysis', *American Sociological Review*, **71** (3), 426–49.

Semyonov, Moshe, Y. Haberfeld, R. Raijman, K. Amit, S. Dolevn, A. Bollotin-Chachashvili and S. Heilbrunn (2007), *Ruppin Index for Immigrants' Integration in Israel – 2nd Report*, The Institute for Immigration and Social Integration, Ruppin Academic Center, Publication no. 2 (Hebrew).

Sethi, H. (1993), 'Survival and democracy: ecological struggles in India', *New Social Movements in the South: Empowering the People,* Wignaraja, Ponna (ed.), New Delhi: Vistaar Publications, pp. 122–48.

Shafir, G. and Y. Peled (2002), *Being Israeli. The Dynamics of Multiple Citizenship*, New York: Cambridge University Press.

Shaw, P. (1973), *Report to the Minister for Immigration, the Hon. A.J. Grassby, M.P., on Good Neighbour Council Participation in the Observance of Australia Day 1973*, Canberra: Department of Immigration.

Silver, H. (1994), 'Social exclusion and social solidarity: three paradigms', *International Labour Review,* **133** (5–6), 531–78.

Smyth, P. and B. Cass (1998), *Contesting the Australian Way: States, Markets, and Civil Society,* Melbourne: Cambridge University Press.

Soysal, Y.N. (1994), *Limits of Citizenship. Migrants and Postnational Membership in Europe*, Chicago: The University of Chicago Press.

Spilerman, Symor and Jack Habib (1976), 'Development towns in Israel: the role of community in creating ethnic disparities in labor force characteristics', *American Journal of Sociology*, **81** (4), 781–812.

Statistics Canada (2003), *Ethnic Diversity Survey, Portrait of a Multicultural Society*, available at: http://dsp-psd.tpsgc.gc.ca/Collection/Statcan/89-593-X/89-593-XIE2003001.pdf (accessed 8 April 2009).

Steketee, Mike (2009), 'Liberals wrong on refugees', *The Australian*, 16 April, p. 12.

Stephan, W.G. and C.W. Stephan (2000), 'An integrated threat theory of prejudice', in Stuart Oskmap (ed.), *Reducing Prejudice and Discrimination,* Mahwah, NJ: Lawrence Erlbaum, pp. 23–46.

Sudanese Lost Boys Association of Australia (n.d.), available at: http:// www.lostboys.org.au/index.php (accessed 17 June 2010).

Tavan, Gwenda (2004), 'The dismantling of the White Australia policy: elite conspiracy or will of the Australian people?', *Australian Journal of Political Science*, **39** (1), 109–25.

Tavan, Gwenda (2005), *The Long Slow Death of White Australia*, Carlton North: Scribe Publications.

Thomson, P. (2005), 'Simon's journey', *Australian Mosaic*, **11** (3), 47–8.

Toren, N. (2003), 'Tradition and transition: family change in Israel', *Gender Issues*, **21** (2), 60–76.

UNHCR. The UN Refugee Agency (2010), 'Israel', available at: http:// www.unhcr.org/cgi-bin/texis/vtx/page?page=49e4864b6 (accessed on 17 June 2010).

Waldinger, R. and J. Perlman (1998), 'Second generation: past, present, future', *Journal of Ethnic and Migration Studies,* **24** (1), 5–24.

Walmsley, Jim, Fran Rolley, Raj Rajaratnaan and Alsion McIntosh (2007), 'Settlement patterns and experiences', in Kerry Carrington, Alison McIntosh and Jim Walmsley (eds), *The Social Costs and Benefits of Migration into Australia*, Armidale, NSW: Centre for Applied Research in Social Science, pp. 8–24.

Will, Louise (1997), *Australian Non-English Speaking Background Immigrants' Income Adjustment*, PhD Thesis, Canberra: ANU.

Withers, Glenn and David Pope (1993), 'Do migrants rob jobs? Lessons of Australian history 1861–1991', *Journal of Economic History*, **53** (4), 719–42.

Yaish, Meir (2001), 'Class structure in a deeply divided society: class and ethnic inequality in Israel', *British Journal of Sociology*, **52** (3), 409–39.

Yaish, Meir and Vered Kraus (2003), 'The consequences of economic restructuring for the gender gap in Israel, 1972–1995', *Work Employment and Society*, **17** (1), 5–28.

Yarwood, A.T. (1967), *Asian Migration to Australia*, Carlton: Melbourne University Press.

Yishai, Y. (1998), 'Civil society in transition: interest politics in Israel', *The ANNALS of the American Academy of Political and Social Science*, **555** (1), 147–62.

Yitzhaki, Shlomo (1987), *Ethnic-Based Stratification and Inequality in Israel*, Survey No. 63: 31–42, Jerusalem: Bank of Israel (Hebrew).

Index